The Working Class in American History

A list of books in the series appears at the end of this volume.

ANOTHER CIVIL WAR

ANOTHER CIVIL WAR

Labor, Capital, and the State
in the Anthracite Regions
of Pennsylvania
1840–68

GRACE PALLADINO

UNIVERSITY OF ILLINOIS PRESS
Urbana and Chicago

This book is printed on acid-free paper.

LIBRARY OF CONGRESS CATALOGING-IN-PUBLICATION DATA

Palladino, Grace.
    Another Civil War : labor, capital, and the state in the
anthracite regions of Pennsylvania, 1840–68 / Grace Palladino.
        p.   cm. — (The Working class in American history)
    Bibliography: p.
    Includes index.
    ISBN 0-252-01671-8 (alk. paper)
    1. Coal miners—Pennsylvania—History—19th century. 2. Coal
mines and mining—Pennsylvania—History—19th century. 3. Labor
movement—Pennsylvania—History—19th century. 4. United States—
History—Civil War, 1861–1865—Draft resisters. I. Title.
II. Series.
HD8039.M62U6493   1990
331.7′622335′0974809034—dc20   89-32837
                                                       CIP

For my mother and in memory of my father

Contents

Acknowledgments   xi

1. Introduction   3

2. The Industry: Speculation, Competition, and Control,
   1820–60   16

3. The Miners: Economic Centralization and Class
   Formation, 1840–60   43

4. The Region: Class, Ethnicity, and Political Allegiance,
   1840–60   70

5. Opposition to Conscription in the Coal Regions,
   1862–63   95

6. Labor Organization in the Wartime Economy,
   1862–65   121

7. The Return to Order: The Provost Marshal and
   Organized Labor, 1862–65   140

8. Conclusion   166

Bibliography   177

Index   191

Acknowledgments

Like most products of "individual enterprise," this book could not have been published without the assistance of family, friends, colleagues, and institutions, and it is a pleasure to acknowledge their many contributions. The Mellon Foundation, through the University of Pittsburgh, and the Joseph Skinner Fellowship, administered through Mount Holyoke College, financed the dissertation upon which this work is based. I am especially grateful to my advisor, David Montgomery, and to teachers like Laurence Glasco and Ted Muller, of the University of Pittsburgh, and Charles Trout, formerly of Mount Holyoke and now Provost at Colgate College, who all encouraged my efforts.

A postdoctoral fellowship at the National Museum of American History, Smithsonian Institution, not only allowed me to revise the dissertation, but also provided ideal working conditions and an intellectually stimulating environment. Pete Daniel and Francis Gadsen guided me through the museum's extensive mining collection; Jim Roan helped me to locate and borrow numerous microfilmed newspapers and manuscript collections; and my fellow fellows, especially Colleen Dunlavy and Stephanie McCurry, proved to be both effective critics and good friends. I am grateful also to my colleagues at the Gompers Papers, especially Stuart Kaufman and Peter Albert, who not only encouraged me to take the fellowship, but have continued to support my work in practical and satisfying ways. The Library of Congress also significantly aided this project, providing work space and expert research assistance. Bruce Martin, of the Research Facilities Office, and Charles Kelly, of the Manuscript Division, proved especially helpful.

Numerous friends and colleagues have offered substantial

help along the way. Patricia Cooper, Wayne Durrill, Eric Foner, Eugene Genovese, Steven Hahn, Cornelia Levine, and Sean Wilentz read and commented on various drafts of this work. Jacqueline Goggin not only shared with me her extensive knowledge of archival sources but boosted my confidence at a time when I really needed it. Peter Gottlieb saved me from traveling to Pennsylvania one last time by providing me with typewritten transcripts of a crucial manuscript. Celia Gray expertly deciphered my handwritten drafts and "processed" the bulk of this manuscript. I owe a huge debt to Larry Lynn, who led me kicking and screaming into the world of computer technology and also challenged me, more than once, to defend the basis of my ideas. Bob Danton, who knew me long before I became a historian, provided a welcome, and usually necessary, respite from the academic world. I am grateful also to Becky and John O'Brien, who demonstrated the meaning of friendship at a critical period in my life.

Throughout the long gestation of this book, my family has stood behind me, offering the kind of moral and practical support I needed to complete this work. My sisters, Christine Bridges and Rosemary Palladino, together with Jennifer Liang, Katie Bridges, Walter Bridges, and Marianne Brennick, managed to keep my spirits up and generously provided transportation and hospitality. My aunt, Phyllis Baiori, who always applauds her nieces' efforts, remains my most enthusiastic booster. My mother, Frances Palladino, whose high standards of family commitment and community involvement continue to impress me, has always made it possible for me to pursue whatever paths I've chosen. I regret that my father, Anthony Palladino, did not live to see me complete this work, but he let me know, early on, that he knew I could do it. Finally, I am grateful to Brad Piepmeier, who not only helped me through the final stages of this project, but managed to convince me that the future can be more interesting than the past.

ANOTHER CIVIL WAR

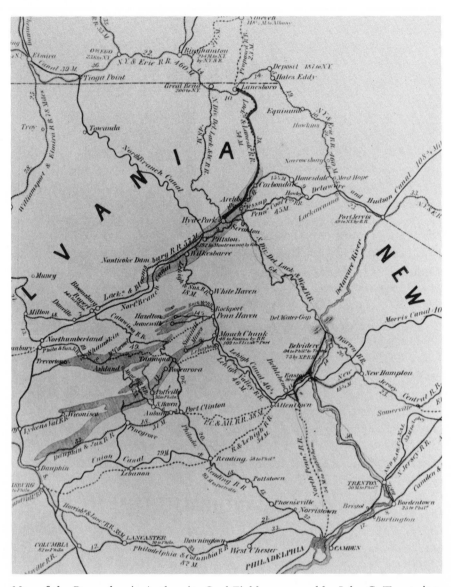

Map of the Pennsylvania Anthracite Coal Fields, prepared by John C. Trautwine, 1856. (Courtesy of the Division of Geography and Maps, Library of Congress. Photograph by Brad Piepmeier.)

1

Introduction

By the time that Charles Sharpe and James McDonnell ascended the gallows outside the Carbon County Courthouse in January 1879, eight other "Molly Maguire" convicts had preceded them there. A mysterious secret society allegedly determined to rule or ruin the coal industry, the Molly Maguires were blamed for the serious social disorder that racked the anthracite regions of Pennsylvania in the mid-nineteenth century. Sharpe and McDonnell, however, would be hanged for crimes more complicated than those usually attributed to the group. Although their alleged victim was a mine superintendent, a common target in these years of labor strife, their crime had transpired some fifteen years earlier, when George K. Smith was shot to death in his Carbon County home. The *Mauch Chunk Democrat* clarified the significance of the case. "During the Civil War, in 1863, when the drafts were being enforced," the paper explained, "Carbon County and some of its neighbors were scenes of riots and bloodshed." Attributing Smith's murder to his role in implementing the draft, the paper linked evidence of organized terrorism in Pennsylvania's coal regions to violent resistance not only to conscription but to the Union cause itself.[1]

The *Democrat* offered no new analysis here; on the contrary, the paper merely confirmed an interpretation that contemporaries had long endorsed. Frequent and alarming reports of wartime "outrages" — riots, murder, and arson — had convinced numerous residents that a sinister, well-organized, alien force threatened life, property, and social order in the coal regions. "When I was District Attorney of Schuylkill County [during the war]," Franklin B. Gowen, well-known prosecutor of the Molly Maguires and later president of the Philadelphia and Reading

Railroad, remembered, "I made up my mind from what I had seen in innumerable instances that there existed . . . a secret organization banded together for the commission of crime. . . ." Other residents of the coal regions shared this opinion. When miners shut down a Schuylkill County colliery in 1862, for example, observers blamed a traveling band of armed strangers for the trouble. "It seems to have been a movement originating in Cass Township," a notorious trouble spot, a local paper explained, "where a secret association termed the Molly Maguires exists. . . ."[2] The apparent increase of violent crime in the coal regions, at the same time that the federal government required increasing supplies of coal, lent credence to the notion that Pennsylvania's miners—at least her Irish Democratic miners— were part of a treasonous network determined to sabotage the Union's war efforts.

Reports of violent opposition to conscription further substantiated this belief. "I think the organization to resist the draft in Schuylkill, Luzerne and Carbon Counties is very formidable," Governor Andrew Curtin informed the Secretary of War in October 1862, soon after a group of miners stopped a trainload of conscripts on the way to Harrisburg. Although he expressed his desire not to exaggerate the problem, he nonetheless insisted that some five thousand miners were armed and in league ready to resist the draft.[3] This and similar reports of well-organized, violent resistance ultimately convinced the federal government to base a standing army in the coal regions and employ coercive state power against the allegedly dangerous, treasonous coal miners.

Historians, for the most part, agree that widespread draft resistance in Pennsylvania's anthracite regions required such action. Basing their analysis largely on the documents comprising the *Official Records of the Civil War,* they generally confirm contemporary assessments of these wartime conflicts. Eugene C. Murdock, citing the miners' Democratic loyalties, for example, explained that "when the war came [the miners] adopted a vigorous anti-war, anti-administration stance." Arguing that they utilized a secret protective society as a basis for organized opposition to conscription, he added that the "notorious 'Molly Maguires' of post-war fame cut their terrorist teeth on the draft machinery of the Civil War." J. W. Coleman, William Itter, and Arnold Shankman all agree that Pennsylvania's mining regions harbored virulent critics of the war who organized "serious affrays" when the government attempted to conscript soldiers in 1862 and 1863. "So serious did resistance become," Itter added, "that . . . the Department of the Susquehanna [a division of the Union Army] set up a separate military district . . . for the purpose of maintaining and enforcing the draft."[4] Fred A. Shannon, who offers perhaps the most informed reading of this conflict, likewise premises his analysis on the fact of organized, violent resistance. Noting that the miners had terrorized so-called "law-abiding portions of the community," he concludes that by the summer of 1863, "it is certain that the rebellious element was entirely too strong for the small force at the disposal of the provost marshal."[5]

These historians are certainly correct that opposition to conscription proved widespread in Schuylkill, Luzerne, and Carbon Counties. In fact, in most northern communities that housed a largely foreign-born, Democratic population, this proved to be the case. But the sustained violent resistance cited by contemporaries and historians alike to justify the presence of military troops cannot be documented for the coal regions.[6] To be sure, residents of all three counties regularly threatened the lives of those charged with making the enrollment in 1862 and 1863, so much so that it proved impossible to retain enrollers in certain "disaffected districts." But these threats were more often carried out in agricultural, not mining, districts. It was Democratic farmers, more than miners, who forcefully helped friends and relatives contest the draft. In the coal districts, residents generally took advantage of the mountainous terrain to evade or escape, not combat, enrollers. In fact, only two major skirmishes involving groups of miners erupted, both during the 1862 enrollment (an enrollment later discredited for including aliens not liable to the draft). Both occurred in the midst of a heated political campaign (a campaign that encouraged Democrats and Republicans to manipulate the enrollment process in order to elect their candidates). Such evidence cannot explain the fact that the army remained encamped in the coal regions for the duration of the war. On the contrary, it suggests that these home-front conflicts proved more complicated and more historically significant than is generally acknowledged.[7]

If the level of violent draft resistance cannot account for the presence of a standing army, the level of labor organization and the increasing frequency of successful strikes between the years 1862 and 1865 shed important light on the subject. Reporters of violent draft resistance — especially those with ties to the anthracite industry — regularly conflated evidence of labor organization and workplace struggles with evidence of opposition to conscription and to the war itself. When Charles Albright, a Republican lawyer in Carbon County well connected to the coal industry, described draft resistance, for example, he offered proof of labor discontent and labor organization to document his case. "They dictate the prices for their work," he informed Abraham Lincoln in 1862, "and if their employers don't accede they destroy and burn coal breakers, houses, and prevent those disposed from working."[8] His contention that opposition to the coal operators' authority in the mines equaled opposition to the Union cause was not unusual. In fact, as this study will demonstrate, provost marshals, the local administrators of the draft, construed evidence of labor organization to be evidence of organized resistance to conscription in all three anthracite districts. Whether this action reflected confused observations, deliberate misrepresentation, or both, it allowed these agents of the federal government to acquire the military force necessary to execute a draconian draft in the coal regions. In the process, however, it also provided industrialists and their supporters with the federal force necessary to override whatever local economic and political power the miners had thus far managed to achieve.[9]

The recognition of this official duplicity — intentional or otherwise — raises questions about the historical significance of these home-front struggles. Are these "outrages" best understood as the product of ignorant, negrophobic Irishmen in the clutches of demagogic Democrats, as many historians have asserted? Is there evidence to sustain the alleged connection between these episodes and a secret treasonous society? Was it opposition to the war that triggered miners' strikes, and contempt for the Union that induced miners to shirk their wartime duties? Can the conventional historical interpretation adequately explain the provost marshals' decision to join forces with the operators and equate strike activity with disloyalty?

Certainly a strong case can be made that strikes undertaken during war—especially in an industry central to the prosecution of that war—constitute treason. But this view assumes that war-related issues of national importance, like the decision to emancipate the slaves or conscript an army, provoked these strikes. It also assumes a correlation between the Irish miners' support for the Democratic party and their alleged support for the Confederacy. The conventional view presents the miners' strike activity as a manifestation of their solidarity with the South.

This view, however, overlooks the deep-rooted social, economic, political, and cultural tensions that had long informed everyday life in the coal regions—tensions present before, during, and after the war. It also ignores a pattern of industrial conflict already well established by the outbreak of the war, and it obscures the industrialists' historical role in that conflict. At the same time, it underestimates the social and economic ties between local wartime agents of the Republican administration and leading coal operators, and it ignores evidence that provost marshals willingly provided military assistance to those employers, who were anxious to be rid of troublesome organized miners. Although their critics argued that wartime strikes were undertaken to embarrass the Union, the history of economic development, class formation, and industrial conflict in the coal regions and elsewhere suggests otherwise. The fact that workers of all political persuasions and ethnicities struck to assert their rights and interests throughout the war-torn North forces us not only to reassess the conventional interpretation of draft resistance during the Civil War, but to reconsider the actual process of such historical transformations as industrialization and political centralization and their relation to these wartime conflicts.

In fact, it is only when these conflicts are viewed solely in the context of the war itself that the conventional interpretation makes sense. When they are viewed in the context of the region's social, political, and economic history, however, then class formation and industrial conflict, not draft resistance and disloyalty, emerge as central considerations. Indeed, when these conflicts are analyzed in light of the development of the anthracite industry and the evolution of a hierarchical class system, the social and economic roots of the miners' aversion to centralized political power in general, and to the Republican program for economic growth and cultural reform in particular, become more clear. From this vantage point these conflicts assume greater historical significance, for they reveal the crucial role the military played not only in enforcing the political centralization necessary to prosecute the war but in extending the benefits of that centralization to industrialists seeking to demolish labor's claims to industrial and social equality. Wartime "outrages"—and especially their resolution—have more to tell us about the development of the industrial capitalist system, its relation to class conflict, and the process of building a national state than they do about disloyalty.

In order to reassess these conflicts in their broader historical context, I begin with an examination of the industry, focusing especially on the process of economic centralization and its effect on miners and operators in Pennsylvania's three anthracite regions: the Wyoming or northern field, located primarily in Luzerne County; the Lehigh or middle field, in Luzerne and Carbon Counties; and the Schuylkill or southern field, primarily in Schuylkill County. In each of these regions, particular geographical, geological, and economic conditions shaped the structure of the industry. In the Schuylkill region, for example, where coal was more accessible and therefore cheaper to produce, independent landowners, operators, and shippers developed the industry. More centralized and better-capitalized transport corporations, combining mining, shipping, and landowning rights, developed the trade elsewhere. These two business forms originally complemented each other: in the early days of the trade, Schuylkill's independent operators gladly supplied the market with coal while the transport companies, interested in keeping the price of coal high, restricted production in favor of constructing canals and railroad lines.

Beginning in the 1840s, however, those transport companies able to control both the mining and shipping of coal competed among each other to dominate the trade. Driving prices so low that independent operators could barely survive, and in the process encouraging overproduction, overinvestment, and economic instability, this competition contributed to a social and industrial environment riddled with class conflict.[10] If this competition to dominate the market took its toll on independent entrepreneurs, its consequences fell hardest on the miners and mine laborers, whose wages were regulated by the price of coal. Responding to the same competitive environment that rewarded operators who were able to centralize their control of the industry, miners likewise sought to organize their forces. Although the social geography of the industry severely limited the scope of labor organization, miners nevertheless attempted to define and assert their class interests in the face of this economic assault. Forming local unions as early as the 1840s, miners in Schuylkill, Luzerne, and Carbon Counties waged strikes to increase wages and improve working conditions long before the outbreak of civil war.[11]

Although miners and operators had worked together as producers to develop the trade, by the 1860s miners generally comprised a propertyless and subordinate wage-earning class. In spite of significant changes in the structure of the industry and a decline in the miners' social status and condition, however, miners retained the producer ideology that shaped their vision of industrial relations and informed their decision to organize unions. From the miners' point of view, it was their labor that imparted any value to the product, and they saw themselves as equal contributors with capitalists to social wealth. Thus they organized to protect their claim to an equal share of the industry's profits and to an equal right to determine wage rates, safe working conditions, and work rules.

Their employers, on the other hand, who considered their right to manage a property right of capital, sought to enforce an industrial hierarchy based on their unilateral and unquestioned authority in the workplace. If they recognized labor as a partner in industry, theirs was a partnership premised on dependency, not equality. From the operators' point of view, it was the employers' right to set the terms of the wage bargain, establish hiring and firing policies, and enforce work rules without interference. Those employees who disputed this had the right to seek work elsewhere. When miners challenged this no-

tion of managerial prerogative and organized strikes to press
their claims, the operators made it clear that they would not
acknowledge the miners' position, regardless of the grievance
involved. Stigmatizing strike activity as an inherent threat to
life and property, the operators regularly sought and received
military protection and usually paid for it. By the time the federal
army took up residence in the coal regions in 1863, the pattern
of employing force to inhibit labor organization and to protect
those miners willing to break a strike was already well established.

Local industry supporters, especially those committed to small-
scale, individual enterprise, generally applauded such action.
From their point of view, the presence of unruly, undisciplined,
and mob-oriented miners weakened the structure of republican
society, which, they argued, rested on continuous and unen-
cumbered economic growth. Ignoring evidence of economic
centralization in the industry, these boosters considered strikes
to be the cause of class conflict, not the result of it. Thus, in
their view, labor organization threatened future investment in
the region at the same time that it restricted the employers'
ability to utilize resources as they saw fit. Eager to counteract
the collective spirit that animated organized miners in the workplace and in the community, Whig, and later Republican, critics
of labor organization endorsed programs for social and moral
reform that promoted individualistic "American" values consistent with their vision of a productive economy. Such programs
together with a protective tariff would, they argued, improve
the material conditions of worker and employer alike, as long
as workers conceded their employers' economic integrity, avoided
liquor, worked longer hours in the mines, and voted against the
Democrats. These political spokesmen fully expected the working class—or at least its "right-thinking" component—to en-
dorse their platform, eschew collective activity, and thereby reap
the benefits of productive republican industry.[12]

When a majority of miners continued to repudiate this view—
in the workplace and at the ballot box—their critics were
dumbfounded. Republicans, who recognized no systematic justification for the miners' position, could only assume that Democratic politicians pandered to Irish voters by promoting class

conflict. In fact, for the most part, Republican spokesmen blamed any evidence of social discontent on the Democrats' control of the Irish and the party's low-tariff position. Demagogic Democrats, in their view, and not the industrial system, fueled labor unrest; ignorance and depravity, not the Republicans' well-documented anti-Irish, anti-labor rhetoric, accounted for the Democrats' electoral success. The outbreak of war in 1861 produced a crisis that significantly transformed the idiom, but not the substance, of this critique. In the context of war, onetime "demagogues" and party hacks became copperhead traitors sympathetic to the South. When the coal regions continued to post Democratic majorities despite the national crisis, it was but a small step for critics to identify the miners' economic struggles with disloyalty. The Democrats' denunciation of war measures like emancipation and the suspension of habeas corpus seemingly substantiated the charge.

Although Democrats in Pennsylvania opposed a number of Republican war measures, especially the Conscription Act of 1863, this opposition did not necessarily indicate disloyalty. Rather, it demonstrated the Democrats' deep-rooted, if self-serving, aversion to centralized political authority. Democrats did not dispute the idea of military service; they opposed aspects of the conscription legislation itself. They focused their criticism on the Conscription Act's inherent inequality in allowing individuals to purchase their way out of the draft, but more especially they focused on its administrative features. Section five of the Conscription Act especially worried them. It called for the President to appoint a provost marshal in every congressional district, "who shall be under the direction and subject to the orders of a provost marshal general." From the Democrats' point of view, this aspect of the law promised to revolutionize relations between individuals and the state, as it strengthened the law-enforcement capabilities of the federal government. "Look at these provisions," Congressman Charles Biddle of Philadelphia proclaimed, "a provost marshal in every congressional district . . . arresting summarily under this act or under no act, but under some order or proclamation, anyone who may be obnoxious to him or his superiors."[13] These district provost marshals not only administered the draft but possessed the power to arrest deserters, seize spies, and confine traitors. Through the Provost Marshal General, his assistant state marshals, and the district provost marshal and his well-armed guard, conscription would be enforced and treason identified and controlled without interference from state and local government.[14] "You must not put the life and liberty of the citizen under the whim and caprice of every upstart officer who may take upon himself," Congressman Hendrick B. Wright of Luzerne County pleaded, ". . . to judge what is treason and what is not treason." In the eyes of these Democrats, the Conscription Act of 1863 not only threatened their power base, since it would bring the machinery of federal government directly into the lives of local citizens, but it might also pave the way for military despotism in those areas traditionally Democratic.[15]

For the miners the implementation of this clause posed a more immediate threat: the provost marshals in all three anthracite regions represented not just the interests of the Republican administration but the interests of the major coal operators as well. In fact, in Schuylkill County, the alleged center of draft resistance, the provost marshal held significant investments in the industry. Thus the separate struggles to impose centralized political authority and centralized economic control became joined in the person of a provost marshal who identified the economic interests of the operators with the political interests of the nation.[16]

In the midst of a national civil war, then, miners and operators continued to fight another civil war—a war to determine whose vision of "republican" industry would prevail. Miners demanded an industrial system wherein organized labor might exercise authority in the workplace; operators, however, willing to deal with their employees only as individuals, defined their right to manage to be a property right of capital. Both sides exploited wartime economic conditions to press their claims. For the miners, the government's insatiable demand for coal offered them their first real chance to amass, and then exert, their economic power as a class. That same demand offered operators, large and small, a similar chance to profit handsomely from a heretofore unstable business. Both sides used the war to make up for past deprivation and to advance their social and economic interests. But the operators also used the powers generated by the Conscription Act to shore up their class position. Taking advantage of their social and economic ties to representatives of the federal government, the operators utilized troops intended to enforce conscription to nullify the miners' legitimate claims and to dismantle their labor organizations. Under the guise of preserving the Union, industrialists and provost marshals acquired the military force necessary to intimidate striking miners into submission, to disperse leaders of the miners' committees, to protect strikebreakers, and to impose managerial prerogative by force of law.

Unlike the war between the states, this civil war was not ended at Appomattox. On the contrary, the very same struggles that racked the coal regions between the years 1862 and 1865 were played out over and over again in other industrial centers, especially as employers in large-scale industry extended their control over production. But if the particular coalition of provost marshals, military leaders, and industrialists that defended the employers' sovereign rights ended with the war itself, its success during the 1860s nevertheless decisively shaped the social order of industrial capitalism for years to come. At Pittsburgh in 1877, as in the coal regions fifteen years earlier, for example, railroad officials easily procured military troops to "restore order," although striking workers had maintained the peace. Not surprisingly, it was the arrival of the troops that provoked violence and allowed the military to break this first nationwide strike. Likewise, at Homestead in 1892, as in the coal regions three decades earlier, the courts agreed with employers that a strike in and of itself constituted violence, if not treason. Thus they justified the use of troops not only to disperse striking workers and protect social order but, significantly, to escort strikebreakers into the mills. And at Pullman, Illinois, in 1894, as in the coal regions in 1864, corporate lawyers and government officials creatively interpreted the law in order to imprison leaders of a strike and thereby cripple a growing union. Indeed, despite strong evidence of their own predilection to organize and to manipulate the market whenever their interests required it, and despite fierce local opposition to their efforts, industrialists retained a remarkable ability to command the coercive power of the state to protect their particular economic interests and to disrupt and discredit organized labor for the remainder of the century.

NOTES

1. *Mauch Chunk Democrat,* Jan. 18, 1879. For a discussion of the Molly Maguires and their link to opposition to the draft see Francis P. Dewees, *The Molly Maguires: The Origin, Growth and Character of the Organization* (Philadelphia, 1877); J. Walter Coleman, *The Molly Maguire Riots* (Washington, D.C., 1936); Wayne G. Broehl, *The Molly Maguires* (Cambridge, Mass., 1964).

2. Franklin B. Gowen, "Argument in the Case of the *Commonwealth* v. *Thomas Munley,*" Court of Oyer and Terminer of Schuylkill County (Pottsville, Pa., 1876), 15; *Miners' Journal,* Dec. 20, 1862. For a biography of Gowen, who was elected District Attorney in 1862, see Marvin W. Schlegel, *Ruler of the Reading: The Life of Franklin B. Gowen, 1836-1889* (Harrisburg, Pa., 1947).

3. Curtin to Stanton, Oct. 22, 1862, in *The War of the Rebellion: A Compilation of the Official Records of the Union and Confederate Armies* (Washington, D.C., 1889–1901), ser. 1, vol. 19, pt. 2, 268; Stanton to Curtin, Oct. 23, 1862, ibid., 473; Curtin to Stanton, Oct. 24, 1862, ibid., 473.

4. Eugene C. Murdock, *One Million Men: The Civil War Draft in the North* (Madison, Wis., 1971), 44; Coleman, *The Molly Maguire Riots;* William Itter, "Conscription in Pennsylvania during the Civil War," Ph.D. diss., University of Southern California, 1941, 141; Arnold Shankman, *The Pennsylvania Anti-War Movement, 1861–1865* (Rutherford, N.J., 1980).

5. Fred A. Shannon, *The Organization and Administration of the Union Army,* 2 vols. (Gloucester, Mass., 1965), 1:222.

6. For a general discussion of draft resistance see Colonel James B. Fry to Edwin Stanton, *Final Report,* Mar. 17, 1866, Reports and Decisions of the Provost Marshal General, RG 110, National Archives Microfilm Publication M621. See also Adrian Cook, *The Armies of the Street: The New York City Draft Riots of 1863* (Lexington, Ky., 1974); William Marvel, "New Hampshire and the Draft Riots of 1863," *Historical New Hampshire* 36 (1981): 58-72; Robert Sterling, "Civil War Draft Resistance in the Middle West," Ph.D. diss., University of Illinois, 1974; William G. Carlton, "Civil War Dissidence in the North: The Perspective of a Century," in *Essays on the Civil War and Reconstruction,* ed. Irwin Unger (New York, 1970), 265–74; James W. Geary, "Civil War Conscription in the North: A Historiographical Review," *Civil War History* 32 (1986), 256–67. Unfortunately, Iver Bernstein's recent work on the New York draft riots was not available to me at the time I wrote this book.

7. See chapter 5.

8. Cited in David Montgomery, *Beyond Equality: Labor and the Radical*

Republicans, 1862–1872 (New York, 1967), 112. For a discussion of strikes during the war see pages 91–101.

9. See chapters 6 and 7.

10. See chapter 2 for a discussion of overproduction in the industry and Clifton K. Yearley, Jr., *Enterprise and Anthracite: Economics and Democracy in Schuylkill County, 1820–1875* (Baltimore, 1961); for overinvestment see Harold Aurand, *From the Molly Maguires to the United Mine Workers: The Social Ecology of an Industrial Union, 1869–1897* (Philadelphia, 1971).

11. See chapter 3.

12. See chapter 4.

13. *Congressional Globe*, 37th Cong., 3rd sess., 1863, vol. 41, pt. 2:1215 (cited hereafter as *CG*).

14. The text of the law can be found in *United States Statutes at Large*, 13:731–37. The *Final Report* also describes the machinery and duties of the Provost Marshal General's Bureau.

15. *CG*, 1225. See also pages 816, 960, 976, 987, 1306, 1363, 1371, 1454, 1494, and 1525 for the Senate debates over conscription, and pages 1029, 1149, 1175, 1213, 1220, 1225, 1248, 1249, 1251, 1258, 1288, 1289, 1291, 1292, and 1478 for the House debates.

16. See chapter 7.

2

The Industry: Speculation, Competition, and Control 1820–60

"If ever a nation had occasion for thanksgiving," the Philadelphia *Public Ledger* proclaimed in November 1863, "we are that people." Despite the devastation of "a gigantic war," the paper explained, industrial production had reached new heights, particularly in Pennsylvania. "Our iron, our coal, the timber of our forests . . . have all been abundantly produced . . . ," the paper proudly announced, "and at prices the mighty remunerating." The Pottsville *Miners' Journal* concurred. Rejoicing that the year 1862 had "yielded a greater coal production than had then been known" and that the tonnage in 1863 had proved "also enormous," the paper promised even higher returns in 1864. Encouraged by reports that "new and expensive shafts are being sunk, lateral railroads being built, [and] coal cars constructed in fabulous numbers," the *Miners' Journal* confidently predicted that this vast expansion would provide "profit enough for all." Such optimism notwithstanding, one branch of the industry still seemed hell-bent on destroying prosperity: miners and laborers, who had recently "urged a bloody resistance to the draft," were now in the throes of a serious strike wave.[1]

In fact, around the same time that the market for coal began to stabilize in 1862, miners throughout the coal regions had begun to organize their forces. "They claim that at short notice they can rally three thousand men to engage in their unlawful work," the *Miners' Journal* reported, adding that the owners were at the mercy of this labor "combination" that claimed the right to "dictate who should be employed and who shall not, what mines shall be worked and what shall be abandoned." Even more troubling, however, was the fact that, by 1864, these miner combinations had exacted "such wages as were never before known in a coal mine." Used to paying their hands about twenty cents per ton in a good year, operators were now being forced to pay four times that rate. "If these high-handed outrages are permitted to go on unchecked," the paper feared, "property will depreciate in value and life will be more unsafe than it is among the savage guerrillas of the south."[2]

Unable to reconcile this seemingly self-destructive behavior with evidence of prosperity and future expansion, observers blamed outside agitators and disloyal Democrats for stirring up industrial conflict. Miners, however, needed no such prodding. According to their experience, expanded production and industrial growth in no way guaranteed that employers would share the fruits of economic prosperity equally. Already by the summer of 1863, in fact, the operators had confirmed the miners' suspicions by securing a plentiful supply of newly arrived immigrants who would undercut wages at the same time that production rates soared ever higher. Nor was this experience a new one. Whether the operators and their supporters cared to recognize it or not, the logic and the history of the anthracite trade itself encouraged miners to organize their forces if they intended to benefit from industrial expansion.

"If it is properly managed, the coal business will settle down into a regular system," the *Lehigh Pioneer* predicted in 1831, "producing a fair return to the enterprising men who have introduce[d] to market . . . a new article of commerce. . . ." But, the paper warned, if competition to dominate the trade led to ruinous overproduction, that "fair return" could not be guaranteed. "Give the people no more coal than they will purchase at equitable prices," the *Pioneer* advised, "do not hold out the delusive idea that it will be sold for a *song* and make a Croesus of him who sells it."[3] Although independent operators and shippers would hear the same advice in one form or another over the next fifty years, they could not easily abandon their speculative dreams: rapidly increasing demand for anthracite, for both domestic and manufacturing purposes, together with a general belief in the inexhaustibility of Pennsylvania's coal supply, buoyed hopes that vast fortunes would be made in the coal regions.

The industry's spectacular takeoff seemingly confirmed these "delusive" ideas. Beginning with barely 400 tons in 1820, the coal trade boasted 174,734 tons in 1830, and almost five times that ten years later. In fact, between 1820 and 1840 some five million tons of anthracite had been mined and sent to market.[4] At the same time, real estate values in the coal regions increased dramatically—land that sold for $9,000 in 1824 brought $40,000 in five year's time. "Speculation," one landowner noted in 1829, "is running high. . . ." Although the consequences of this speculation would lead to destructive price competition and eventual corporate domination by the 1870s, in these early years the industry rewarded both small and large investors alike.[5]

Anthracite had been discovered in all three major fields— the northern, middle, and southern—late in the eighteenth century, but at least three decades elapsed before it found more than a local market. Although industry pioneers had early recognized the commercial prospects of this resource, the remote location of the coal fields together with the novelty of the product itself seriously impeded the evolution of the trade. In fact, before Jacob Cist and Charles Miner of Wilkes-Barre could sell the two arkloads of coal they had painstakingly shipped to Philadelphia in 1813, they first had to convince a cynical public that "stone coal" would actually burn. Distributing handbills in both English and German that described various methods of burning coal, they also personally visited private homes and establishments to instruct potential customers in the uses of anthracite. "We were sometimes obliged to bribe the journeymen to try the experiment fairly," Miner recalled, "so averse were they to learn the use of a new sort of fuel." Nor was their story unique. Only when war cut off supplies of foreign coal, raising the price of charcoal, did Pennsylvania anthracite begin to find a ready market.[6]

In one sense, natural advantages—geography and geology— determined the timing and structure of the industry's development. Although financial and political advantage also played important roles, in the earliest days of the trade, location and easy access to coal proved paramount. Trade districts in the southern field—especially around Pottsville in Schuylkill County and Mauch Chunk in Northampton (later Carbon) County— possessed the necessary attributes, and regular commercial traffic first developed there. But if the Schuylkill and Lehigh trade districts shared similar advantages and grew almost simultaneously, the industry in each nevertheless developed along very different lines.

Trade in the Lehigh district was initiated in 1791, after the Lehigh Coal Company opened a mine and built a rough road to link the mine and the river. Failing to ship coal successfully to Philadelphia, the company soon leased its mines to various independent operators, none of whom proved any more successful. In fact, by 1815 the last of these had abandoned the business. Three years later the situation changed significantly when Josiah White and Erskine Hazard, both organizers of the Schuylkill Navigation Company, joined with George F. Hauto to take over the Lehigh Company lands. Organizing the Lehigh Navigation Company and the Lehigh Coal Company in 1818, and merging them two years later, they inaugurated the commercial coal trade when the company shipped 365 tons of anthracite to Philadelphia in 1820. Eventually incorporating in 1822, with Hazard and White at the helm, the Lehigh Coal and Navigation Company possessed the legal rights to own coal lands, coal mines, and transport facilities, and thus exercised a virtual monopoly on the Lehigh trade.[7]

In the Schuylkill district, on the other hand, no single company dominated all three phases of the business. The Schuylkill Navigation Canal began operation as "an open highway free to all the world" and transported the coal tonnage of all who paid the toll. Single proprietors, partners, and unchartered companies developed the industry in Schuylkill County, where the law prohibited coal landowners or shippers from mining or selling coal. If corporate interests early acquired the most productive lands in the Lehigh and Wyoming regions, independent operators in Schuylkill County leased the lands they worked from independent landowners. Such "individual enterprise" not only encouraged industrial expansion, these operators contended,

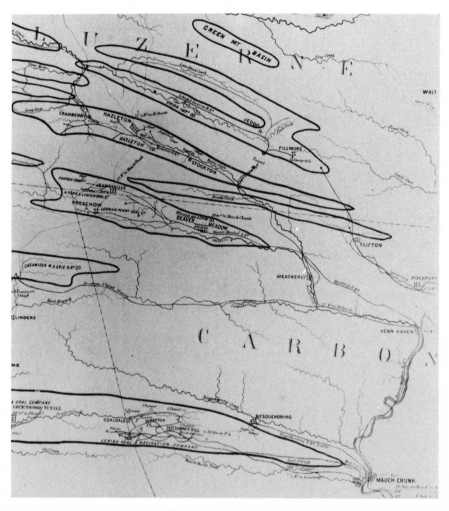

A map of the Anthracite Collieries, by P. W. Sheafer, 1859. (Courtesy of the Division of Geography and Maps, Library of Congress. Photograph by Brad Piepmeier.)

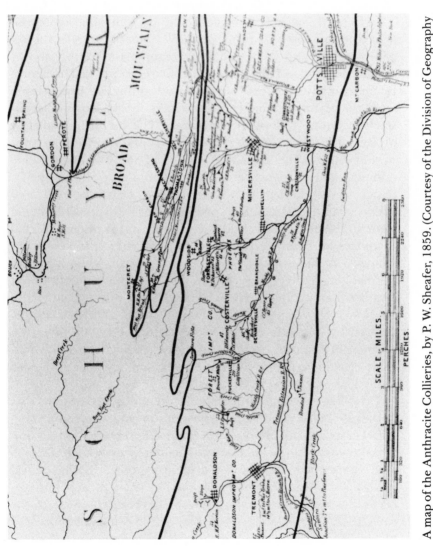

A map of the Anthracite Collieries, by P. W. Sheafer, 1859. (Courtesy of the Division of Geography and Maps, Library of Congress. Photograph by Brad Piepmeier.)

but offered miners and laborers a choice of workplaces, further ensuring independence. Thus the industry in Schuylkill County seemingly provided a republican alternative to the "monster" corporations that developed the trade elsewhere.

In the early, expansive days of the trade, individual enterprise proved a suitable organizing principle, especially given the region's topography. "The Schuylkill region," the *North American Review* observed in 1836, "seems to have been marked by nature for individual enterprise." Outcrops of anthracite nearly burst from the seams, making it economically feasible for numerous small investors to develop the trade. "The coal is immediately perceived *breaking out today* in the *roads* and *ravines* in beds of *streams* and on the *sides* and *summits* of the mountains," one mining prospectus exclaimed. "It does not cost $50 to open a mine," since "the facility with which coal . . . can be excavated [is] peculiarly great." In fact, promoters of the Schuylkill region went so far as to boast that the mining and transport of coal "requires little or no capital." The coal, these promoters explained, "is dug out of the bowels of the earth, without the aid of steam engines and it is conveyed to the water's edge without a railroad at a trifling expense." At the same time, Schuylkill's operators enjoyed a natural monopoly on red ash coal, a variety favored by domestic consumers. Because the region offered a distinct, high-quality product, the market for Schuylkill's tonnage remained strong between 1825 and 1835 and allowed individual enterprise to flourish.[8]

Unwilling or unable to recognize the specific conditions that bolstered their economic success, industry promoters in Schuylkill County instead elevated "individual enterprise" into a universal theory of individualism and economic growth. In Schuylkill County small-scale, individual enterprise embodied a political philosophy and an economic vision as much as a form of business organization. When the Pennsylvania legislature noted in the early 1830s, for example, that incorporated companies mirrored "the domination of despotism and tyranny" and possessed the power to usurp and trample upon "the liberties of the people," individual operators in Schuylkill County concurred. "The general objections to wealthy corporations acquire additional force in a republican country," one group of operators explained, "as their natural tendency is to create privileged classes and thereby endanger the stability and permanence of our republican institutions." Companies that controlled all aspects of the trade might also control the "numerous dependents" in their employ, thereby acquiring an "undue influence" in local politics. Despite the operators' political pretensions, however, the initial success of Schuylkill's industry had less to do with liberty or republican virtue than with the region's natural, if ultimately exhaustible, advantages.[9]

This initial success, in fact, generated a rivalry between promoters of decentralized industry and their more centralized competitors. Benjamin Bannan, self-appointed defender of the faith of individual enterprise, used his newspaper, the *Miners' Journal,* to fuel the fight. Monopolies, including the Lehigh Company, he explained, employed "anti-republican" policies. They relied on "usurious management," "pillage," and "extortion [of] the consumers" to enrich the "favored few" at the expense of the common good.[10] Monopolies not only undermined the social basis of American republicanism and thwarted the development of industry in general, but they also slowed the social and economic development of the coal regions in particular. In both the Lehigh and Wyoming regions, Benjamin Bannan asserted, the fruits of monopoly were evident: "The result has been that where business is in the hands of a few, there exists that want of bustle and activity which checks the vitality of the trade. . . ." Such was hardly the case in Schuylkill County, however, where the industry welcomed the "enterprise of all." Here, Bannan explained, "a population has grown up, a village has been raised which bids fair to rival the inland towns of our country."[11]

Independent operators in Carbon County agreed. Arguing that the legislature had been far too generous in granting privileges to the Lehigh Company, these operators sought to restrict its power. In fact, when the company approached the legislature, seeking to increase its capital and finance improvements in 1828, public disapproval forced it to negotiate a loan. Such disapproval continued well into the 1830s, as individual operators continued to blame the Lehigh Company for discouraging investment in the middle anthracite fields. Charging that it manipulated toll rates to prohibit competition, these operators complained that the Lehigh Company "scoffs at the citizens" by declaring "we have the power and will exclude you from the market." Supporters of decentralized industry suggested that the company be stripped of its mining or carrying rights, but the legislature failed to act on their petitions.[12]

The *Lehigh Pioneer* disputed these arguments, rightly pointing out that if individual operators had "anything to value," they owed it all to the "legislative charters which they now despise" since individuals had not financed the canals and improvements that made the trade possible.[13] And, far from undermining republicanism, the paper made it clear, the Lehigh Coal and Navigation Company actually strengthened the community since its stock was owned by some three hundred individuals, including widows and orphans. "The wages of the hands are good; the pay is prompt and regular, and hundreds have rendered themselves comfortable in a pecuniary point of view," the *Pioneer* contended. "If, then, the Lehigh Company, by extraordinary exertions, has introduced anthracite coal into market, if it has promptly and well paid those in its employ, if it has been the means of causing a competency to be realized by many and is still sustaining by its operations some two or three thousand people . . . if such are the fruits of monopolies," the *Pioneer* concluded, ". . . give us more of them."[14]

The *Pioneer's* criticism was well taken. Despite their claims to the contrary, individual operators owed their current prosperity less to economic and political superiority than to the "monopolistic" corporate policies that had kept supplies low and prices high. Throughout the first fifteen years of the industry, in fact, the trade had favored this arrangement, which allowed low-capitalized individuals to stock the market while capital-intensive corporations built up and improved their works. Both the Lehigh Company and the Wyoming region's Delaware and Hudson Canal Company, saddled with debt in their early years, had restricted production in favor of high prices and high profits, which benefited operators and miners alike.[15] These companies designed their policies to suit their particular needs, however, not to protect or advance individual enterprise, and when those needs changed, independent operators suffered accordingly.

When shippers refused to lower tolls to help out individual operators in 1831, for example, Benjamin Bannan chastised the corporations for practicing unfair competition. But, as the *Lehigh Pioneer* pointed out, there was nothing "unfair" in the contest. "In business each man *acts for himself* and if a businessman can undersell his competition, he does so," the paper declared, adding that "if we can get our [coal] to market cheaper—supply that market and do so at a less price we will do it without reference to the effect it may produce upon our rivals and why not?" Quoting the time-honored adage that "every man . . . should 'Take care of *number one,*'" the *Pioneer* made it clear that competition, both within and between regions, and not cooperation for mutual benefit, would direct industrial development.[16]

As long as these rivalries were conducted by newspaper editors and confined to political rhetoric, supporters of individual enterprise made a strong case for their position. When industry leaders entered the fray and used their power to manipulate the price of coal, however, they ultimately demonstrated the impotence of small-scale, individual enterprise in a contest with well-capitalized, centralized competitors. At the same time they exposed the limits of republican economic ideology in action. Although small independent companies numerically dominated the industry, their rivals determined the price structure and exerted considerable influence on economic policies as early as the 1840s. Indeed, in the anthracite industry corporate interests and corporate policies regulated the supply and the price of coal. The independent operators' inability to do business at those prices and still post a profit resulted in an unstable, unsafe industry, beneficial only to well-capitalized, centralized competitors.

The Philadelphia and Reading Railroad's challenge to the Schuylkill Canal and Navigation Company's control of the carrying trade in the 1840s well illustrates the social and economic ramifications of this competition. On the surface, the incorporation of the railroad boded well for individual operators since increased competition promised to lower shipping costs. In reality, however, this competition heralded the demise not only of the canal but of individual enterprise as well. Although the effects of this competition would not be immediately apparent, the railroad's control of shipping in the Schuylkill region and its attempt to undercut competing carriers in other regions dealt a severe blow to the independents, if not to the trade in general.

By 1840 the Schuylkill Navigation Canal carried as much tonnage as the combined totals of its competitors and thus dominated not merely the Schuylkill trade but the entire anthracite trade. The Philadelphia and Reading Railroad (P & R), eager to claim this tonnage for its own, immediately lowered carrying charges, and the canal soon followed suit. This competition proved to be more than a "fair and square" price war, however. In 1845 the P & R managed to rent a number of the Navigation's boats, which it then kept idle, limiting the canal's carrying capacity. And since the P & R supplied the operators with the cars that delivered coal to the boats, the canal's tonnage was severely decreased. The Navigation Company fought hard to retain its position, improving the canal, purchasing coal cars, and acquiring docks and landings at various ports, but to no avail. When these expenditures brought the Schuylkill Canal and Navigation Company to the brink of bankruptcy, the company was forced to come to terms with the railroad. In 1849 a truce of sorts brought an end to this rivalry when the Navigation Company agreed to cede all but one-third of the tonnage to the railroad, and the P & R agreed to raise shipping rates.[17]

In the meantime the P & R also worked to extend its influence beyond the limits of the Schuylkill region. Intimations that the P & R intended to monopolize "the whole trade" surfaced as early as 1840, when an anonymous writer, "X," sought to discredit the Lehigh Company's plans to improve the Lehigh Canal. With the support of the *Miners' Journal*, X castigated the company's management, asserting that it operated at a loss and explaining that the railroad offered the only means to save the Lehigh trade. The charges and countercharges exchanged between X and the Lehigh's supporters "Truth" and "Honestus" demonstrated not only an interregional competition but a competition pitting investors in the railroad against those who favored canals.[18]

Although the Lehigh Company apparently won that early round, the price war started by the P & R nevertheless disrupted the Lehigh trade. "If the Reading Railroad and the Schuylkill Canal Company are, like the Kilkenny cats, determined to devour each other, why let them," the *Carbon County Gazette* advised its readers in 1844. The competition may have lowered shipping rates, the paper explained, but at the same time, it also lowered the wholesale price of coal offered by transporters who purchased the tonnage of independent operators. Yet, as the *Gazette* made clear, the competition had in no way lowered production costs. If it had cost independents $2.50 per ton to mine and deliver coal and still pay fair fees and royalties to landowners before the onset of this competition, the paper argued, it did not cost "one penny less" after it. "Whatever may be the result of the strife between rival companies contending for the carrying trade," the *Gazette* insisted, "we can see no necessity for furnishing them with freight for nothing."[19]

Nor were individuals the only operators to suffer through this competition. The Board of Managers of the Lehigh Company also registered complaints. "The effect of this rivalry . . . ," the board reported in 1845, "has been to force upon this Company such a reduction in the price of coal and in the rates of toll, as to render absolutely necessary a great extension of our business in order that the diminished profits per ton may, in the aggregate, produce the amount required to pay the interest and make provisions for the principal of the Company's obligations." Consequently, the company opened more of its land for mining, significantly increasing the supply of available coal. The Delaware and Hudson Canal Company (D & H) responded similarly to the price war. Abandoning its long-time restrictive policy, the D & H countered the railroad's challenge through "wholesale production and wholesale transportation," undertaking extensive improvements and increasing its carrying capacity. Despite the expenses encountered, the D & H survived the price war, posting a 12 percent profit in 1850.[20]

Individual operators, however, could not so easily adjust to these new conditions. The fixed costs faced by these operators left little room for profit even in the best of times, and the low prices induced by this competition stretched them to the limit. When coal sold for $3.25 per ton, for example, operators paid out about 90 cents to mine coal, $1.45 to ship it, and 40 cents in royalty fees. If operators took a 10-cent profit, only 40 cents remained for overhead costs, including maintenance of the mines. Individual operators who were already outproducing their competitors could hardly afford this fight. Although the number of individual operators in Schuylkill County remained high, reaching 120 in 1848, the number of business failures also reached new heights. In fact, as two historians later recalled, in the 1840s there were "but four years of prosperity in the Schuylkill Coal traffic."[21]

Although low prices might have encouraged individual operators to restrict output, the structure of individual enterprise undercut this strategy. The leasing system, for example, that allegedly preserved republican industry, in fact compelled operators to produce regardless of market conditions. Operators, who leased property for a fixed sum, also paid royalties on all coal mined and shipped, and most leases required a minimum annual fee equal to the royalties on forty thousand tons of coal. Since few had access to cash, individual operators had first to sell their coal to meet their obligations. Thus the operators, according to one observer, "rushed into the market in destructive competition with each other . . . as though their object was to break down the market or produce a larger tonnage than their neighbors." Instead of being recognized by the carrying companies as partners or patrons, individual operators "were regarded as machines to provide tonnage . . . that and nothing more." As long as red ash coal—always a marketable commodity—remained available, this excessive production proved profitable; but by 1850 all but one red-ash region in Schuylkill County had been exhausted. Individual operators watched the price of white ash coal drop from almost $6.00 per ton in the 1830s, to $4.00 in the 1840s, to $3.50 in the 1850s. When they had to compete on equal terms with other white-ash producers, they registered surplus coal, not profits, at the close of the shipping season.[22]

Although men like Benjamin Bannan continued to claim that "no company can mine coal as cheap as individuals," in fact, by the mid-1840s individual enterprise had already started on its decline. The depletion of surface coal encouraged by the system meant the end of cheap mining. When investors began to open

new coal regions in Schuylkill County, around the same time
that the P & R Railroad entered the trade, they could not rely
on individual capital to finance the deep mining these new fields
required. Acknowledging the problem of rising costs and lowered prices, these investors championed a new form of enterprise—the improvement company—to sink shaft mines, erect
breakers, and finance the development of these new regions
within the legal limits of individual enterprise.[23] If independents
continued to outnumber these new entities, the emergence of
improvement companies nevertheless testified to the decline of
individual enterprise as a viable business arrangement. The fact
that improvement companies did not mine the lands they developed allowed Schuylkill County's operators to preserve the
fiction of individual enterprise's vitality well into the 1870s. As
the history of improvement companies suggests, however, the
law that prohibited the "combination" of landownership and
mining rights was easily, if not obviously, transgressed.

The Forest Improvement Company (FIC), the most successful
of this new breed, was chartered in 1837. A direct descendant
of the New York and Schuylkill Coal Company, a company that
had made more money in real estate speculation than in coal
mining, the FIC had been developed to open and prepare coal
mines, to construct lateral railroads, and to underwrite major
capital expenditures. With properties stretching over fifteen
thousand acres, the FIC financed and sustained the industry in
the Swatara and West Branch districts of the Schuylkill region.[24]

Although most operators agreed that deep mining required
more than individual capital—not merely to sink the shafts, but
to keep the mines in relatively safe working order—the FIC
nevertheless encountered criticism. In 1846 petitioners complained that the FIC both transported and sold coal and that it
was a "monopoly highly injurious to the individual enterprises
of the citizens of [Schuylkill] County." Two years later a coal
dealer complained about the privileges enjoyed by the FIC.
"This company, which is composed of persons residing in New
York," he wrote to the *Miners' Journal*, "received a charter . . . for
the purpose of making *improvements* in the coal region—thus
conferring corporation privileges upon citizens of other
states . . . while our citizens are compelled to make their own

improvements and open their own mines in the individual capacity." Benjamin Bannan also expressed distrust. "There are
some grave charges made against the Forest Improvement Company," he noted in an editorial. "We would advise the individual
operators to be cautious how they aid a coal company . . . in
gaining a strong foothold in this region. We owe all our prosperity to the triumph of individual enterprise," he added, and
noted that he would expose "corporations clothed with privileges not enjoyed by our individual operators . . . whenever they
come in conflict with individual enterprise."[25]

The Forest Improvement Company did enjoy privileges not
available to individual operators, but the extent of these privileges was not generally known or acknowledged. Although the
law clearly prohibited any merger of mining and landowning
rights, the FIC, through the collieries owned and operated by
the Charles Heckscher family, did mine coal from its own coal
lands, and sold its own coal, too. The extensive mining interests
of the FIC could not be discerned by its charter alone, but both
the improvement company and the Heckscher family mines were
presided over by Charles A. Heckscher, a German-born merchant with wide-ranging financial investments.

Heckscher, together with his nephews Richard Heckscher and
Eugene Borda, owned and operated collieries in the newer coal
regions of Schuylkill County. Although their early operations
were managed by various partners and managers, by 1860 they
operated the five largest, most productive collieries in the region.
The Heckschers' operations grew in Reilly and Foster Township;
however, they chiefly dominated the coal regions in Cass Township, especially the areas known as Heckscherville and Forestville. In 1861 the Heckschers' combined tonnage accounted for
11 percent of the region's total, that is, 284,613 tons. In fact,
the Heckschers' production surpassed that of the thirty smallest
operations combined.[26]

Regional competition and low prices proved less a problem
for the Heckschers than they did for independent operators.
Already by the middle of the 1850s the Heckscher collieries
boasted large breakers and steam engines that produced vast
quantities of cleaner, more salable coal in a variety of sizes, thus

allowing them to meet changing market demands easily. Their well-equipped collieries also allowed them to capitalize on economies of scale and thereby lower production costs. This equipment, which often meant the difference between profit and loss in this variable trade, proved expensive, and few operators in Schuylkill County could afford the $50,000 investment. The Heckschers, however, had little trouble raising the necessary capital since they enjoyed close personal and economic ties to Moses Taylor, a New York financier who had also developed the industry in Scranton. In 1850 Taylor put up $225,000 for FIC bonds signed by Richard and Charles Heckscher to underwrite costly improvements. The Heckschers also had personal and business ties to other financiers including John Austin Stevens, president of the Bank of Commerce in New York, and to politicians like Salmon Chase and Simon Cameron. Financial investments in the iron industry further strengthened the Heckschers' market position. At the same time, Moses Taylor's and Charles Heckscher's financial ties to the Philadelphia and Reading Railroad eased the Heckschers' access to shipping facilities.[27]

The Heckscher coal operations avoided most of the problems associated with individual enterprise thanks to these ties. Nevertheless, they were not completely immune to the problems engendered by this system. For example, at least in the mid-1840s, the Heckschers, like other operators, had to cajole the managers of the Philadelphia and Reading Railroad to provide them with the cars they needed to ship their coal to market. In 1846 the Forestville colliery produced some forty thousand tons and required at least 45 cars at the height of the season and 25 toward the end. Thomas Petherick, colliery manager, spent a good deal of his time convincing John Tucker, the railroad's representative, to provide the cars he needed. "He appears to have no mind of his own," Petherick complained when Tucker failed to reach an early decision, "and I suppose will be influenced . . . by those behind the scenes [in Philadelphia] who played so strongly into the hands of particular operators last year to the prejudice of the trade generally." By 1848, however, the Heckschers had substantially improved their relations with the railroad, when the FIC supplied iron for railroad tracks and thereby gained a reduction in shipping costs. In 1855 Heckscher, Taylor, and

Percy Pyne advanced funds to the railroad to purchase more cars. Heckscher's attorney, Charles Loeser, questioned these ties to the railroad and accused his client of "trying to fix things exclusively for [his] personal pecuniary advantage." In Loeser's view, such cooperation between competing branches of the coal industry "will be the reverse for the balance of the trade of everybody in Schuylkill County."[28] However unpopular their business arrangements, the Heckschers, like their corporate competitors, relied on access to capital resources and transportation rights to build a thriving and relatively stable operation.

Despite changes evidenced by the emergence of improvement companies, local boosters in Schuylkill County still considered individual enterprise to be a viable and competitive form of business organization. "There ought to be at least one beacon light, one monument to show how superior Individual Enterprise is in the development of prosperity...," Benjamin Bannan argued in 1853, "where petty corporations generally governed by petty tyrants do not exist." But if Bannan seemed incapable of testing his ideology against actual economic practice, other residents of the Schuylkill region were not so encumbered. "It is useless to say that individual capital is adequate to carry on the business with success," operator David Brown informed the state legislature. "No colliery that does a business much less than one thousand tons a year... can be made profitable. No colliery capable of producing one hundred tons per annum can ... be put in operation for less than one hundred thousand dollars. No man can judiciously manage ... one hundred thousand tons of coal and place them in the hands of consumers with less than one hundred thousand dollars of working capital and no sane man who is worth two hundred thousand dollars clear of the world," Brown concluded, "would ever invest the whole of it in the coal business."[29]

For Brown incorporation would solve the problems generated by individual enterprise, but this solution found few supporters. Men like Benjamin Bannan, who hoped in vain that corporate privileges elsewhere might be revoked, also believed that a high protective tariff might replicate the expansive days of the trade's infancy, when individual enterprise had thrived. Others, like the editor of the *Mining Register and Democrat*, offered a solution less radical than abandoning individual enterprise but more prac- tical than clinging to past glories: "the coal trade of the Schuylkill especially suffers from want of that reasonable harmony," the paper pointed out, "which, wherever practicable is cultivated among producers in other businesses to guard them against blindly working for mutual destruction. We do not now speak of combinations for prices," which, naturally, the editor despised, "but of union of intellect and concert of action to whatever extent is in mercantile usage legitimate."[30] An association of coal producers to gather market information and then rationally plan and assign tonnage quotas might protect individual operators from destructive competition. Indeed, as the trade operated in the 1850s, only carrying companies were profiting from the business. When the P & R Railroad issued its 1850 annual report, the *Mining Register* publicized the message to individual opera- tors. "The Reading Railroad relies . . . upon the great tonnage we will press into market, avowing that their interest lies not in our obtaining high but low prices! The cat is now fairly out of the bag," the editor explained, that is, "that the Railway expects most of us to go to the wall." If operators and landowners would unite, if colliers could be induced to mine less, not more coal, then, perhaps, prosperity might return. "Instead of boasting, every man how much he can mine and help to overstock the market," the *Mining Register* advised its readers, "the word should be how much can he curtail his production, make coal less of a drug and advance his true interest by working for a profit instead of losing for glory."[31]

Individual operators apparently agreed in theory that the low prices induced by competition and attempts to control the trade proved the root cause of their economic distress. "The only plan we know of to remedy existing evils," one operator ex- plained, is "for all those who are losing money in mining coal . . . to cease work and wait for more propitious times. Noth- ing but a reduction of the quantity sent to market," he con- cluded, "will enhance the price under existing conditions." But despite their apparent belief that collective production control might empower individual operators, and despite the *Mining Register*'s endorsement of the plan, Schuylkill's coal operators could not easily cooperate even in their own self-interest. If the

Coal Mining Association of Schuylkill County argued that "the mining of coal . . . has been conducted without regard to the principle of supply and demand," and therefore claimed the right to regulate the quantity of coal mined, it had no power to enforce production quotas.[32] Stories of the operators' haste to break their commitments to each other were legion throughout the coal regions, and these operators continued to outproduce and undersell each other as if high production somehow generated profits.

Nor were small producers the only culprits. "What others sell at would not matter if [we] five could stick together," Eugene Borda wrote to Richard Heckscher concerning the five largest producers in the region, "but [Johns] alone would spoil it all. . . . This shows what can be expected of the coal trade where five concerned cannot work together when it could be done . . . much to their mutual advantage." When iron companies cooperated to purchase coal below market price, Borda showed no surprise. "With such a set of operators as we have here," he remarked, "the Iron men will be successful [I] have no doubt." Indeed, throughout the 1850s, it was natural disasters, including freshets, floods, and heavy rains, and not the operators' own purposeful action, that remained the most reliable check on overproduction.[33]

Independent operators outside of the Schuylkill region voiced similar complaints. In the northern fields, for example, these operators suffered from the low prices transport companies paid for their coal. Both the D & H Canal Company and the Delaware, Lackawanna, and Western Railroad (D. L. & W.) refused to ship the tonnage of independents, preferring to purchase their output, and individuals had little choice but to accept the prices offered. In the winter of 1853–54 supporters of individual enterprise attempted to rationalize production, just as their counterparts in the Schuylkill region had done. Although operators met in Wilkes-Barre and fixed the price at $1.10 per ton for coal delivered to the boats at the wharves, with the purchaser paying the freight thereafter, a few operators quickly broke the agreement, selling their coal at 95 cents per ton.[34] These operators, the Pittston *Gazette* explained, may have sold the most coal, but those who abided by the agreement "made the most money." In 1856, according to the *Gazette*, a ton of coal brought $1.25, and most operators adhered to this rate. When demand fell off at the close of the shipping season, the paper complained, some operators, "anxious to do business at any cost, began their old practice of forcing sales and adopted a sure measure to reduce the price for the coming season." These operators apparently failed to realize "that every ton forced upon the market, was only placing the knife to their own throats."[35] Although their precarious financial condition no doubt persuaded these operators to sell coal at whatever price they could get, their decision to do so only further weakened their position.

When the North Branch Canal opened new markets in New York in the mid-1850s, independent operators in the northern field expected to exploit them and thereby strengthen their business. Since Pittston was situated nearest the canal, operators there expected Pittston coal to supply the tonnage. Noting that operators to the south of Pittston had a similar advantage in more southern markets, Pittston's operators exhorted those involved in the trade to carve up the expanded market in a reasonable fashion, figuring geographical advantage into the price of coal. The Pittston *Gazette* suggested that a committee be appointed to estimate production capacities and to calculate probable demand in order to assign production quotas. "This will enable all to sell their proportion of coal," the paper promised, "and prevent that ruinous competition [caused] by over anxiety to do business—a business which, unless systematized will never be a source of profit to those engaged in it."[36]

Numerous operators agreed with the *Gazette*'s analysis, but a Wilkes-Barre operator calling himself "Anthracite" insisted that any agreement would prove worthless unless operators could be forced to honor their commitments. "It is easy to see that 'Anthracite' is a bona fide, out and out coal operator," the *Gazette* chided, "for the first move he makes is to abuse some of his neighbors, a plan too often used to effect sales." If operators would stick to their natural outlets and not attempt to dominate the entire trade, the *Gazette* believed, overcompetition might give way to a more systematic, more profitable business.[37]

Although such a plan might have benefited individual operators, carrying companies like the Delaware and Hudson and the Delaware, Lackawanna, and Western were not in the business to supply only their "natural markets." These companies had invested heavily in order to expand their carrying capacity and even employed agents to promote their product and extend their market. High volume and increased sales, not balanced competition, interested them. When Scranton coal appeared on the market in the 1850s, for example, the Lackawanna Coal and Iron Company, the coal-producing arm of the D. L. & W., worked hard to edge out its competitors in the western New York market. One of the company's testimonials proclaimed that "the new Scranton Coal is equal, in every respect, to the Lehigh Coal for foundry purposes." The greatest inducement, however, was "the low rate at which this coal is to be sold, the *price being from 15 to 20 percent less than the Lehigh coal in this market.*" Roswell Hart, the company's agent, "coaxed and treated and bribed" until he succeeded in "getting a fair trial" for Scranton coal. "The result is now I shall sell to all who have not already made contracts or are not too ignorantly stupid to be persuaded even though one rose from the dead. In three years time," he promised George W. Scranton, "Lehigh coal will not be used west of Syracuse [N.Y.] for *any* purpose."[38] Although operators in Pittston were equally close to this market, they could not compete with the Lackawanna Coal and Iron Company and the D. L. & W. Railroad. "The Scranton coal interests has got the Northern and Western market and will hold it so long as Pittston coal has to pay the present rate of freight and tolls . . . ," one observer noted. The problem would be solved, he added, only by increasing the North Branch Canal's capacity and lowering tolls. Then, he concluded, Pittston's operators might "secure the whole western and northern market at once and bid defiance to any anthracite coal interests in the world to take it from them." The dream of selling coal for a "song" and thereby controlling the entire trade died hard among operators, even as they witnessed their own destruction.[39]

Like Schuylkill's operators, individuals in the northern field were in no position to force companies to pay high prices for their coal or to enforce production quotas. "If the coal operators do not enter into an arrangement willingly," the *Gazette* warned in 1857, "they *will be forced into it* at some future period." But another observer, sympathetic to the individual operators' double bind, pointed out that these operators exhibited more than bad faith when they failed to work together. "After investing all their money and probably in debt [and] their creditors clamorous for their just dues," this Wilkes-Barre resident explained, "it is necessary for them to sell at what they can get, hoping for better times, forgetting that every ton sold retards the change so ardently wished for." The best safeguard against failure, in his view, was to sell coal for cash and to "economize in small things."[40] For individual operators, already hard-pressed by low prices, few such "small things" remained; labor costs and mine maintenance seemed to be the only variables in the individual operator's control.

Competition to dominate the trade and the price-cutting this competition generated certainly took their toll on individual enterprise. The real costs of this competition, however, included more than just low profit margins and business failures: unsafe, poorly ventilated mines and inefficient production methods also resulted, as well as habitual cash shortages, undercapitalization of mines, and declining working conditions. These were problems exacerbated by competition, but problems borne by the work force and not the operators. The miners and laborers who produced the coal, and their families, shouldered the heaviest burdens of this anarchistic trade.[41]

"The coal business has become little better than gambling," one Schuylkill County newspaper complained, with the miner playing victim to the operator's role of blackleg. "A man possessing four or five hundred dollars and an old mule, leases a coal mine, gets a store with a hundred weight of sugar or so," the paper continued, "and he is an operator fairly launched in the coal business." The miners on the other hand, "work from month to month and never see the bright face of a dime." Because wages were based on the price of coal, they fluctuated accordingly: a miner earned about $1.25 a day in 1842, but only 80 cents in 1850. Ten years later, contract miners, who were paid by the ton, averaged $10.00 a week, while miners who worked for wages brought home close to $1.00 a day. Considering the seasonable nature of the work, and the fact that mine patches offered no opportunities for women to supplement the family wage except for scavenging fuel, the low prices for coal fell hardest on miners, laborers, and their families—especially on young sons employed as nippers, who operated the doors underground, or as "breaker boys," who manually separated slate from salable coal, or as mule drivers.[42]

Miners may well have been among the most poorly paid workers by the time of the Civil War, but worse yet, many miners rarely saw even their low wages paid in cash. Before an operator could pay his employees, he first had to receive payment for his coal. If collieries hoped to stay afloat, coal miners and laborers had to be satisfied with "store-order" payments in lieu of cash. The store-order system meant that miners took their wages in food and supplies carried by a company store. The system allowed operators to use their cash to ship coal tonnage, and, consequently, kept marginal operators in business and miners and laborers employed. "Stores owned by the operators who by the nature of the business must wait for monthly payments," Benjamin Bannan pointed out, "are positive accommodations to the miners."[43]

Nevertheless, hard-pressed operators could, and did, turn the order system to their own advantage. "Every article sold in White and Brown's store . . . ," one miner complained, "can be purchased at least one-third cheaper at any respectable store unconnected with the coal business." The *St. Clair Sentinel* concurred and charged that workingmen paid 25 to 30 percent more on goods bought in a company store. Other problems between miners and operators were also exacerbated by abuse of the store-order system. Miners questioned the operators' calculation of hours, tonnage, and wages, especially when their purchases outweighed their paychecks. Miners also resented the fact that they had little recourse other than to deal at the employer's store. Even when operators overcharged on work-related items, such as blasting powder, one miner pointed out, "it was no use for a man to speak above board to any of these gentlemen because he knew it was immediate discharge."[44] Individual enterprise may have been, in theory, a democratic experiment, but coal miners and laborers were expected to subordinate their interests and needs to those of the operators so that it might survive.

On the eve of the Civil War, then, the anthracite industry demonstrated a paradox that marked a number of mid-nineteenth-century industries. On the one hand, economic and political leaders in the coal regions preached a "republican" gospel of free enterprise and free labor based on the premise of free competition between equals. On the other hand, the industry was already governed by well-capitalized, centralized, large-scale producers who took advantage of the independent operators' economic instability to dominate the trade. Economic centralization, and the price competition that it led to, did more than alter patterns of economic growth and undermine the structure, if not the myth, of individual enterprise — it also significantly altered patterns of class relations in the coal regions. Because it placed a premium on a tractable work force willing to produce regardless of low wages and poor working conditions, centralization in the industry ultimately required centralization of power in the operators', not the miners', hands. At the same time, however, the process of economic centralization had also effected a radical shift in the social structure of the industry that militated against any easy assumption of that power.

NOTES

1. Philadelphia *Public Ledger,* Nov. 26, 1863; *Miners' Journal,* Feb. 6, 1864 (cited hereafter as *MJ*).

2. *MJ,* Feb. 6, 1864, Dec. 20, 1862.

3. *Lehigh Pioneer,* June 13, 1831.

4. Andrew Roy, *The Coal Mines* (Cleveland, 1876), 238–40. Roy includes statistics of the anthracite trade between 1820 and 1874 collected from Benjamin Bannan's *Coal Reporter.*

5. Clifton K. Yearley, Jr., *Enterprise and Anthracite: Economics and Democracy in Schuylkill County, 1820–1875* (Baltimore, 1961), 33.

6. [The Hudson Coal Company], *The Story of Anthracite* (New York, 1932), 36–37. See also Michael Knies, "Industry, Enterprise, Wealth, and Taste: The History of Mauch Chunk, 1791–1831," *Proceedings of the Canal History and Technology Symposium* 4 (June 1985): 17–45; Howard Benjamin Powell, *Philadelphia's First Fuel Crisis: Jacob Cist and the Developing Market for Pennsylvania Anthracite* (University Park, Pa., 1978); Arthur Chandler, "Anthracite Coal and the Beginnings of the Industrial Revolution in the United States," *Business History Review* 47 (1972): 149–81.

7. By 1825 the Schuylkill trade had also been inaugurated. Around the same time, the Delaware and Hudson Canal Company began the arduous and expensive task of opening the northern anthracite field for

trade with New York. That trade did not begin until 1829. Roy, *The Coal Mines*; John N. Hoffman, "Anthracite in the Lehigh Region of Pennsylvania, 1820–45," in *Contributions from the Museum of History and Technology* (Washington, D.C., 1968), 91–141. Nearly every county in the anthracite region claims the discovery and marketing of coal, but the trade seems to have begun with the Lehigh Coal and Navigation Company. See also "A History of the Lehigh Coal and Navigation Company," included with the *Annual Report*, 1840.

8. "The Anthracite Coal Trade of Pennsylvania," *North American Review* 42 (1836): 248; George F. Hopkins, "A Cursory Review of the Schuylkill Coal Region," pamphlet (New York, 1823), 9–10; see also Eli Bowen, ed., *The Coal Regions of Pennsylvania* (Pottsville, Pa., 1848), and James MacFarlane, *The Coal Regions of America* (New York, 1873), 7–64, for a discussion of topography.

9. Cited in Eliott Jones, *The Anthracite Coal Combinations of the United States* (Cambridge, Mass., 1914), 21. See also Louis Hartz, *Economic Policy and Democratic Thought: Pennsylvania, 1776–1860* (Cambridge, Mass., 1948); Chester Lloyd Jones, *The Economic History of the Anthracite-Tidewater Canals* (Philadelphia, 1908); "Memorial Against an Act to Incorporate the Schuylkill Coal Company to the Senate and House of Representatives of the Commonwealth of Pennsylvania" (n.p., ca. 1822), John N. Hoffman Files, Division of Agriculture and Natural Resources, National Museum of American History; Rowland Berthoff, "Peasants and Artisans, Puritans and Republicans: Personal Liberty and Communal Equality in American History," *Journal of American History* 69 (1982): 579–98.

10. *MJ*, Aug. 28, 1830.

11. Ibid.

12. Jones, *Economic History*, 4, 18–21. Apparently the middle fields were not developed until 1834.

13. *Lehigh Pioneer*, Sept. 13, 1830.

14. Ibid., May 23, 1831.

15. See Michael Shegda, "History of the Lehigh Coal and Navigation Company to 1840," Ph.D. diss., Temple University, 1952, and the company's *Annual Reports*. For the Delaware and Hudson Company, see *A Century of Progress: History of the Delaware and Hudson Company, 1823–1923* (Albany, N.Y., 1925).

16. *Lehigh Pioneer*, May 23, 1831. (This issue is misdated.)

17. Jones, *Economic History*, 133–34; Jules I. Bogen, *The Anthracite Railroads: A Study in American Railroad Enterprise* (New York, 1927), 19–40.

18. Lehigh Coal and Navigation Company, *Annual Report*, 1840. Correspondence between "X" and "Honestus" is included.

19. *Carbon County Gazette*, June 12, 1844.

20. Lehigh Coal and Navigation Company, *Annual Report*, 1845; *A Century of Progress*, 125.

21. Anthony F. C. Wallace, *The Social Context of Innovation* (Princeton, 1982), 134–38; Peter Roberts, *The Anthracite Coal Industry* (New York, 1901), 18; Yearley, *Enterprise and Anthracite*, 58–59; Adolph W. Schalck

and D. C. Henning, *History of Schuylkill County, Pennsylvania* (Harrisburg, Pa., 1907), 108.

22. P. D. Luther, "The Development of the Coal Trade in Schuylkill County," in *A History of Schuylkill County* (New York, 1881), 58, 63. Prices are from Yearley, *Enterprise and Anthracite*, 77.

23. *MJ*, Dec. 22, 1862; Yearley, ibid., 133–42.

24. Yearley, ibid., 42; Charter, Forest Improvement Company, Jan. 12, 1839, in the Charles A. Heckscher Company Papers, the Moses Taylor Collection, Manuscript Division, New York Public Library (cited hereafter as CAH Papers, NYPL).

25. Petition in Charles Loeser Papers, vol. 12, Historical Society of Schuylkill County, 251 (cited hereafter as HSSC); *MJ*, Feb. 19, 1848.

26. Yearley, *Enterprise and Anthracite*, 143. Yearley notes that Eugene Borda, like a few other large producers, sold his own coal. He is apparently unaware of the relation between Borda and Charles and Richard Heckscher. Daniel Hodas, *The Business Career of Moses Taylor* (New York, 1976), 82; *MJ*, Jan. 11, 1862. Total production for the county was 2,511,104; total for the thirty smallest operations was 277,166.

27. Hodas, *Moses Taylor*, 82, 153. The bonds are in the CAH Papers. It should be noted that this collection is, for the most part, unprocessed. See also Alexander Du Bin, ed., *Massey, Lea, and Heckscher Families* (Philadelphia, 1948). Charles Heckscher, according to Du Bin, "was a prominent merchant of New York City. He became associated with Mr. Forrest and Moses Taylor of New York in the Forrest [*sic*] Improvement Company and in the anthracite coal fields" (12). Richard Heckscher "was president of the New York and Schuylkill Coal Company and manager of the Forrest Improvement Company. He developed and opened numerous collieries" (12). Richard married John A. Stevens's daughter. Letters between Charles Heckscher and Salmon Chase in the Chase Papers, Library of Congress, attest to close personal ties between them. For breakers and other improvements see Anthony F. C. Wallace, *St. Clair* (New York, 1987), 36–37.

28. Thomas Petherick to CAH, Apr. 12, 1846, May 5, 1846, CAH Papers, NYPL; Hodas, *Moses Taylor*, 153; Borda to CAH, Feb. 2, 1860, CAH Papers, NYPL.

29. *MJ*, Feb. 5, 1853; "Petition of David Brown and Others for an Act of Incorporation for Sinking a Shaft at their Colliery in Schuylkill County," pamphlet (Pottsville, Pa., 1856), 9–12.

30. *Mining Register and Democrat*, Mar. 16, 1850.

31. Luther, "The Development of the Coal Trade," 63; *Mining Register and Democrat*, Feb. 2, 1850, Apr. 20, 1850.

32. *MJ*, June 1, 1850.

33. The five referred to were Richard Heckscher, William Milnes, George W. Snyder, William H. Johns, and Kirk and Baum. Borda to Richard Heckscher, Jan. 17, 1860, Borda to CAH, Feb. 2, 1860, CAH Papers, NYPL.

34. "Experiences of Albert H. Repp, Coal Miner," in Miscellaneous

Alphabetical Files, Lackawanna County Historical Society, Scranton, Pa.; Pittston *Gazette,* Jan. 30, 1857.

35. Pittston *Gazette,* ibid.

36. Ibid.

37. Pittston *Gazette,* Feb. 6, 1857. See also Feb. 13, 1857.

38. Bogen, *The Anthracite Railroads,* 83; W. David Lewis, "The Early History of the Lackawanna Iron and Coal Company: A Study in Technological Adaptation," *Pennsylvania Magazine of History and Biography* 96 (1972): 424–68. Roswell Hart to George W. Scranton, Apr. 12, 1852, Scranton Papers, Lackawanna County Historical Society.

39. J. Eaton to H. G. Taggert, Aug. 28, 1858, Scranton Papers, Lackawanna County Historical Society. See also, William Kidd, "A Few Things Interesting to Coal Burners," pamphlet, Littell File, Lackwanna County Historical Society.

40. Pittston *Gazette,* Jan. 30, 1857; "Carbon" to Editor, ibid., Feb. 20, 1857.

41. See chapter 3; Yearley, *Enterprise and Anthracite,* 165–80.

42. *St. Clair Sentinel,* Feb. 13, 1862, cited in George Bergner, pub., *Legislative Record: The Debates and Proceedings of the Pennsylvania Legislature* (Harrisburg, 1862), 779; Yearley, ibid., 168. "Nippers" was the name given to doortenders in the mines. See Homer Greene, *The Blind Brother, A Story of the Pennsylvania Coal Mines* (New York, 1887), for a literary portrayal of child labor in the mines. Wages cited in *MJ,* June 1, 1850, and Wallace, *The Social Context of Innovation,* 135.

43. G. O. Virtue, "The Anthracite Mine Workers," *Bulletin of the Bureau of Labor* 2 (1897): 728–74; *MJ,* May 26, 1862.

44. James Foly to *Workingmen's Advocate,* Feb. 13, 1858, handwritten draft in Miscellaneous Manuscripts, HSSC; *St. Clair Sentinel,* Feb. 13, 1862; Joseph Patterson, "After the W.B.A.," *Publications of the Historical Society of Schuylkill County* 4 (1912-14): 179.

3

The Miners:
Economic Centralization
and Class Formation
1840–60

When Philip Hone visited the coal regions in 1831, he described, with obvious pleasure, a typical Sunday in Carbondale. "The rattling of the cars, the explosion of gun powder and the clanking of pickaxes are now as still as the tombs of the Capulets," he noted in his diary, "and the miners who yesterday . . . looked like citizens of the netherworld, are seen this morning on their way to church clean and well-dressed, with long coats and gilt buttons, high shirt collars and brooches in their bosoms." Such symbols of respectability would not have surprised Eli Bowen, who, in 1848, considered the moral condition of the mining population to be "vastly superior to that of the same class in any other country." Benjamin Bannan concurred, and he traced the roots of this respectability to the reciprocal interests that linked miners and operators. "Taken as a whole," he wrote of Schuylkill County's work force, "the miners and laborers . . . are probably quite as intelligent as any body of men in the Union. . . . As citizens," he added, "they are as good as the capitalist, merchant or manufacturer."[1]

This image of a respectable, responsible, and well-remunerated work force reinforced the general belief that the system of industrial capitalism generated mutually beneficial economic growth. Eager to prove that American enterprise need not follow a European class model, industrialists and their supporters promoted an ideal of economic progress grounded in republican virtue. From their point of view, a "harmony of interests" be-

43

tween employers and employed would protect the structure of republican society and guarantee economic security and independence for all who practiced sound investment strategies, temperance, and well-regulated work habits.

As early as the middle 1830s, however, the material circumstances of a wage earner's life belied these egalitarian claims. The consequences of reckless financial speculation coupled with currency inflation fell especially hard on wage earners who were denied steady employment following the economic crisis of 1837.[2] At the same time, industrialization and the expansion of the national market had engendered a new industrial order that not only transformed artisans and craftsmen into wage earners but also undermined their customary rights and culture in the process. As an increasing number of citizens were rendered more vulnerable to the vagaries of a competitive market system, labor discontent surfaced. In New York City and Philadelphia, in Lowell, Massachusetts, and Newark, New Jersey, wage earners tested the employers' concept of republican industry and generally found it wanting.[3] Throughout the industrial North, in fact, evidence of a class-based, social inequality was already explicit by the 1840s.

Although the process of industrialization in the anthracite regions differed from that in established commercial or manufacturing centers, it proved no less complicated. In some cases the advent of the trade itself transformed a "howling wilderness" into bustling coal-producing towns. In others, however, the industry encroached upon areas boasting a long and proud agricultural tradition.[4] If the coal trade rapidly assumed economic ascendancy in eastern Pennsylvania after 1820, residents of these agricultural districts did not always agree on just how far and how fast industrialization should proceed. Some sought to harness growth, assuming that agriculture and anthracite could peacefully coexist. Thus they questioned the legislature's liberal grants of incorporation, and they supported the Democratic party's "pay as you go" economic philosophy against the Whigs' more expansive plans. When the agricultural districts in Schuylkill County, for example, opposed rechartering the Bank of the United States, their attitude startled industry supporters. "We cannot believe for one moment that the people of this county can be induced to oppose a measure which is so fraught with the best interests of the Commonwealth," the *Miners' Journal* argued in 1836. But residents of the agricultural districts were not at all convinced that their interests would be served by the expansion of banking facilities, the infusion of outside capital, or the mushroom growth of mining centers like Pottsville or Mauch Chunk. Neither were they eager to pay any taxes that might accompany these measures. Such different economic aspirations were not easily reconciled in the coal regions or elsewhere, and, especially in the years before the Civil War, they significantly influenced political decision making.

Industry promoters worked hard to convince their critics that the expansion of the industry benefited farmers as much as speculators. When the *Carbon County Gazette* noted that the coal trade had generated some two million dollars worth of wages in a single year, it asked its readers to consider just how those wages might be spent. A full two-thirds of the total, or sixty cents of each dollar, the paper asserted, was "paid out for provisions . . . such as flour, meat, potatoes, garden vegetables, chop, hay and straw. . . . Who will say," the *Gazette* then queried, "that the farmers of Pennsylvania have not a deep interest in the prosperity of the coal trade?" But if thriving industry promoted a thriving market for local farmers, it also altered social and political configurations in the region, threatening the agricultural districts' traditional preeminence. Indeed, the decision to remove Schuylkill County's political seat from Democratic, agricultural Orwigsburg to Whig, cosmopolitan Pottsville testified to the revolutionary consequences of this transformation.[5]

Industrial expansion likewise restructured class relations in the coal regions, undermining the industrial "harmony" that had characterized the industry's formation. Practical miners had proved scarce in these early years, and they generally commanded the respect of independent operators, or colliers, who often worked alongside them in the mines. With new mines being driven nearly every week, labor remained scarce, and companies imported English, Scotch, and Welsh miners to man the works.[6] Experienced in the trade, these immigrants accepted a certain level of industrial discipline—early starting times and the strict measurement of output, for instance—in exchange for a certain level of industrial privileges, including adequate housing and a free supply of fuel. No great differences in status separated these miners from their employers; they shared, for the most part, similar ethnic and religious backgrounds and an apparent belief in mutually beneficial economic growth. Satisfactory wages and working conditions sustained this belief throughout the 1820s and early 1830s, and the vision of "republican" industry—or at least financial independence—seemed a real possibility.[7]

This industrial harmony was further sustained by the temporary abundance of easily accessible coal that made it possible for miners to employ relatively safe technology. In the Schuylkill region, for example, where drift mines, or tunnels, were driven horizontally into coal veins, miners relied on hand tools, not blasting powder, to bring down the coal. Although shaft mines were sometimes sunk, these rarely reached below water level in the early days; if they did, miners extracted the coal and water that collected by means of buckets brought up by a hand windlass or horse gin. The entire process required, at most, a half-dozen men to produce the forty buckets deemed a good day's work. Similarly, in the Summit Hill and Room Run mines of the Lehigh district, operators employed an open-pit quarrying system manned by laborers who removed the coal with pickaxes and driving wedges. In the days before deep mining, although hand labor proved arduous, the miners' job was not yet excessively dangerous or demanding. Experienced miners earned $1.00 a day in 1828 and laborers earned 80 cents; one year later, miners earned about $1.25 for producing 1½ tons of coal per day— about the same as wages paid to skilled craftsmen.[8]

Already by the mid-1830s, however, the miners' position in the industry began to decline, and wages failed to keep pace with these early levels. At a time when authorities agreed that workingmen required at least $6.00 a week to live comfortably, wage rates dropped to about 87.5 cents per day for miners and 70 cents for laborers. Since wage rates were mediated by the price of coal, the increasing competition among carrying companies that lowered prices likewise lowered wages. Even when wages rose slightly in the 1840s, the fact that miners were expected to produce three tons of coal per day—about twice their expected output in the 1830s—meant that they worked at lower rates than they had previously. At the same time, charges for work-related items including kerosene and blasting powder were increasing, thus further lowering the miners' real wages.[9] A vast expansion of the mining population also weakened the miners' position in the industry. In Schuylkill County alone the number of miners increased from about 600 in 1830 to 3,500 in 1842 and tripled over the next ten years.[10] At the same time that the miners' job grew increasingly more dangerous and the market price for coal became more unstable, this increased labor supply seriously constrained the miners' efforts to increase their wages or improve working conditions.

Despite these obvious changes in the structure of "republican" industry, supporters nevertheless continued to assert that the system of industrial capitalism generated a harmonious social order of competitive, independent producers. Even as cut-throat competition between rival transport companies lowered prices to the point where only large, well-capitalized collieries could succeed, these critics saw no connection between the industrial system, the rise of economic centralization, and the miners' recognition of their own class interests as separate from those of their employers. Whether they realized it or not, however, the low prices induced by unchecked competition together with the overproduction of coal that resulted had already destroyed the social and geological basis of republican industry in the coal regions.[11] Small independent producers could not operate on a cash basis and expect to stay in business at such prices. These independent operators, who produced the bulk of the industry's tonnage, survived only by paying their work force intermittently, and even then in store orders or scrip, thus demonstrating the class discrimination built into the economic system. Although industry boosters like Benjamin Bannan insisted that this store-order system benefited the miners as much as it did their employers, in fact it laid bare the workers' subordinate position in the industry and in the community. Especially when some operators abused the store-order system, overcharging their employee/customers, miners challenged the inequality at the base of this so-called republican order.

Although residents boasted that labor strife had not marred

economic development in the coal regions, by the 1840s coal miners and laborers began to question the direction of industrial development and to assert their interests in an industry that had seemingly reneged on its promised reciprocity. One "hard worker," writing to the *Pottsville Emporium,* criticized the social changes that had accompanied industrialization and called public attention to the "increasing contempt for the working classes" expressed by those deemed "entrepreneurs." "It is enterprise when a company issues shin plasters . . . to pay their workmen and then employs a broker to shave the same at an enormous discount," he protested, "but it is *outrageous* for those cheated . . . to expose and condemn such illegal conduct."[12] Miners in Schuylkill County could readily sympathize with this complaint, especially as the store-order system flourished, and in July 1842 they launched the industry's first regional strike. These striking miners, about 1,500 strong, called a meeting on July 7 to plan their strategy and publicize their position.[13] "We protest . . . against the present order system . . . ," they proclaimed, "because we lose one-third if not one-half of our hard earnings . . . ; because we are obliged to deal in places where we do not wish to deal . . . ; because we cannot get such goods as we want and we are obliged to take such as we do not want. . . . Finally," they added, they protested the order system "because it is an immoral mode of doing business and more especially, because it takes from us the only pleasure enjoyed by the workingman of spending his earnings where and in what manner he pleases."[14]

If operators and their supporters disputed these complaints, contending that only a very few abused the system, it was not abuse alone that provoked the strike: miners based their protest on the fact that the order system ensured their dependence on the operator and confirmed their subordinate social and economic position. Striking miners, who constituted about one-third of all those employed in the region, did not challenge the system that linked wages to the price of coal, nor did they demand a wage increase. They struck to call attention to increasing inequality, to assert their interests as producers, and to restore the reciprocal basis of industrial "harmony." Although critics would interpret their efforts as evidence of violent threats against life and property, the "republican" underpinnings of the miners' strike, the belief that miners and operators had equal rights and obligations, as well as an equal interest in the industry, fueled strikes in the anthracite region at least until the end of the century.[15] Miners, more than their employers, apparently believed that republican industry could work, but only when labor and capital met as equals. The miners, like other industrial workers, attempted to organize their forces to amass the power required to assert such equality. To the operators, however, the very notion of labor organization smacked of unfair coercion, and they promptly asserted their own power to protect their indisputable authority in the industry.

When striking miners marched along the Norwegian Railroad on Saturday, July 9, the situation heated up. The marchers, who were largely Irish and armed with "clubs and other weapons," according to the *Miners' Journal*, convinced laborers along the line to quit work. The citizens of Minersville were allegedly so "alarmed for their safety on account of divers threats and demonstrations of intended violence" that the sheriff called on local militia captains to order out their troops. Around midnight some 150 armed soldiers arrived in Minersville only to find "everything quiet," and they marched out the following morning. The next day, two companies were ordered to Pottsville, where, as the *Miners' Journal* explained, the sheriff "held them in readiness to act with our own military should circumstances require it." By this time, some 1,000 men had gathered about three miles from Pottsville. As they marched toward the town, they were met by the sheriff and the chief burgess, both of whom had issued proclamations defining the limits of the law and explaining the acts which constituted a riot. When officials requested that the strikers dispose of all "clubs and sticks," they apparently complied peacefully. "Indeed," Benjamin Bannan noted, "their behavior throughout the whole day was characterized by moderation and decorum."[16]

After assembling in Pottsville and listening to more speeches, the strikers appointed a committee to confer with the operators. A few miners, no doubt fearing for their jobs, declined nomination, and the group then named Democratic party spokesmen Thomas Brady, Edward Cochran, Edward O'Conner, and Robert Palmer to the committee. As the *Miners' Journal* made clear, however, the operators "very properly refused to have any communication" with this group. One of the colliers, the paper explained, "very wisely told them that when he wanted guardians to take charge of his business he would get the court to appoint them." According to the *Miners' Journal*, the operators would have acceded had the committee advised the strikers to meet individually with their employers. "But on the contrary, with the most consummate effrontery and impudence," the paper complained, "they strut forward between the operator and his men, as monitors or dictators, to advise and instruct him in the management of his private business and foolishly supposed that such meddling influence would be tolerated."[17] Managerial prerogative—that is, the operator's claim to sole authority in the workplace—apparently took precedence over any grievance a miner might harbor.

When the strike continued into the next week, the chief burgess of Pottsville issued another proclamation urging citizens to arm themselves in anticipation of any attempts to violate the law. He also promised to protect any miners wishing to "pursue their occupation," that is, break the strike. Although the *Miners' Journal* suggested that turbulent miners determined the decision to employ armed force, only sporadic episodes of violence or "outrages" were reported in its pages. In Wadesville, for example, a group compelled miners there to join the strike, and the sheriff arrested a few "ringleaders." The following week, on July 22, miners apparently threw stones at a house where strikebreakers resided, intending, according to the *Miners' Journal*, "to tear down the building and murder the inmates." When a foreman who lived nearby arrived on the scene, he fired two shots into the crowd, thereby settling the matter. The next morning the sheriff arrested one "ringleader," who had been identified "by his dress and voice, as well as strong circumstantial evidence . . . such as having used threats and foretelling the shedding of blood." Reporting another arrest one week later, the *Miners' Journal* applauded this victory for law and order. "There is a full determination evinced to arrest every man who has been prominently engaged to any of these outrages," the paper explained, "for the purpose of making an example to prevent future occurrences of the kind."[18] The decision to employ armed force in anticipation of violence, not in defense, and the operators' ease in securing this military assistance, provided clear evidence of an industrial social hierarchy well in place by the 1840s. It also suggested that, without the help of coercive power, the operators might have been compelled to consider their employees' grievances rather than intimidate them into submission.

Although declining wages, status, and working conditions, as well as an increasingly dangerous and unstable industry, might well have explained the outbreak of the strike, the *Miners' Journal*, representing the interests of independent operators, offered a different view. It was the strike itself, and not the conditions that led up to it, that had provoked dissatisfaction, and the paper blamed Democratic politicians, not the order system, for stirring up trouble. "Turnouts . . . are productive of ill-feeling and jealousy between the employer and the employed," the paper made clear, "[and] at such times . . . the amicable footing which before existed is suddenly destroyed." From the journal's point of view, the order system represented not the subordination of labor's interests to capital's needs, but the shared interests that linked miners and operators. Only those with the most jaundiced view could suppose that operators would not pay equitable wages if they were able to do so; indeed, the paper insisted, operators had devised the order system merely to keep miners employed despite hard times, not to survive the cutthroat competition that threatened the independent operators' survival. And if some operators abused the system, a fact that even the *Miners' Journal* reluctantly acknowledged, a strike could not settle grievances. "After using remonstrances and other orderly means without avail, the proper plan," the paper explained, "would have been to seek employment elsewhere and not to remain with any man who would so far forget the bounds of right and justice, as to oppress you." And where grievances existed, the journal urged miners and laborers to seek redress through their individual contracts, always remembering "that your interests are identical and that whatever benefits [the operator] will also benefit you."[19]

The termination of the strike in no way resolved the issues that provoked it. Neither did it silence critics of the store-order system or the social imbalance that the system represented. Some five months after the strike, Thomas Brady, A. W. Leyburn, and Robert Palmer restated the miners' position and reevaluated the operators' actions during the strike. "When moral combinations among the sufferers seemed to expose the [store-order system's] hideousness if not to threaten its overthrow," they pointed out, "we beheld with what violence of language and threats of blood its supporters attempted to crush the incipient feeling of dissatisfaction." Insisting that the military presence denied the strikers their constitutional rights, they added that truth "was suppressed and falsehood circulated—everything was done to draw on the sufferers the current of public malevolence." The operators' derogation of the miners' complaints and their reliance on armed force to impose order suggested to these writers that a dangerous social revolution was well underway.

The *Pottsville Emporium* reiterated this theme and linked labor strife and social inequality to the operators' "intemperate" business methods. Likening their dependence on the store-order system to "drinking moral rum," the paper questioned the social consequences of a system that encouraged overproduction while enslaving workingmen. "The [laborer] feels no longer any moral obligation towards his oppressor . . . ," the *Emporium* warned its readers. "The hope of bettering his condition . . . by laying up his little savings is the only tie that binds a laborer to the tail of society . . . and having removed this bond," the paper wondered, "how can we expect them to respect the rights of those who trample them and their just claims in the dust?"[20]

Increased labor activity throughout the coal regions, as elsewhere, underscored the *Emporium*'s point. When operators reduced wages in 1846, miners employed by Henry Heilner and Gideon Bast in Schuylkill County turned out to restore wages and protest store-order payments. After a three-week strike the employers compromised, raising weekly wages to seven dollars instead of the six originally offered. This apparent concession alarmed other operators. "After what has taken place . . . ," one colliery manager complained, "we must soon put up our prices but I wish to do what must be done without the appearance of compulsion and to delay it as long as may be prudent." At least in this case neither the market price of coal nor the operator's economic position was at issue: this manager sought to maintain his absolute right to control wages regardless of his ability to afford an increase.[21]

The operators' reluctance to raise wages when their prices increased belied their commitment to "shared interests" and testified to their very different understanding of "republican" industry and society. Where the miners claimed social and economic equality based on equal contributions to production and the labor theory of value, operators continued to identify their particular economic interests with the public good and claimed sole authority in the industry to protect those interests. Critics of this short-sighted reasoning castigated these "illiberal" capitalists who, as the *Mining Register and Democrat* put it, refused to raise wages when prosperity raised prices, thus compelling workmen to strike for their share of the increase. "We feel no hesitation in saying that the movements of laborers in the fluctuations of prices are infinitely more justifiable than those of capitalists who," the paper asserted, "can combine more rapidly and more secretly and . . . can always protect themselves against unjust claims."[22]

Although successful strikes proved rare in the anthracite regions in the 1840s and 1850s, numerous workers in the trade continued to turn out. Boatmen employed on the Schuylkill Navigation Canal struck for higher wages in 1847 around the same time that railroad workers in Carbon County walked off the job. The following year miners in Schuylkill County organized a union, and in 1849 members of the Bates Union suspended production for three weeks' time. The operators met this suspension with a lockout and the union soon disbanded, but miners nevertheless continued to protest low wages and operators continued to view these strikes as unwarranted attacks on property rights.[23] When some miners capitalized on rising coal prices to demand higher wages in 1852, for example, operators saw no justice in their claim. "Our men feel so independent that they are quite uncontrollable," one operator complained, "and the mining costs us more than it could be done for in previous circumstances."[24] Such operators, more interested in controlling overhead costs than in promoting "republican" industry by paying fair wage rates, deliberately sought to keep wages as low as the market would bear. Their economic interests rested squarely on their ability to control labor costs and on the recognition of the employers' right to set the terms of the wage bargain. Labor organization and "turnouts," then, struck at the very heart of this new industrial order.

Although English and Welsh miners had a long tradition of labor organization and were known to employ the strike weapon whenever conditions warranted it, it was Irish miners, especially those of the famine immigration of the 1840s, who were charged with disrupting social order. An ethnic group that tended to organize economic and community life around an extended family network, the Irish were considered to be a particularly "clannish" people. If these family ties often ensured economic survival for recent immigrants, however, they took on new meaning in the coal regions, where Irish immigrants constituted the largest group of new miners and laborers. By the 1850s observers drew sharp distinctions between the "turbulent" Irish miners and their more respectable "right-thinking" English and Welsh counterparts. The Irish, according to Benjamin Bannan, demonstrated a "tendency to retain a distinct, exclusive nationality"—a tendency eschewed by the "quieter and better class of emigrants." If Bannan was willing to admit that "it would be unjust to charge all the difficulties on the Irish population," he nevertheless contended that "all the open outrages, as far as we can learn, are committed by Irishmen and just in proportion as the Irish element predominates in any district, the outrages increase."[25]

Because Irish immigrants lacked the funds to set themselves up as contract miners, they tended to be employed by centralized, well-organized companies that needed to attract large numbers of men to their often geographically isolated, and largely undeveloped, mining towns. Thus Irish immigrants, whose cultural and political values often clashed with those of their employers, comprised the bulk of the work force in newer coal districts like Cass Township in Schuylkill County, Hazleton in Luzerne County, or Jeansville in Carbon County. Entering the industry at the very moment when price competition among transporters proved most fierce, these miners seemed particularly threatening when they stood together to assert their class interests.[26] For example, after a Boston newspaper reported that "a new and exclusively Irish secret organization called the Molly Maguires" had come into power, the *Miners' Journal* prominently reprinted the article, implying that strikes among Irish miners emanated from a sinister, well-organized foreign force.[27]

The coincidence of this increased Irish presence with increased strike activity in the newer coal districts encouraged critics to blame social conflict on Irish intemperance and culturally derived disorder, not on economic "combination" and the operators' wage policies. Ignoring the material and social circumstances of labor discontent, these observers instead insisted that moral depravity had induced the strikes and that moral reform would resolve the problem. Industrial harmony, these critics insisted, would flourish as soon as operators banned liquor from their property.[28] But it was not "rum" that had stirred unrest in the coal regions. The Irish miners' ethnic solidarity and minority status may well have enhanced their ability to stand together in labor disputes, but it was an unbalanced economic system and an unsafe, unstable industry that provoked strikes in the coal region, regardless of the ethnic identity of the strikers.

In fact, although Irish immigrants surely contributed their fair share of strikers and labor agitators, they by no means controlled the supply. Reports of strikes were widespread in the mid-nineteenth century and came from a variety of regions and industries, suggesting that the wage system and the social subordination of labor to capital, and not character deficiencies, induced turnouts. When the Associated Mechanics of Schuylkill County organized a protective union in 1853, for instance, there was nothing particularly "Irish" about the group, although its demands echoed those voiced by miners some ten years earlier. Calling attention to the fact that their wages did not allow mechanics to purchase their own houses or to "secure the means of moral cultivation" necessary in a republican social order, they reminded master mechanics that they "*ought to sympathize* with their craft" and support all reasonable demands. These mechanics declared the first Monday in April to be the date for a wage increase and resolved to strike against those employers who did not acquiesce peacefully. Convinced of its just and unassailable position, this association also resolved that, should any employer refuse the increase, it would "be taken as a sundering of all present interests between them and us as employer and employed."[29] These mechanics, like the miners, organized themselves to assert their rights under an economic system that would otherwise have rendered their labor power a commodity like any other. They organized not to dismantle republican industry, as critics charged, but to achieve that much-talked-about "harmony of interests." Mechanics, miners, railroad workers, and the like, Irish or not, had learned firsthand that labor and capital defined the "common good" differently. They had also learned—and would continue to learn—that economic and social power, not logic, republican theory, or employer goodwill, would determine their position in the industrial order.

If increased labor activity exposed economic and social inequities inherent in the industrial system, the financial panic of 1857 and the depression that followed demonstrated the social costs of such inequities. As the price of coal dropped and wages hit a new low, strikes and turnouts continued. This time, however, the strikes proved more violent and the strikers more adamant in their demands. When miners in Schuylkill County struck the Heckscher works in the spring of 1857, calling for the removal of an obnoxious boss, colliery manager Eugene Borda informed county prosecutor Charlemagne Tower that the miners "just now are threatening to burn the breakers and have threatened the Engineer . . . who is [afraid] to remain at work." Instructing Tower to call upon the sheriff to provide "a strong force to protect our works," and, incidentally, to protect strikebreakers, Borda made it clear that the company would pay for such military protection. "Let the force be strong," he added, "and have instructions given them not to leave . . . until they have arrested all the men (Irish) . . . whose names can be given by the boss. . . ."[30] Foreshadowing his future performance as provost marshal for Schuylkill County, Tower made good use of his political power to carry out the operators' demands.

The military presence, however, provided only a temporary respite from industrial unrest. As the economic depression deepened, the specter of whole communities of underemployed, underpaid miners and their desperate families haunted the keepers of social order. "Hunger knows no law and it begins to tell dreadfully in many parts of [Schuylkill] County," Borda explained later that same year, "where men have had but little work this summer and are idle now with nothing coming and positively starving." Confessing that he had never before witnessed such widespread unemployment and such high prices for food, Borda questioned his superior's decision to lay off the work force without paying them. "We are in a powder keg," he explained, "and a spark will be enough to bring ruin all around. You must not therefore tell me discharge hands and do not pay them, it cannot be done without increasing risks. The operators must come together in faith [and] distribute food in the shape of bread. . . . The future is dark with difficulties," he concluded, "which we must face coolly. . . and not wait until the worst comes."[31]

The story was much the same throughout the coal regions. Especially in towns where large companies dominated the local economy, residents expected those companies to keep them afloat. For example, when company stores in Carbon County would no longer extend credit in the spring of 1858, residents of Summit Hill apparently burned down or threatened to burn down the offending stores. "It is not pretended that any of the laborers were wronged by their employers or others," the *Mauch Chunk Gazette* explained. "But although many of them are already largely in debt, they ask for more, and it being refused [they] seek revenge by burning the principal businessmen out of house and home." Fearing further disorder, local citizens watched over the coal works and stores. When four men approached the McClean and Company coal breaker, allegedly carrying combustible materials, namely straw, one watchman opened fire. The superintendent, awakened by the shots, grabbed his loaded gun and fired on the men who, nevertheless, escaped. Following this "outrage," local residents organized the Carbon Guards, a sixty-man uniformed force commanded by Captain A. J. Wintersteen and "amply prepared" for any emergency. "The real cause of this trouble is, doubtless, a large laboring population without employment," the *Gazette* noted, "and as long as they persist in voting down . . . every measure calculated to protect American Industry . . . they must blame none but themselves if our . . . mines are closed for want of demand for our coal." Unable, or perhaps unwilling, to perceive a more systemic problem—even in the face of arson and uniformed armed citizens—critics blamed Irish miners and their Democratic loyalties for a national financial crisis.[32]

The trouble did not end here, however. In June miners in neighboring Jeansville, Beaver Meadow, and Yorktown struck for higher wages. Yet even the *Carbon Democrat* deplored their efforts. "We never knew any good to result to the laboring population from these turnouts," the paper contended. "A strike at this time is particularly uncalled for, and evinces such a want of feeling as well as appreciation of what is right that we cannot forbear alluding to it." Although the *Mauch Chunk Gazette* insisted that the majority of miners desired to work and were "prevented from doing so by a few mischief makers," several hundred miners held a meeting at which they resolved to remain on strike. That same day officers arrested John Gallagher, a "ringleader" at the Yorktown Colliery, for threatening violence on strikebreakers. These officers, the *Gazette* explained, expected to return to Yorktown to "nab a few more," and within a week the Yorktown miners were back at work "of course at the old prices."[33]

In Schuylkill County miners employed in Ashland also turned out for higher wages late in May 1858. These miners apparently marched throughout the county, according to the *Miners' Journal,* "coercing men who are satisfied with their situation" to stop work. "The situation of all classes is such in this region," the paper pointed out, "that they must work or starve and the prudent portion prefer working even at low wages, to standing idle. . . ." After the strike spread into St. Clair, coal operators presented their case to the sheriff, who then deemed it necessary to request military assistance to maintain law and order. With the help of the First Regiment, five ringleaders were arrested and held on five hundred dollars bail. Ironically, at the same time that the operators and the sheriff were containing what they preceived as a violent threat to social order, miners in Ashland convened a meeting where they set out their view of the problem. Explaining that they could no longer support their families on the low wages offered, and unable to afford the blasting powder, paper, cotton, and oil essential to their work, these miners resolved to cut back production in hopes of raising prices since "nothing less than a general strike by all persons employed in and about the anthracite collieries of Pennsylvania will give to us remunerating wages for our hard labor." They also resolved that in the process of the strike they would not "get drunk, bellow, make threats, give insults, [or] stop those who wish to work . . . so that," they concluded, "our employers or any evil disposed persons may not find any blame in any of our actions during our 'strike' for our rights." Although the *Miners' Journal* deeply sympathized with their plight, the editor offered only philosophical balm. "Half a loaf," Benjamin Bannan suggested, is certainly "better than no bread at all." Like his colleagues in Carbon County, he agreed that only a protective tariff could solve the miners' problems.[34]

By June 12 the strike was effectively over, and within a week the "Ashland Gang" that had been arrested in St. Clair was brought to trial. Three of the five arrested were found guilty and were imprisoned for thirty days. In a similar case tried around the same time, two other miners were charged with conspiracy "in endeavoring in an unlawful manner to raise the wages of workingmen." Although the jury found the defendants guilty, they recommended leniency on "account of their being ignorant and misguided by designing persons." This jury apparently blamed Democratic spokesmen, especially the editor of the *Workingmen's Advocate,* for leading the miners astray.[35] "Every word spoken or published tending to alienate employee and employer," Benjamin Bannan explained, "is like casting a fire brand among inflammable material." Although Bannan acknowledged the miners' suffering, he added that the operators suffered just as severely. "There should be harmony of feeling between miner and operator," he had long urged. "The interests of both require it."[36]

For men like Bannan, however, it was ideological harmony— that is, a shared faith in the integrity of the economic system— that would produce the material harmony conducive to a republican social order. When labor granted capital the benefit of the doubt, when employees assumed the good faith of employers, then strikes and dissatisfaction would cease. Despite evidence of a pattern of insufficient wages, an abusive store-order system, increasing accidents, poor ventilation in the mines, and the operators' reliance on the military to settle hard-fought strikes, Bannan held fast to his conviction that the industry recognized and fairly compensated the contributions of both labor and capital. All evidence to the contrary, he continued to insist that in those aberrant cases where employers proved unjust, a committee of workmen could "wait upon their employers and insist firmly but courteously upon redress of their grievances." His model of conciliation and face-to-face negotiation was one that long inspired the labor movement and one that miners attempted to implement; nevertheless, throughout the nineteenth century labor possessed few legal rights that capital was bound to respect, and coal operators were loath to acknowledge committeemen unless they were being arrested.[37]

Indeed, not even in Schuylkill County, where the industrial structure at least approached Bannan's conception of individual enterprise, could his vision of republican industry be sustained. Nor could ideological "disharmony" account for the strife there. Although it was true that the *Workingmen's Advocate* publicized the miners' complaints and supported strike efforts, labor discontent continued long after the editor was jailed for libel and the paper ceased publication.[38] If the anthracite industry had generated employment for numerous workingmen and fueled the development of whole townships and regions, the system of industrial capitalism nevertheless produced an unbalanced social structure that contributed to labor strife. Rather than fostering an independent wage-earning class able to seek the highest wages from competing individual entrepreneurs, the industrial system encouraged economic centralization that allowed a few employers to set the price of labor much in the same way that they controlled the price paid for coal. Numerous independent collieries may have dotted Schuylkill County's industrial landscape, but by 1860 a few large well-connected collieries dominated the regional economy (see table 1).[39]

In fact, of the almost four thousand miners employed by the county's major producers, 45 percent worked in the collieries owned by the Charles A. Heckscher Company and 71 percent of these worked in Cass Township. The Heckscher collieries,

TABLE 1. Major Employers and Their Control of the Work Force, 1860

Town	Operator	Number Employed	Number in Town	Percent of Local Work Force	Number of Collieries in Town
Cass	Heckscher	1,200	1,590	75	5
St. Clair	Milnes	400	1,130	35	5
Foster	Monterey	150	304	49	3
Reilly	Hecksher	500	980	51	4
Blythe	Richert	200	1,580	13	16
East					
Norwegian	Snyder	400	810	49	5
Branch	Miller &				
	Goyne	300	490	61	3
Ashland	Pioneer	250	650	38	3
New Castle	Repplier	350	1,350	26	10

Note: Figures based on the manuscript for the U.S. Census of Manufactures for Schuylkill County, Pennsylvania, 1860.

the most productive in the county by 1860, were also the most centralized, and they boasted strong ties to the Philadelphia and Reading Railroad and to well-placed financiers and politicians. Although this company, like others, suffered through the economic depression of the late 1850s, it was better able to withstand the price competition that crippled marginal independent operators. Yet miners in Cass Township fared no better than miners in less prosperous coal towns. Only 3 percent of the miners in Cass owned real property—a total far below the 16 percent of land-owning miners countywide. Critics may have chided Cass Township's Irish miners for their intemperate ways, but this low rate of property ownership better reflected the Heckscher Company's domination of real estate. Neither was personal property more widely distributed in Cass, suggesting that wages were sufficient merely to keep a working-class family working and were not high enough for these workers to save part of their pay or to move on when hard times hit the industry. More than half of the adult male population claimed less than $25 in cash in 1860, and almost 80 percent claimed less than $50. Thus the industry in Cass Township—the most successful in the Schuylkill region—generated a propertyless, wage-earning class, whose members had little opportunity to improve their situation as individuals (see table 2).[40]

TABLE 2. Mining Towns Ranked by Percentage of Miners Holding Property, 1860

Town	Number of Miners Owning Property	Percent
Tremont	66	38
Tamaqua	99	36
St. Clair	141	30
Minersville	78	29
Ashland	56	28
Schuylkill	39	26
Frailey	21	17
East Norwegian	31	15
West Penn	8	12
Blythe	31	10
Branch	10	9
Reilly	35	8
Cass	28	3
Foster	2	1
Newcastle	2	1

Note: Figures based on the manuscript for the U.S. Census of Population for Schuylkill County, Pennsylvania, 1860.

The social structure in Cass Township did not differ significantly from that of other major anthracite centers. In Lackawanna and Foster Townships and the borough of Hazel in Luzerne County, over 90 percent of the miners owned no property. A full 70 percent of miners employed in the northern field and 92 percent in the middle field owned no property in 1860. In Carbon County a mere 9 percent of miners claimed property. Although property-holding rates varied for different ethnic groups of miners, the overall low rate made these differences insignificant, suggesting that "cultural depravity" cannot account for the lack of property (see table 3).[41] Nevertheless, observers consistently linked poverty and labor discontent not to inequities inherent in the economic system, but to the degree of Irish concentration in particular coal towns. Towns dominated by Irish miners, like Jeansville and Lausanne in Carbon County and Cass in Schuylkill County, had by this time gained reputations as notorious trouble spots. They had also managed to organize fledgling labor unions in the late 1850s and the early 1860s.

TABLE 3. Property-owning Miners as Percent of Ethnic Mining Groups, 1860

Ethnic Origin	Number of Property-owning Miners	Percent of Ethnic Mining Group	Percent of All Property-owning Miners
English (707)	133	19	20
German (413)	170	41	26
Irish (1,881)	153	8	24
Welsh (656)	132	20	21
U.S. (337)	39	12	6
Other (149)	20	13	3

Note: Figures based on the manuscript for the U.S. Census of Population for Schuylkill County, Pennsylvania, 1860.

"Cass Township," the *Miners' Journal* attested early in 1863, ". . . is one of the most lawless spots in the county." The most productive coal township in Schuylkill County and the center of labor unrest, its notoriety no doubt reflected the miners' relatively successful efforts to organize a union in 1860. Contrary to popular opinion, however, this organizational bent hinged neither on the Irish miners' cultural predisposition for conflict, their taste for whiskey, nor their willingness to wield the Molly Maguires' famous "coffin notices."[42] Rather, Cass Township boasted a high degree of ethnic concentration and a similarly high degree of economic centralization that effectively created conditions suitable for labor organization. By 1860 Cass Township housed not only the largest number of miners and laborers in Schuylkill County but also the largest concentration of Irish miners. Thirty-eight percent of all Irish miners in the county resided in Cass, a figure more than triple that of the next highest concentration.[43] Although Irish miners could be found in nearly every mining township, often constituting a majority of the work force, in no township in Schuylkill County did a single ethnic group employed in a single industry and by a single company so dominate a community as it did in Cass. And in no other mining township in Schuylkill County were the miners so able to organize their forces.[44]

It was this coincidence of ethnic concentration and economic centralization in Cass and similar communities throughout the coal regions that provided the material basis for labor organization in the years before the Civil War, regardless of the ethnic group involved. Given the social and geographical isolation of these mining towns, their residents early learned to rely on each other to organize and build communal wells, grist mills, and ovens to supply their families with water and bread, to construct the churches in which they worshipped, and to work together in times of crisis to protect the mines that employed them against fire and floods. They looked to each other for financial and moral support in times of accidents or death, and they paraded the streets together celebrating religious holidays—the Irish on St. Patrick's Day, the Welsh on St. David's. Pooling their resources by means of benevolent societies or extended family networks, the miners depended on an ethic of mutuality in their everyday lives that was readily extended to the workplace. Indeed, the very danger of the work itself required miners to rely on each other to protect the safety of the group and to stand together when that safety was threatened by orders from superintendents or operators unfamiliar with the job.[45]

"Unionism has always been popular" with the anthracite miner, one miner later explained. "He is ever ready to fight valiantly for the uplift of his class, for he never expects to get out of it; its condition will be his condition."[46] Because miners had nothing but their labor to sell, their livelihood and their future depended on their ability to command adequate wage rates. That ability, in turn, rested on their organizational prowess: unless wage earners could stand together and resist the employers' efforts to replace them with others more desperate for work, they could not hope to achieve economic security. Because the operators successfully pitted ethnic groups one against the other, labor solidarity across ethnic lines proved difficult to achieve, especially in the early stages of industrialization.[47] But in mining communities dominated by well-organized companies, where class, ethnicity, politics, and religion usually converged, labor organization could take root. Thus at the same time that the industrial system attempted to reduce wage earners to the status of interchangeable "hands" to be purchased at the lowest possible rates, it also generated a structure that made labor organization possible. Although critics would continue to blame outside agitators and foreign influences for the discontent manifested in the coal regions, it was the values and practices of the new industrial order, as well as the process of industrialization itself, that provided both the basis and the remedy for the "outrages" in the coal regions.

In fact, evidence of labor organization in the northern anthracite fields further demonstrated that it was the industrial system in action, and not cultural depravity or outside agitation, that sparked labor organization. Miners in Pittston, for instance, made a most reasonable and respectable bid for shared authority in the workplace, making it clear that it was their concern with their own safety that forced them to impose work rules and challenge the operators' sole rights to hire and fire personnel. "No man has taken a more active part [in bringing to the surface heretofore hidden and useless treasure] than the practical miners," one group explained in the Pittston *Gazette,* "and no man, we think, is esteemed less than the one that leaves his home in the morning, not knowing that he will return to see those which are ever dear to him. . . ."[48] These miners, who also organized a benevolent association in 1860, emphasized the dangers of their profession, especially when operators employed men "not acquainted with mining" to supervise the works. "We think it is our duty as a class of miners, for the sake of our numerous widows and orphans . . . to form in a combination," they announced, "for an amendment of what we consider a disgrace to the moral and social condition of man in civilization." Convinced that the public would undoubtedly sympathize with their "great struggle," they called upon miners throughout the coal regions "to go hand in hand" in their demand for fair prices and safe working conditions. Not only did this group agree that miners should refuse to dig coal for less than 50 cents per ton under any circumstances, but they added that 3 cents for every ton produced should be deposited in a bank "for the benefit of the bereaved widows and orphans." This miners' association also urged combination to secure the employment of only "practical and experienced superintendents. . . . If otherwise," the group made it clear, "the miners shall . . . substantiate his deficiencies [to the employer]." Should the operator fail "to discharge his duty and not dismiss him, the miners shall then stop until all things are amicably settled."[49] These miners, like the large, well-organized operators who continued to dominate and centralize the trade, attempted to organize the work force locally and regionally to centralize their influence in the industry.

Critics of labor organization, however, especially those who continued to believe that individual enterprise and "republican" industry fueled the American economy, consistently blamed Democratic politicians and their Irish supporters for all the industry's ills. It was Democratic demagoguery, not the miners' recognition of competing class interests, that allegedly convinced these supposedly turbulent, intemperate, and clannish wage earners to question the workings of the industrial system. And it was the Democrats' low tariff policy, these critics insisted— not economic centralization, boom-bust economic cycles, market manipulation, or the subordination of labor's interests to capital's—that gave rise to an unstable industry unable to pay fair wages to employees. "The best counsel that can be tendered [the workingman] under the circumstances," the *Miners' Journal* reiterated in 1858, in the face of economic depression and labor unrest, "is to bear the heavy burden patiently, and at the Fall election to strike one united blow for 'Protection' to their industry. . . ."[50]

When "clannish" Irish miners, especially those who dominated the newer coal regions, cast a bloc vote against this advice, however, Republican keepers of social order feared for the future. Chastising office-seeking Democrats who supposedly pandered to their ignorant constituents' mistaken view of industrial oppression, the *Miners' Journal* charged its opponents with fanning the partisan flames of labor discontent and thereby threatening the rights of property in the coal regions. Although these charges had been raised over and over again in the 1840s and 1850s, they would nevertheless take on new significance in the 1860s. By the time of the Civil War, the miners' continued attempts to organize to protect their interests —and the Irish miners' allegiance to the Democrats—would be reinterpreted as evidence of disloyalty to the Union.

NOTES

1. Allan Nevins, ed., *The Diary of Philip Hone* (New York, 1927), 1:45; Eli Bowen, ed., *The Coal Regions of Pennsylvania* (Pottsville, Pa., 1848); *MJ*, Nov. 28, 1848.

2. Edward Pessen, *Jacksonian America* (Urbana, Ill., 1985), 146–48; Eric Foner, *Free Soil, Free Labor, Free Men: The Ideology of the Republican Party before the Civil War* (New York, 1970).

3. Sean Wilentz, *Chants Democratic: New York City and the Rise of the American Working Class* (New York, 1984); Susan E. Hirsch, *Roots of the American Working Class: The Industrialization of Crafts in Newark, 1800–1860* (Philadelphia, 1978); Bruce Laurie, *Working People of Philadelphia, 1800–1850* (Philadelphia, 1980); Jonathan Prude, *The Coming of Industrial Order: Town and Factory Life in Rural Massachusetts, 1810–1860* (Cambridge, 1983); Thomas Dublin, *Women at Work: The Transformation of Work and Community in Lowell, Massachusetts, 1826–1860* (New York, 1979); Michael Hanagan and Charles Stephenson, eds., *Proletarians and Protest: The Roots of Class Formation in an Industrialized World* (Westport, Conn., 1986).

4. Henry C. Bradsby, *History of Luzerne County, Pennsylvania* (Chicago, 1893); Oscar Jewell Harvey and Ernest Greg Smith, *A History of Wilkes-Barre, Luzerne County, Pennsylvania* (Wilkes-Barre, 1930); Hendrick B. Wright, *Historical Sketches of Plymouth, Luzerne County* (Philadelphia, 1873); Daniel I. Rupp, *History of Northampton, Lehigh, Monroe, and Schuylkill Counties* (Harrisburg, Pa., 1845); Frederick Brenckman, *History of Carbon County* (Harrisburg, Pa., 1913); Frederick Hitchcock, *History of Scranton and Its People* (New York, 1914); *A History of Schuylkill County, Pennsylvania* (New York, 1881); Adolf W. Schalck and D. C. Henning, *History of Schuylkill County, Pennsylvania* (Harrisburg, Pa., 1907).

5. Horace Hollister, M.D., *History of the Lackawanna Valley* (Philadelphia, 1885), 370, 382; *MJ*, Feb. 6, 1836; *Carbon County Gazette*, May 8, 1844. See also *Gazette*, May 14, 1844, June 21, 1847; *Pottsville Emporium*, July 24, 1847; *MJ*, Jan. 30, 1847, Feb. 20, 1847; William A. Gudelunas, Jr., and William G. Shade, *Before the Molly Maguires: The Emergence of the Ethno-Religious Factor in the Politics of the Lower Anthracite Region, 1844–1872* (New York, 1976).

6. Clifton K. Yearley, Jr., *Enterprise and Anthracite* (Baltimore, 1961), 166.

7. Yearley, ibid.; Fergus G. Farquhar, "The Coal Trade" (n.p., n.d.), typed transcript in John N. Hoffman Files, Division of Agriculture and National Resources, National Museum of American History, Washington, D.C.. See also Anthony F. C. Wallace, *St. Clair* (New York, 1987), 177–79.

8. Yearley, *Enterprise and Anthracite*, 109–10; John N. Hoffman, "Anthracite in the Lehigh Region of Pennsylvania," in *Contributions from the Museum of History and Technology* (Washington, D.C., 1968), 103–4; Harold Aurand, *From the Molly Maguires to the United Mine Workers* (Philadelphia, 1971), 33–43; Robert Allison, "Early History of Coal Mining and Mining Machinery in Schuylkill County," *Publications of the Historical Society of Schuylkill County* 4 (1912): 134–55.

9. Yearley, *Enterprise and Anthracite*, 168–69.

10. Ibid., 165–66.

11. See chapter 2.

12. *Pottsville Emporium,* June 20, 1840.

13. *MJ,* July 9, 1842.

14. *Pottsville Emporium,* July 16, 1842.

15. For a discussion of the miners' "republicanism" in the last half of the century see Mark Hirsch, "Coal Miners and the American Republic: Trade Union Ideology in the Anthracite Regions of Pennsylvania, 1875–1902," Ph.D. diss., Harvard University, 1984.

16. *MJ,* July 9, 1842, July 16, 1842.

17. *MJ,* July 16, 1842.

18. *MJ,* July 23, 1842.

19. Ibid.

20. *Pottsville Emporium,* Dec. 10, 1842, June 24, 1843.

21. Thomas Petherick to Charles A. Heckscher, Jan. 5, 1846, in Charles A. Heckscher Company Papers, Moses Taylor Collection, New York Public Library (cited hereafter as CAH Papers, NYPL).

22. *Mining Register and Democrat,* Apr. 30, 1852. This paper did not always support strikes, though. See May 4, 1850, and Mar. 26, 1853, for less sympathetic expressions.

23. *Carbon County Gazette,* Mar. 11, 1847, Mar. 3, 1847; Aurand, *From the Molly Maguires to the United Mine Workers,* 66.

24. Eugene Borda to Charles A. Heckscher, Sept. 25, 1852, CAH Papers, NYPL.

25. *MJ,* Jan. 2, 1864. For a discussion of various ethnic groups in the coal regions, see Wallace, *St. Clair,* 133–41, 180–83.

26. Wallace, ibid., 133–35, 177–79, 180–81.

27. *MJ,* Oct. 3, 1847.

28. *MJ,* Jan. 18, 1851, May 29, 1851, Mar. 4, 1854.

29. See note 3 above. See also Norman Ware, *The Industrial Worker, 1840–1860* (Chicago, 1964); John R. Commons et al., *History of Labor in the United States,* vol. 1 (New York, 1918); John R. Commons et al., *A Documentary History of American Industrial Society,* vol. 8 (Cleveland, 1910), among many others; *Mining Register and Democrat,* May 4, 1850, Apr. 27, 1850, Mar. 2, 1850, June 28, 1851.

30. Eugene Borda to Charlemagne Tower, Apr. 7, 1857, Charlemagne Tower Papers, Butler Library, Columbia University, New York.

31. Borda to Richard Heckscher, Oct.1, 1857, CAH Papers, NYPL.

32. *Mauch Chunk Gazette,* Apr. 22, 1858, May 27, 1858.

33. *Carbon Democrat,* cited in *Mauch Chunk Gazette,* June 17, 1858; *Mauch Chunk Gazette,* June 24, 1858.

34. *MJ,* May 22, 1858; May 29, 1858; June 12, 1858.

35. *MJ,* June 19, 1858. Gideon Bast, a land owner and operator, charged the *Workingmen's Advocate* with libel in Dec. 1857. See *MJ,* Dec. 5, 1857.

36. *MJ,* July 3, 1848.

37. *MJ,* May 28, 1858.

38. *MJ,* Mar. 11, 1858, July 3, 1858.

39. See chapter 2.

40. Population statistics from the manuscript of the Eighth Population Census, National Archives Microfilm M653; industrial statistics calculated from the manuscript of the United States Census of Manufactures, National Archives Microfilm T956. Total number of miners is 3,750.

41. Ibid. See James Henretta, "The Study of Social Mobility: Ideological Assumption and Conceptual Bias," *Labor History* 18 (1977): 165–78, for a discussion of property holding among the Irish.

42. *MJ*, Jan. 11, 1863. For examples of "coffin notices" see Francis P. Dewees, *The Molly Maguires* (Philadelphia, 1877).

43. Reilly Township housed 11 percent of the county's Irish miners.

44. There are references to a Workmen's Benevolent Union in Forestville, Cass Township, organized in 1860 or 1862. Charles Hewett, an operator, told Charlemagne Tower that a union had been formed in Cass and Foster Townships in May, 1862. Hewett to Tower, Feb. 2, 1864, Letters Forwarded, Tenth District, Pennsylvania, RG 110, National Archives.

45. Wallace, *St. Clair*, 139–41, 174; John P. Gallagher, *A Century of History: The Diocese of Scranton, 1868–1968* (Scranton, Pa., 1968), 71–77.

46. Joseph F. Patterson, "After the W.B.A.," *Publications of the Historical Society of Schuylkill County* 4 (1912): 183.

47. For a discussion of ethnic conflict see Wayne G. Broehl, *The Molly Maguires* (Cambridge, Mass., 1964) and Anthony F. C. Wallace, "The Miners of St. Clair: Family, Class, and Ethnicity in a Mining Town in Schuylkill County, 1850–1880," in *Hard Coal, Hard Times: Ethnicity and Labor in the Anthracite Region,* ed. David L. Salay (Scranton, Pa., 1984), 1–16.

48. Pittston *Gazette,* Nov. 29, 1860.

49. Ibid.

50. *MJ*, May 28, 1858.

4

The Region:
Class, Ethnicity,
and Political Allegiance
1840–60

"What is our duty as patriotic men—as sons descended from Revolutionary ancestors?" Charles Albright asked delegates to Carbon County's Peoples Convention in July 1862. For Albright the answer was clear: to close solidly and firmly around Abraham Lincoln. Although men might differ on "minor matters" or "political details," the exigencies of war left little room for party politics or partisan debates. "There is but one way of saving the country," Albright insisted, "and that is by supporting the President."[1]

Democrats, who considered themselves patriotic men despite their differences with the administration, disputed this claim. From their point of view, it was Republicans who had put party before nation and Republicans whose war policies had weakened the northern will to fight. Supporters of the administration, one Democratic editor complained, not only "avowed themselves bent upon emancipation, though the road should lead through blood bridle deep," but abandoned constitutional restraints whenever such restraints "stand in the way of their schemes." Democrats, this editor suggested, were concerned with the restoration, not the reconstruction, of the Union. "Let us not allow a faction at the North to accomplish without a struggle," he implored, "that very overthrow of our government which southern rebels have attempted with force of arms."[2]

From the Democrats' point of view, both parties contested the means, and not the ends, of this war for Union. Congres-

70

sional Democrats, even so-called peace Democrats, for example, voted financial support for war measures, despite their belief that war could have been averted. "This is no time for us to be fiddling," Democratic senator Henry Rice of Minnesota explained. "It is no time for us to be swapping jack-knives when the ship is sinking." Democrats, only a very small number of whom favored peace at any price, believed that the Union should be preserved and the Constitution defended; they did not concede, however, that slavery need necessarily be destroyed or civil liberties temporarily suspended in the process.[3] Neither did they acknowledge any contradictions inherent in this position.

The Democratic party's essential racism, its conservative belief in a "natural" social order, and its conviction that compromise might still reconcile North and South—no matter how abhorrent to modern-day critics—attracted significant numbers of northern voters. Although Pennsylvania had elected a Republican governor and cast its electoral ballots for Lincoln in 1860 and 1864, some 25 percent of the state's electorate favored a nonmilitary resolution of the struggle.[4] These Democrats—many of whom resided in the anthracite regions—supported local autonomy over what they called Republican despotism and measured national issues in terms of local consequences. When Democrats in Luzerne County, for example, debated the issue of slavery, they viewed it as a regional, not a national issue, and certainly not as a moral question. "Had our puritanical cousins minded their own business, instead of interfering with the concerns of the South," the *Luzerne Union* lamented, "we should have had no war."[5]

The social structure, social relations, and even social geography of the anthracite regions very much shaped the provincialism that defined the region's politics. Miners more readily recognized their employers, and not the slaveholders of the South, as the real threat to the republic, and the miners' economic struggles, even in the midst of civil war, proved their primary concern. Practical circumstances, local conflicts, and hard-fought struggles for economic survival tempered the miners' parochial political vision—and shaped their political alliances. The structure of the industry and the ethnic-based, working-class communities that evolved in the newer coal regions encouraged miners to depend on each other to improve their living and working conditions as a class and to stand together in political, as well as economic, fights. But if their preference for local autonomy and their rejection of centralizing war measures demonstrated a well-developed distrust of the Republican party's economic vision, especially among Irish miners, their tendency to cast a bloc vote alarmed their opponents. Although the roots of this political behavior were grounded in ethnic and class-related conflicts older than the war itself,[6] opponents nevertheless interpreted evidence of the miners' dissatisfaction with the industrial system as evidence of their sympathy for the South.

"Schuylkill is a great county—," Benjamin Bannan boasted in the summer of 1863, "she is great in her enterprise . . . great in sending volunteers to fight for Union and liberty. . . great in the loyalty of the mass of her citizens. . . ." In fact, as Bannan saw it, the county was flawed in only one respect. "She is cursed," he regretfully explained, "by the presence of a humbug of the meanest dirtiest and most God-forsaken Copperheads that ever disgraced humanity. . . ."[7] Given the brand of nativist politics that Bannan peddled, first as spokesman for the Whigs and then for the Republicans, the strong Democratic contingent in the county's mining districts could have come as no surprise to him. Almost half of Schuylkill County's four thousand miners were Irish in 1860, and they dominated the county's largest, most productive coal towns. Together with the long-time Democratic agricultural towns, these constituted the party's strongholds. In Carbon County and Luzerne County similar patterns emerged: Irish miners and German farmers cast dependable Democratic votes.[8]

Whigs had early welcomed immigrants throughout the 1840s, perceiving in their growing number a sign of economic prosperity. But they also advocated naturalization reform as a sensible, republican precaution. Clamorous and turbulent men "who come here with distorted views of liberty," the *Miners' Journal* explained, "should be taught their place and their duties, and learn to understand our institutions before they are admitted to the privileges of citizens." In fact, as other Whigs freely admitted, the Irish immigrants' political behavior had already demonstrated the need for political reeducation. "There is no use disguising the fact that some of our naturalized citizens are bent upon mischief," one Whig explained, "and it is made apparent by the undue advantage of numbers brought together . . . by appealing to national prejudice independent of the term American citizen. . . . Let our citizens act independently," he cautioned. "Clanship and prejudice are but blind guides to the confidence of patriotism."[9]

As long as the Whigs won local elections—as they did in the late 1840s—the *Miners' Journal* praised immigrant voters for doing "their own voting and thinking." The paper denigrated those immigrants who continued to favor the Democrats, however, bemoaning this as evidence of "abject slavery" that weakened the very fabric of the republic. When Whig presidential candidate, Zachary Taylor, carried Schuylkill County in 1848, for example, the *Miners' Journal* complained that his majority would have been greater had "Irish adopted citizens" been permitted "to follow their inclinations." Charging local party leaders with coercing the Irish vote, the paper likened Democratic control of the coal regions to the "oppression of the English Government in Ireland." According to editor Benjamin Bannan, those Irish miners who had cast a Democratic ballot had either been physically threatened or had bartered away their rights as freemen "to secure paltry offices . . . from a corrupt and dishonest party."[10]

This early concern with the Irish Democratic vote foreshadowed the strong anti-Irish, anti-Catholic political campaigns waged by opponents of the Democratic party throughout the 1850s and 1860s. To be sure, political nativism informed political campaigns nationwide, but this nativism expressed more than a generalized antipathy to foreign cultures or an abstract and timeless aversion to strangers. The nativist attack on the Irish, in the coal regions as elsewhere, communicated the fears of small propertyowners and independent producers in the face of an unpropertied, wage-earning class. The emergence of such a class tested the limits of the Whigs' "free labor" ideology and seemingly refuted their vision of the republic. At the same time, it forced these petty producers to realize that they, too, might share this fate.[11]

Whig political campaigns in Schuylkill County illustrate this
point well. Party spokesmen adopted particularly inflammatory
nativist rhetoric—owing in part to Benjamin Bannan's acerbic
personality and in part to the fact that independent producers
proved most prevalent, and most vulnerable, in Schuylkill
County.[12] Whether the campaign focused on cultural issues, like
temperance or keeping the Sabbath holy, or on the means of
economic growth, Schuylkill County's Whigs articulated a belief
that political consensus could mediate class differences that otherwise threatened the republican social order. When these means
failed, as they surely did, these producers eventually joined with
the large industrialists they disdained and looked to the strong
arm of the state to enforce consensus.

If the Whigs had demonstrated their political aversion to the
Irish throughout the late 1840s, in 1852 they expected their
commonsense, high-tariff economic program to attract "right-
thinking" miners, as it had a number of Democrats. In fact, as
Benjamin Bannan saw it, the election of 1852 would test the
question of protection versus free trade, the question of fostering
"home manufactures and . . . the remunerative prices of American labor" or encouraging "foreign manufactures and the introduction of the rates of European wages." Irishmen, the *Miners' Journal* advised, "can act much more effectively. They have
only to cooperate with the large majority of native citizens and
establish the Whig protective system to pull down the manufacturing and commercial supremacy of England. . . ."[13]

Although Bannan lambasted so-called "locofoco" Democrats
for their low-tariff platform, pointing out that "England was in
the field for [Franklin] Pierce," local Democrats also favored a
protective tariff. Given the region's dependence on the coal and
iron industries, no politician, Democrat or not, could argue
otherwise. "The Democracy," the *Mining Register* explained, "has
always advocated a tariff . . . to afford protection to all the leading interests of the country." In fact, as the *Carbon County Gazette*
had earlier noted, the protective tariff "was the only principle
upon which both parties in the state appear united." But when
the Democrats elected Franklin (Free Trade) Pierce, with
Schuylkill County's help, Bannan argued that anti-tariff forces
had manipulated the Democratic vote. "We will never appeal

to the Catholic vote again so long as we conduct a newspaper," the *Miners' Journal* pledged. "We are now satisfied that the controlling power of the Catholic Church does not want Protection to American Industry in this country. . . ." Irrational, manipulative forces, not the Whigs' obvious aversion to the Irish, in Bannan's view, had induced a Democratic victory. Those same irrational forces would be blamed whenever social conflict arose or economic reversals threatened the survival of "individual enterprise."[14]

True to his word, Bannan and the *Miners' Journal* began a virulent campaign aimed against Catholics in general and Irish Catholics in particular. Like similar nativist campaigns, Bannan's stressed cultural reforms, especially temperance, as the key to political unity and economic stability. The temperance movement popularized through the *Miners' Journal,* however, implied more than a generalized quest for sobriety as a positive social good; it proved rather to be a quest for Irish sobriety as a political and economic good. Neither Democrats nor the Church could manipulate temperate Irishmen, and their sobriety could only increase the county's coal production. As it was, Bannan estimated, one-quarter of the work force spent more time in the beer shops than in the mine breasts, costing the coal trade one thousand tons and one thousand dollars a day. The allegedly high wages paid to intemperate miners compounded the problem. Instead of mining more coal and doubling their pay, as right-thinking miners should, intemperate miners worked fewer hours, spending the remainder "at [rum] establishments." And, as Bannan pointed out, they had plenty of establishments from which to choose. In 1853 the coal region alone housed 636 liquor establishments, one for every 9½ voters.[15]

Just to make sure that his readers knew which miners were right thinking and which were intemperate, Bannan emphasized the fact that it was only the "Romish element" that seemed hell-bent on destroying the county's economy. "Now what is the policy of the Roman Catholic Church on the temperance issue?" Bannan asked his readers. Did not the priesthood dismiss the Maine Law as "Whig humbug," thereby endorsing drunkenness? "Who is not conversant," he inquired, "with the piece of scandal currently circulated . . . that [a] fast young man [set] his jolly reverence to dancing in his stocking soles, for the amusement of a barroom crowd?" Bannan advised those readers who still doubted the connection to "travel through our county and see if there is not a difference, a marked difference even in the exterior domestic habits of the people, where Protestants and Romish elements respectively predominate." Using poorhouse statistics to bolster his argument, Bannan pointed out that the Irish led the ranks of those impoverished through intemperance, and the burden fell to the "sober *hardworking* taxpayers [who] have to foot the bill." When the Democratic *Mining Register* challenged this anti-Catholic crusade, Bannan stood his ground. "If to advocate reform, social and political; to oppose the Church and State machinations of popery; and to stand by the sacred institutions of our glorious republic [is to] be 'destined to do evil to this place,' " Bannan chided his accusers, "then we will singly plead guilty."[16]

Although German "Pennsylvania Dutch" Democrats were also taunted as grogshop owners and tipplers, they escaped the rhetorical vehemence that the Whigs reserved for the Irish. In part, this reflected the fact that Germans embodied neither a homogeneous religious group, social class, nor political faction. If German farmers continued to drink or vote Democratic, their social habits and political organization only vaguely threatened economic growth. The campaign against "foreign influence" increased in direct proportion to the foreigner's relation to the coal industry. Nativist politics in the coal regions were directed at the wage-earning Irish, not the propertied Germans, and they had as much to do with conceptions of economic growth and prosperity as they did with religious worldviews or cultural orientation.[17]

In fact, one need not delve far beneath the surface of Benjamin Bannan's Whig rhetoric to discover the economic underpinnings of his political faith. A staunch supporter of individual enterprise and a caustic critic of "monster" corporations, Bannan believed that free and unrestrained competition among independent operators, landowners, and transporters guaranteed all men an equal chance for economic independence. The fulfillment of this goal depended on a dynamic economy, marked, in this case, by the proliferation of mining establishments, high production rates, and a strong protective tariff. As long as miners and operators recognized that their interests were one and the same and that any dysfunction resulted from personal depravity and not from the economic system itself, harmony and prosperity would ensure economic mobility.[18]

The harmony of interests described by Bannan, however, rested on an acceptance of existing social hierarchies, not on any concept of equality. Although, as Bannan gratuitously explained, "capital always controls labor," he contended that their interdependence nevertheless required "a spirit of mutual conciliation between both." Harmony, mediated by market forces, could be ensured by operators who paid fair wage rates and miners who respected their employers' calculations. Right-thinking miners, who by definition accepted this premise, recognized their employers as patrons, not adversaries, and understood that strikes could only destroy prosperity, not increase wages. Bannan offered an example of the Whigs' "right-thinking" road to economic advancement in 1854, when he commended two miners who, by sheer hard work, had earned three times the going daily wage rate. "It is true they work from twelve to thirteen hours a day," he explained, at a time when miners fell victim to noxious gases in poorly ventilated mines, "but it only shows what can be done by steady men."[19]

The miners' experience in the industry, especially in the lean years of the late 1850s, belied the harmony or economic mobility that Bannan's Whig philosophy asserted. With operators often unable to meet wage obligations for months at a time, miners struck to improve their condition. To Bannan, such actions did not demonstrate conflicting class interests nourished by the economic system but rather showed the Irish miners' typical inability to react as American citizens. Their refusal to wait out this downturn in the market gracefully, their inability to make do with the wages offered, reflected their intemperate ways, not the failings of undercapitalized, anarchistic individual enterprise. The miners' willingness to band together to force the operators' hand was derived, in Bannan's view, from foreign clannishness and sinister manipulation, not from the very social conditions generated by the industry itself.[20] If the producers' republic envisioned by men like Bannan had any hope of enduring, clannish foreigners would have to "melt into our population as snowflakes in a river . . . leaving Americans to guard the national tradition of freedom and guide the country to its glorious destiny." Otherwise, he made it clear, the force of law would compel their compliance. When clannish miners in Cass Township assaulted a foreman in 1855 and the sheriff arrested some twenty-eight men, although only three had been implicated, Bannan praised this powerful demonstration of law and order. "The prompt action of the authorities . . . ," he explained, "will have a proper effect upon this class [of miners] and teach them that there is a superior to that which they arrogate to themselves."[21]

Opponents of the Democratic party in Carbon County, if less belligerent, generally offered the same political message. When serious labor conflicts disrupted coal production in 1858, the *Mauch Chunk Gazette* blamed Democrats not only for the violence that accompanied some strikes but also for overall economic decline. Convinced that the Democrats' free trade position had prostrated the iron and coal business in Pennsylvania, the paper urged miners to "STRIKE FOR A PROTECTIVE TARIFF" at the coming election. "As for any other kind of 'strike,' " the *Gazette* added, "we say you are wrong." By voting for Republicans, the miners might "lay the axe to the root of the evil" and thus enable operators to pay high wages. But Irish voters judged the matter differently. "Every mother's son of them who either expects to be Sheriff, Register, Prothonotary, Legislator or Township . . . officer," the *Gazette* complained, "will submit to the arrogance of the slave power, so as to preserve 'the harmony of the Democratic Party,' for without harmony they might be defeated by the 'Black Republicans' " (Democrats used this term to express contempt for their opponents' agitation on the slavery issue).[22]

By contrast, the Democrats seemed much more aware of conflicting class interests and appeared less convinced that high production or the tariff might resolve them. "Open plenty of mines," the *Mining Register and Democrat* advised in a parody of "ruinous" Whig economics, "run in debt all you can—screw down your men and gouge them by store orders if you can't do it any other way. Dang the odds about whether the market will want your coal or not—as for paying your debts, pooh!!

Nonsense!! If this ain't Whig talk, it is Whig acts," the editor noted at a time of economic decline, "and Schuylkill County owes its downfall . . . entirely to this practical application of extravagant Whiggery by the coal merchant, the canal and Railroad directors nearly everyone of whom are Whig. . . ."[23] Local Democrats argued that senseless competition and overproduction, not the tariff, intemperance, or Irish depravity, proved the roots of this economic reversal. "None so well understand the true merits of the matter as the laboring men of Schuylkill County," the *Mining Register* remarked, "who suffer the most . . . and it is in vain," the paper continued, "that our political opponents struggle by empty sophistry, nicknames, and low language, to divert the working men from the convictions they feel. . . ."[24]

Democratic spokesmen offered Irish miners a far more hospitable political haven than their opponents did. "The Democratic party welcomes these 'oppressed and starving poor' whether Roman Catholics or Protestant to the shores of . . . our prosperous country," the *Emporium* had announced in 1847, "where they need no longer be oppressed. . . ." Not only did the Democrats criticize Whig attempts to slow Catholic immigration or to extend the period of naturalization, but they annointed the pope as "the biggest Democrat alive."[25] To be sure, such rhetoric merely demonstrated the Democrats' determination to attract the Irish Catholic vote. Their strategy, however, reflected an assumption that economic and social classes were inevitable and that their conflicting interests could be mediated through political pragmatism and compromise. Gubernatorial candidate Francis Shunk displayed the Democrats' style in 1844 when he attempted to reconcile conflicting religious values in a manner quite different from the Whigs' conformist "American" plan. "In schools where the parents of children differ with regard to the use of the Bible as a schoolbook, it is well," he advised, "rather than make that holy book an occasion of unholy strife, not to insist upon its use for the purpose."[26]

More interested in avoiding conflict than in imposing a particular viewpoint, Democrats sought to achieve compromise whenever possible. Their opponents, however, sought to avoid conflict by acculturating groups to some national norm through cultural reform and education. "Nothing will tend sooner to improve our national character, to break down the ficticious distinctions of social life, and to make us what we should be, republicans at heart," the *Miners' Journal* explained in an editorial favoring common schools. By eradicating artificial class and ethnic differences, the common schools would "render us as a nation, an intelligent and thinking people, and . . . give a general impetus to business, science, and morality." From the point of view of the *Miners' Journal,* this was just practical, even pragmatic, advice to minority groups who had to face the social facts of life. Irish Catholics, the paper boldly stated, "are in the Power of the Protestants, and must ever remain so as long as [they] remain in this country." Such advice no doubt strengthened the Irish Catholics' support for the Democrats.[27]

One need not subscribe to the "ethno-cultural" interpretation of American politics to acknowledge that the Democrats and their opponents appealed to, and attracted, different segments of the electorate. If the Democrats could count on the Irish Catholic and German Lutheran vote, the Whigs, and then the Republicans, benefited from the Protestant Welsh and English vote. Although the religious orientations of these groups may have predisposed them to favor the "Evangelical" Republicans' political crusades, or the "Orthodox" Democrats' more passive style, the practical dynamics of party politics also reinforced these ties. At the same time that Republicans denounced their opponents as "swindling Irish-toadying Demagogues" and the Democrats charged Republican employers with controlling their employees' votes, both parties used patronage and campaign funds to court various groups of voters.

The decentralized structure of the antebellum state and the strong local political institutions that resulted from it rendered voting blocs a particularly valuable commodity to competing political parties. When Republicans in Schuylkill County, for example, sought to attract German voters, they traded a promise of future patronage for editorial support in a German newspaper. When they sought the votes of various working-class groups, they used even more practical means. "We have a list of one hundred boatmen, seventy of whom we know and have promised to vote the 'Union ticket,' " one party organizer re-

ported. "They . . . are men of very limited means," he added,
"and in order to get them back [in time to vote] we must pay
their fares."[28] Party politicians also paid the taxes of other "men
of very limited means" to enable them to vote. Even Benjamin
Bannan, the erstwhile protector of "individual" voting, was not
above appealing to ethnic groups of voters. "There is a large
Welsh population in this county, and in all the mining districts
of the state," he wrote to Henry Carey in 1856. "My impression
is that if the Republican committee would get out Welsh documents . . . they will secure more votes from that class. . . ."
Republicans in Carbon County employed similar strategies with
good results. Although, as E. H. Rauch pointed out, Irish Catholics "to a man" opposed "Republican-Americans," the party
had secured the votes of "a goodly number of Protestant Welsh
and daily hear of new converts among the Germans to our
side."[29]

Republicans sharply criticized the Irish for their "slavish"
devotion to the Democrats, but the patron-client relation that
linked the two did provide some benefits to the Irish. Roman
Catholic voters in Democratic towns controlled a certain amount
of patronage, and this patronage provided them with at least a
leg up into the party network itself. In Schuylkill County, for
example, Irish Catholics constituted 7 percent of the Democratic
party's leaders between 1844 and 1853, and 43 percent between
1855 and 1872. In 1855 almost one-quarter of the delegates to
the Democratic County convention were Irish, but no Irish
Catholic Whig leaders could be counted. The Democrats may
not have offered the Irish any better solution to social inequality
and exploitation than the one advanced by their opponents, but
they did offer them at least a modicum of representation in the
party. Irish Democrats often campaigned and won elections with
party support—a claim that Republicans could not, and indeed
would not, make.[30]

Once in office Irish Democrats addressed Irish class interests
in terms calculated to retain political support. When James Ryon
favored a bill that would force operators to pay miners' wages
before liquidating other debts, his fellow Irishmen could applaud
his speech. "Sir," he addressed his opponents, "labor forms the
basis of every sound system of society . . . [and] when labor is

depressed and a preference given to capital at that moment your government degenerates into aristocracy. . . . The capitalists of Schuylkill County have grown rich and richer," he concluded, "and the poor men . . . have grown poorer and poorer every year." Ryon may well have been appealing to his constituents' self-interest, but he was also airing the miners' grievances in a political forum. The *Miners' Journal,* in contrast, offered a very different reading of the bill. According to that paper, "every thoughtful workingman in the region" considered it unnecessary, and not only that—the bill was "mischievous" since it attempted to place "the power in the hands of a small number [of workers] who are always complaining to stop the collieries at their pleasure."[31] Any reader at all familiar with Bannan's style knew to which miners he referred. If, in the long run, the Irish-Democratic coalition served to ensure the party's survival and not to improve the miners' social or economic status significantly, the party nevertheless offered Irish miners more support than any other political party at the time. Given the choice between the Whigs' anti-Catholic proscriptions and the Democrats' patronage and rhetoric, the Irish miners' affiliation with the Democrats made immediate political sense.

The outbreak of civil war tested the limits of the Democratic party's pragmatism. It also exposed the narrow self-interest and provincial political vision of its electorate. When Horatio King, a Democrat from Maine, wrote to President James Buchanan, a Pennsylvanian, soon after Lincoln's election in 1860, he demonstrated the dimensions of his political universe. "The die is cast and Lincoln is elected," he waxed rhetorical. "What course should we, here in the District of Columbia pursue?" Noting that all his assets were tied up in real estate in the nation's capital, he added that "with us, everything depends on the union being preserved."[32]

A similar sense of patriotism may well have motivated Francis W. Hughes's strong preservationist instincts. As Schuylkill County's most conservative Democrat and a candid supporter of John C. Breckinridge, the pro-slavery candidate, Hughes had wide-ranging investments in the South as well as a nephew who fought for the Confederacy. A prominent lawyer and wealthy coal land speculator, Hughes had written to presidential candidate James

Buchanan in 1856, already wary of abolition disunionists. Calling these Republicans "traitorous hordes who are now rallying under the false pretense of 'freedom' and non-extension of slavery," Hughes supported the concept of "popular sovereignty," which, as he saw it, proved the basis "of all American liberty." Some five years later Hughes entertained the idea of taking Pennsylvania into the Confederacy to protect her manufacturing interests. Were Pennsylvania to remain in the Union, he argued, she could only lose out to New York. By joining the Confederacy, however, Pennsylvania would emerge "as the great manufacturing workshop for a people now consuming annually $300,000,000 worth of products and manufactures from and imported through Northern cities."[33]

Although fellow Democrats convinced Hughes to shelve this treasonous suggestion, his belief in the primacy of states' rights and the possibility of peaceful secession proved consistent with his political philosophy. Like many other citizens, Hughes did not envision secession as a necessary deathblow to the Union. James Buchanan argued similarly soon after Lincoln's election. "I would sacrifice my own life at any moment to save the union . . . ," he explained, "but this great and enterprising and brave nation is not to be destroyed by losing the Cotton States; even if this loss were irreparable which I do not believe unless from some unhappy accident."[34]

For leaders of Pennsylvania's Democratic party, the secession crisis exposed the fragility of the Union—a Union, in their opinion, based on consent, not coercion. "Bayonets can't keep a state in the Union," Luzerne County's George Woodward wrote to his colleague Jeremiah Black late in 1860, and both agreed that reason, not force, had kept the nation intact. "I have always known, for I studied Mr. Calhoun when I was a young man," Woodward explained, "that our Union . . . when pressed to extremes would be found a rope of sand—but I have never said much about it," he confessed, "for I thought it was the part of a good citizen not to press it to its ultimate principles." Party supporters voiced similar beliefs. "The blinded want to make, or establish a union with the Bayonet, and that is impossible," D. T. R. Wohlfarth, a Schuylkill County Democrat feared. "When all is done with our forces, the Union is destroyed."[35] It was not only Breckinridge supporters or backward-looking "locofoco" Democrats who believed that compromise might reconcile North and South. "The sentiments of the substantial citizens of this section," Thomas Foster, a Democrat who supported Stephen Douglas, insisted, "is for the peaceful settlement of the difficulties . . . by the passage of some such measure as the Crittenden compromise."[36] Thus even these less conservative Democrats were willing to guarantee the constitutionality of slavery in exchange for preserving the Union.

If Pennsylvania's Democrats had difficulty perceiving the depth of the conflict between the North and the South, this may have reflected the party's policy of keeping slavery out of political debate. For example, when Governor William Johnston discussed his opposition to the extension of slavery in his 1850 annual message, his Democratic opponents in the state legislature attempted to suppress publication of the speech. Later that same year Richard McAllister, a Democrat from Harrisburg, explained his position. "At a crisis like the present when designing demagogues and mad fanatics are devising schemes to destroy the fair fabric of this glorious Union . . . ," he wrote to James Buchanan, "it is refreshing for patriots to take counsel together and to strengthen each other's resolution to 'live and die in the Union.' . . . Instead of always talking of Northern rights and Southern dictation," he suggested, "let us cultivate a feeling of fraternal regard. . . ." The Harrisburg *Patriot and Union* applauded this strategy, proclaiming the Democratic party to be neither pro- nor anti-slavery. In fact, in this paper's view, the party intended "to deal with two distinct classes of society without bringing them into antagonism."[37]

If local politicians did not go so far as this, they did, in general, consider slavery from the perspective of local interests. When the *Mauch Chunk Gazette* expressed its anti-slavery sentiments, it did so in the context of the tariff. "All we need is a protective tariff," to recover from the 1857 depression, the editor noted, "which, however, we cannot have as long as we are ruled by the cotton slave lords of the South." A few months later the paper argued, "Democracy is synonymous with slavery. . . . The Government is drifting hopelessly into debt and bankruptcy. Trade is depressed, the arm of Labor is paralyzed, and industry seeks in vain for employment."[38] Daniel Larer, a Peoples party organizer in Schuylkill County, approached the question similarly. "Our strong fort," he noted in the midst of the 1860 election campaign, "is to prove we are the Tariff Party and to prove that the democrats are in favor of nigger labour in opposition to white labour. . . ." Even Eli Bowen, one time coeditor of the *Miners' Journal,* judged the "irrepressible conflict" in terms of his state's manufacturing interests. "The people are ripe for another party . . . ," he wrote to Simon Cameron early in 1861. "They are tired—sick—disgusted to their very souls with Democracy, with Republicanism, with Americanism. . . . The next step," he argued, "will be to set up for the Union—to give the South all they want and then, in return, make them give us what *we* want—a Tariff."[39] In light of the parochialism expressed by political leaders of both camps, and the apparent reluctance of each to face up to the complexities of the conflict, it is small wonder that residents of the coal regions displayed similar shortcomings.

When hostilities erupted, however, Democrats and Republicans in the coal regions, as elsewhere in the North, rushed to answer Lincoln's call for 75,000 troops. The Democratic districts in Schuylkill, Luzerne, and Carbon Counties recruited companies as quickly as their Republican counterparts, and Irish, Welsh, and German volunteers led the ranks. "Thus we see that our adopted citizens, who have left behind the disadvantages of the . . . despotic government of the old world . . . ," Benjamin Bannan remarked, "are not ungrateful for [the advantages of the new] nor unmindful of the duty they owe government now in this hour of danger." English, French, German, Scotch, Irish, and Welsh, much to his delight, "have banished all differences and [are vying] with each other in their expressions of loyalty to the country of their choice."[40] The Pittston *Gazette* seconded this praise and singled out Luzerne County's Irish, who were ready and willing "to defend the stars and stripes" and who actively participated in Union meetings held in mining towns. Indeed, when Democratic congressman Hendrick B. Wright presided at Luzerne County's first war meeting, only "one universal purpose prevailed," and that was to "Go to War."[41]

Schuylkill County's Democratic leaders also waved the flag

at a bipartisan "Patriots arouse!" meeting. Democrat Franklin B. Gowen explained that war expenses would fall on the rich and not the poor and announced himself the "uncompromising enemy of men now waging war . . . against the government." Meyer Strouse, another Democrat whose "patriotic manner" earned him the approval of the *Miners' Journal,* put his nation before his party and "declared himself . . . for the maintenance of the Government."[42] But if Democrats fully recognized their obligation to defend the Union, they did not accept any obligation to confiscate southern property or emancipate slaves in the process. As Congressman Wright made clear in a speech to the House of Representatives in 1862, he favored prosecuting the war upon the issue for which it was inaugurated. "This war was not a war of conquest and subjugation," the *Luzerne Union* quoted him as saying, "but a war to put down the rebellion and to respect the rights of property." Although Wright acknowledged that he was no advocate of slavery, he "was willing to take the constitution as our fathers gave it to us." One Mr. Ludwig, writing to the *Easton Argus,* put it more succinctly. As the paper reported, this "sound young Democrat" went "to fight for the Union but not for the nigger."[43]

Republicans, on the other hand, fully accepted emancipation as a necessary war measure by 1862, although not all Republicans had favored the idea previously. In the mid-1850s, in fact, the *Miners' Journal* had clearly distanced itself from the "abolitionist fraternity." Bannan noted in 1855, "While we are opposed to the further extension of slavery . . . we believe strongly in the policy of state rights." Because it was a "local matter entirely," he continued, "we think it should rest alone with [the States concerned] for action, either for or against its continuance." As Republican Charles Albright explained, however, the war changed all this, rendering emancipation the key to national survival. Arguing that the Emancipation Proclamation was the "greatest act" of Lincoln's administration, Albright added that "it will be without virtue and effect if the Union army does not march through the seceded states victoriously and bear down all opposition." Benjamin Bannan concurred. "In my opinion," he advised Abraham Lincoln, "this Rebellion cannot be crushed without a general emancipation of the slaves. Let me tell you," he continued, "that *you* can *never conquer and hold the south so long as slavery exists except at an expense that no nation can sustain. . . .*"[44]

These Republicans had no vision of social equality with blacks, free or slave, and no intention of living side by side with them. "Emancipation will cause a decrease of the negro race in the United States," the *Miners' Journal* explained (no doubt to ease its readers' fears) since "systematic breeding" would be discontinued. "We advocate emancipation," the paper added, "to throw open the millions of acres of rich soil of the South to white laboring men. . . ." As for the emancipated slave, he would be forced "still farther south and out of the country by colonization." Indeed, in Bannan's view, emancipation would not only crush the rebellion but inaugurate a free-labor wage system in the South quickly and peacefully. When emancipated slaves demanded wages, he explained to Abraham Lincoln, rebel soldiers, fearing conflict, would desert and return home. Rebel slaveholders would flee the area, and their plantations would be broken up and sold to Union soldiers. Loyal slaveholders would be remunerated for their property and thus have the means to pay black laborers. Apparently Bannan did not even consider the possibility that freedmen might purchase property.[45]

Military necessity or not, moves toward emancipation renewed the Democrats' cries against Republican despotism. Leading Republican papers, the *Easton Argus* noted, were agitating to change "our form of government and favor the idea of establishing a Dictatorship." The *Luzerne Union* carried on the campaign. "The Republicans always stoutly denied of any sympathy with the abolitionists," the editor complained in the spring of 1862. "They go into power and what have they done? Abolished slavery in the District of Columbia . . . and have made negroes eligible to carry the mails of government." Republicans, he continued, obviously regarded the Constitution "as a rope of sand to be swept away when it conflicts with measures sought to be carried out by them."[46]

However negrophobic, the Democrats' anti-emancipation, popular-sovereignty campaign demonstrated more than racism pure and simple. Democrats held no franchise on racism in Pennsylvania or elsewhere; they did, however, claim a particular strand of racist rhetoric that stressed interracial labor competition and the high cost of emancipation. The *Easton Argus,* for example, crafting its message for a rural readership, noted that "though white freemen should be sorely taxed and the Treasury empty," Lincoln nevertheless intended to emancipate "that poor dear Negro!" White men, at the same time, would have to fend for themselves. "Agitate the slavery question," the editor exhorted, "squander the treasures of the nation . . . create thousands of sinecures—pile on the taxes—send along your tax gatherers and excise commissioners. . . . One thing alone we would entreat you not to do: Don't deceive the people; don't attempt to convince them that all these luxuries—war, emancipation, etc., can be long engaged without a proportionate increase of taxation."[47]

The *Wayne County Herald,* another paper aimed at rural Democrats in the coal regions, raised similar issues. "Besides our State, county, township, poor and other taxes, the direct war tax will amount to eight dollars per head for every man, woman, and child in the loyal states. . . . down with public robbers high and low," this paper raged, "down with abolition fanaticism, down with sectionalism in all shapes and guises." But emancipation would do more than raise taxes. Already, the *Herald* reported, black farmhands employed in Pennsylvania's southern border counties worked for five dollars a month—less than half the rate paid to white workers. The *Easton Argus* followed up on this line. In an article entitled "The Niggers are Coming—Fine Prospects Ahead," the paper reported that ninety-seven fugitive slaves had arrived in Philadelphia and abolitionists intended to employ them at arsenals and in the navy yards. "Pleasant prospects for the Irish, German, and American laborer! Sambo to get all the work; poor white man to be thrown out of employ . . . and to be well-taxed to make up Sambo's pay. . . ." The *Luzerne Union* added that abolitionists fully intended to "transplant unskilled and rude black laborers from the south to the north and bring him into direct competition with white laborers. . . . How would Pennsylvania be benefitted," the editor inquired, "if her mines were worked by negroes, her foundries filled by this class of laborers, her fields dotted all over with ignorant persons who have nothing in common with our citizens, who know nothing as to the workings of our institutions, yet by abolition fanaticism have been raised to a political and social equality with the white man?"[48]

During the war Democratic politicians employed the same political tactics they had used for two previous decades: they judged national issues in terms of local consequences and directed their political message to those groups most burdened by their opponents' policies. In the context of war, however, especially war for union, those tactics took on new meaning. When Democrats drew attention to the high costs of Republican war measures or stressed their discriminatory policies, Republicans impugned their patriotism and linked support for the Democratic party to support for the South. "The copperhead leaders of Schuylkill County, those deadly enemies of the Government," the *New York Tribune* informed its readers, had "poisoned the minds of miners and laborers and stimulated them to form combinations dangerous to public welfare." Not only had Democratic copperheads encouraged their supporters to seek "extortionate wages," but their "defiant repudiation of law" had stirred up "bloody resistance to the draft."[49] Republicans in Carbon County voiced similar complaints, one noting that Democratic newspapers "were weekly filled with malicious falsehoods and shameful abuse of the administration. Some of them," he added, "called upon the citizens . . . to arm themselves and oppose [enrollment] officers of the Government in the performance of their duties, pronouncing them tyrannical and unconstitutional."[50] By 1863, in fact, Republicans promoted the idea that a treasonous "copperhead" conspiracy linked Democrats throughout the North and orchestrated opposition to the Republican administration.

But the Democrats, who considered themselves loyal advocates of local autonomy over centralized authority, neither envisioned nor endorsed any opposition to the government more effective than voting a straight party ticket. When the Democratic party carried the coal regions in 1862, it hailed this victory for "popular sovereignty." At least in Pennsylvania, the *Luzerne Union* rejoiced, "the revolutionary spirit of fanaticism has met a terrible rebuke; the tyranny of lawless and arbitrary power has been denounced in a manner that showed clearly that the popular heart is still for the government and constitution of our fathers."[51] The strength and meaning of this commitment would be severely tested in the coming year, however, as the exigencies of war compelled the federal government to override "popular sovereignty" in the North as well as in the South.

Political contests in the coal regions during the 1850s and 1860s demonstrated the Republicans' fears of working-class political and economic organization: struggles over temperance and nativism, although couched in cultural terms, at bottom sought to mitigate any social power organized miners might wield in the workplace or in the community. Republicans became especially alarmed when Democratic miners, capitalizing on class and ethnic concentrations fostered by the development of centralized industry, employed their political strength to defeat the economic program and the individualist values espoused by Republican spokesmen. The outbreak of civil war significantly raised the political stakes of these contests, especially as increasing demands for coal, decreasing supplies of men, and the operators' desire to run at full capacity, created a situation favorable for miners interested in improving their wages and advancing their legitimate authority in the industry. At the same time, however, the enactment of a conscription law and the development of the Provost Marshal General's Bureau provided the operators and the Republicans with a solution to their problems. Supporters of the Republican administration relied on military power to quell this threat to their interests—so they hoped—once and for all. The Civil War, then, created a battleground not only for Democrats and Republicans to thrash out the meaning of Union, but also for the operators and the miners to test the rights of property against the claims of organized labor.

NOTES

1. *Mauch Chunk Gazette,* Aug. 7, 1862. The speech was delivered on July 14, 1862.

2. *Wayne County Herald,* Jan. 23, 1862.

3. Jean Baker, "A Loyal Opposition," *Civil War History* 25 (1979): 143–44.

4. Joel H. Silbey, *A Respectable Minority: The Democratic Party in the Civil*

War Era (New York, 1977); John F. Coleman, *The Disruption of the Pennsylvania Democracy, 1848–1860* (Harrisburg, Pa., 1975); Arnold Shankman, *The Pennsylvania Anti-War Movement, 1861–1865* (Rutherford, N.J., 1980); Bruce Collins, "The Ideology of the Antebellum Northern Democrats," *Journal of American Studies* 11 (1977): 103–21.

 5. *Luzerne Union*, Dec. 24, 1862.

 6. For ethnic rivalries see Wayne G. Broehl, *The Molly Maguires* (Cambridge, Mass., 1964); Harold Aurand, *From the Molly Maguires to the United Mine Workers* (Philadelphia, 1971). For a different view of this rivalry see Anthony F. C. Wallace, "The Miners of St. Clair: Family, Class, and Ethnicity in a Mining Town in Schuylkill County, 1850–1880," in *Hard Coal, Hard Times: Ethnicity and Labor in the Anthracite Region*, ed. David L. Salay (Scranton, Pa., 1984), 1–16.

 7. *MJ*, June 27, 1863.

 8. William A. Gudelunas, Jr., and William G. Shade, *Before the Molly Maguires: The Emergence of the Ethno-Religious Factor in the Politics of the Lower Anthracite Region, 1844–1872* (New York, 1976); Shankman, *The Pennsylvania Anti-War Movement*, 134–37.

 9. *MJ*, May 3, 1845; [John M. Crossland] to Editor, *MJ*, Dec. 30, 1843.

 10. *MJ*, Nov. 11, 1848; Gudelunas and Shade, *Before the Molly Maguires*, 54.

 11. My thinking on free labor ideology has been influenced by Barbara Fields and Leslie Rowland, "Free Labor Ideology and Its Exposition in the South during the Civil War and Reconstruction," paper delivered at the annual meeting of the Organization of American Historians, 1984.

 12. See chapter 2 and Clifton K. Yearley, Jr., *Enterprise and Anthracite* (Baltimore, 1961). For a sketch of Benjamin Bannan see Samuel T. Wiley, *Biographical and Portrait Cyclopedia of Schuylkill County* (Philadelphia, 1893), 213–15.

 13. *MJ*, Aug. 14, 1852.

 14. *Mining Register and Democrat*, Nov. 15, 1851; *Carbon County Gazette*, July 16, 1846; *MJ*, Nov. 6, 1852; William A. Gudelunas, Jr., "Nativism and the Demise of Schuylkill County Whiggery: Anti-Slavery or Anti-Catholicism?" *Pennsylvania History* 45 (1978): 229.

 15. *MJ*, July 16, 1853. One week later Bannan mentioned that the excessive heat that summer generated such foul air in the mines that miners could hardly work in them.

 16. *MJ*, June 25, 1853; see also William A. Gudelunas, Jr., "The Lower Anthracite Region Votes: An Electoral History of a Turbulent Region," *Proceedings of the Canal History and Technology Symposium* 4 (1985): 45–68; *MJ*, July 8, 1854, June 24, 1854. Poorhouse statistics can be found in *MJ*, Feb. 25, 1853, and June 25, 1853. Bannan makes no mention of the fact that Pottsville, and not the coal districts, led the list. Bannan, who was treasurer of the local prohibition organization at this time, employed the rhetoric described by Ian R. Tyrell, *Sobering Up: From Temperance to Prohibition in Ante-Bellum America, 1800–1860* (Westport, Conn., 1979), especially 274–78; *MJ*, July 22, 1854.

17. For a discussion of ethno-cultural politics in Schuylkill County, see Gudelunas, "The Lower Anthracite Region Votes." According to Gudelunas, German Lutheran farmers had formed the backbone of the Democratic party in Schuylkill County. For a critique of this discussion see Grace Palladino, "The Poor Man's Fight: Draft Resistance and Labor Organization in Schuylkill County, 1860–1865," Ph.D. diss., University of Pittsburgh, 1983, chapter 4.

18. Bannan's philosophy is evident in his column "The Coal Trade" and in editorials in the *Miners' Journal.*

19. *MJ*, Aug. 12, 1854, Apr. 8, 1854; "An Observing Miner" to Editor, *MJ*, Sept. 1, 1852, describes the design problems that resulted in poor ventilation and offers a better plan; *MJ*, Apr. 29, 1854, reports that "the miners contend that it is impossible to work ten hours a day in a Colliery particularly where the atmosphere is bad and gas prevails." See Anthony F. C. Wallace, *The Social Context of Innovation* (Princeton, 1982), for a critical discussion of the application of ventilation technology in Schuylkill County mines.

20. See chapters 2 and 3.

21. *MJ*, June 17, 1854, Apr. 7, 1855, Mar. 31, 1855. According to the *MJ*, Apr. 7, 1855, twenty-eight miners were arrested; the March 31 edition reports only three miners involved in the assault. Reports of such assaults and mysterious murders appeared periodically in the *Miners' Journal,* especially when a strike was in progress or elections were near. Since the arrests rarely stuck, such crimes are now difficult to investigate. Similar crimes happened outside the coal region and were reported in the *Miners' Journal.* Whether or not the incidence of crime was higher in Schuylkill County than in any other industrial center remains questionable.

22. *Mauch Chunk Gazette,* Dec. 3, 1857.

23. *Mining Register and Democrat,* June 1, 1850. Also cited in *MJ,* May 4, 1850.

24. *Mining Register and Democrat,* ibid.

25. *Pottsville Emporium,* June 12, 1847, Nov. 27, 1847.

26. *Pottsville Emporium,* Sept. 21, 1844.

27. *MJ,* May 1, 1852, Apr. 23, 1853.

28. *MJ,* Sept. 26, 1854; Frailey to Simon Cameron, Oct. 29, 1859, Simon Cameron Papers, Historical Society of Dauphin County; T. Z. Zulick to Simon Cameron, Oct. 27, 1856, ibid. For a discussion of ethno-cultural politics see Gudelunas and Shade, *Before the Molly Maguires.* See also Lee Benson, *The Concept of Jacksonian Democracy: New York as a Test Case* (Princeton, 1961); Michael F. Holt, *Forging a Majority: The Formation of the Republican Party in Pittsburgh, 1848–1860* (New Haven, Conn., 1969); Robert Kelley, *The Cultural Pattern in American Politics: The First Century* (New York, 1979); Paul Kleppner, *The Cross of Culture: A Social Analysis of Midwestern Politics, 1850–1900* (New York, 1970).

29. Walter Sedgwick to Simon Cameron, Oct. 28, 1856, Simon Cameron Papers; Benjamin Bannan to Henry Carey, July 25, 1856, in Henry

C. Carey Papers, Edward Gardiner Carey Collection, Historical Society of Pennsylvania; E. H. Rauch to Lemuel Todd, July 15, 1857, Edward McPherson Papers, Manuscript Division, Library of Congress, Washington, D.C.

30. Gudelunas and Shade, *Before the Molly Maguires*, 117. See also the Hendrick B. Wright Papers, Wyoming Geological and Historical Society, which include extensive correspondence from various Irish Democrats, especially around election time. This correspondence makes it clear, however, that the Irish were not satisfied with the party's recognition of their voting power.

31. Cited in George Bergner, pub., *The Legislative Record Containing the Debates and Proceedings of the Pennsylvania Legislature for the Sessions of 1860–65* (Harrisburg, Pa., 1860–65), 265. The bill referred to was the "Wages of Labor Bill #123"; *MJ*, Mar. 29, 1862.

32. Horatio King to James Buchanan, Nov. 7, 1860, Horatio King Papers, Manuscript Division, Library of Congress.

33. F. W. Hughes to James Buchanan, Oct. 26, 1856, reel 29, James Buchanan Papers, Historical Society of Pennsylvania. Hughes's resolution on joining the Confederacy is cited in the *MJ*, Oct. 4, 1862. See also Arnold Shankman, "Francis W. Hughes and the 1862 Pennsylvania Election," *Pennsylvania Magazine of History and Biography* 95 (1971): 383–93.

34. James Buchanan to Royal Phelps, Dec. 22, 1860, Horatio King Papers.

35. George Woodward to Jeremiah Black, Dec. 10, 1860, Carl B. Swisher Papers, Manuscript Division, Library of Congress; D. T. R. Wohlfarth to Charles Buckalew, Sept. 5, 1861, Charles R. Buckalew Papers, Manuscript Division, Library of Congress.

36. Thomas Foster to Simon Cameron, Jan. 20, 1861, Simon Cameron Papers.

37. The unsuccessful attempt to suppress publication of the speech is described in John Miller to Thaddeus Stevens, June 13, 1850, Thaddeus Stevens Papers, Manuscript Division, Library of Congress; Richard McAllister to James Buchanan, Dec. 10, 1850, reel 16, Buchanan Papers; *Patriot and Union*, Sept. 2, 1857.

38. *Mauch Chunk Gazette*, Mar. 1, 1858, Aug. 12, 1858.

39. Daniel Larer to Simon Cameron, Mar. 24, 1860, Simon Cameron Papers; Eli Bowen to Cameron, Jan. 22, 1861, ibid.

40. *MJ*, Apr. 27, 1861, May 11, 1861; "Schuylkill County in the Civil War," *Publications of the Historical Society of Schuylkill County* 7 (1961): 33, 35, 42, 65.

41. Pittston *Gazette*, May 2, 1861, May 30, 1861; Henry C. Bradsby, *History of Luzerne County Pennsylvania* (Chicago, 1893), 179–80.

42. *MJ*, Sept. 7, 1861. Bannan called these remarks "the happiest we ever heard him deliver."

43. *Luzerne Union*, Jan. 29, 1862. The speech, which can be found in Wright's papers, was delivered January 20, 1862; *Easton Argus*, Oct. 30, 1862.

44. *MJ*, Nov. 17, 1858; Charles Albright to Abraham Lincoln, Oct. 20, 1862, Abraham Lincoln Papers, Manuscript Division, Library of Congress; Benjamin Bannan to Abraham Lincoln, July 24, 1862, ibid.

45. *MJ*, Feb. 22, 1862, July 19, 1862; cf. Barbara J. Fields, "Ideology and Race in American History," in *Region, Race, and Reconstruction*, ed. J. Morgan Kousser and James M. McPherson (New York, 1982), 143–78; Benjamin Bannan to Abraham Lincoln, July 24, 1862, Abraham Lincoln Papers.

46. *Easton Argus*, Sept. 11, 1862; *Luzerne Union*, May 7, 1862, June 25, 1862.

47. *Easton Argus*, Apr. 3, 1862.

48. *Wayne County Herald*, Jan. 23, 1862, Jan. 30, 1862; *Easton Argus*, Apr. 4, 1862; *Luzerne Union*, Feb. 25, 1863. Cf. Albon P. Man, "Labor Competition and the New York Draft Riots of 1863," *Journal of Negro History* 36 (1951): 375–405.

49. *New York Tribune* is cited in *MJ*, Feb. 6, 1864.

50. Samuel Yohe to James B. Fry, "Historical Report," Eleventh District, Pennsylvania, RG 110, National Archives.

51. *Luzerne Union*, Dec. 24, 1862.

5

Opposition to Conscription in the Coal Regions 1862–63

During the summer of 1862 Abraham Lincoln endorsed the theory that only total war—war waged to destroy the structure of southern society—would resurrect the Union. His decision to draft an Emancipation Proclamation that July clarified his conviction. "These enemies must understand," he explained to August Belmont, "that they cannot experiment ten years trying to destroy the government and if they fail . . . come back into the Union unhurt."[1] The revolutionary consequences of total war, however, would not be confined to the South: Lincoln's strategy for a Union victory required northern compliance with Republican war aims and a central government strong enough to enforce that compliance.

The reluctant response to Lincoln's July call for three hundred thousand recruits underscored the fragile basis of northern support for the war. "We are coming, Father Abraham, three hundred thousand more," a New York editor boldly promised, but his countrymen were slow to pick up the refrain. By mid-July it was already clear that volunteers would not reman the Union army. The Republican administration designed a solution that, it believed, would solve the twofold dilemma of raising men and enforcing compliance: those states failing to meet assigned quotas through volunteering would conscript the difference.[2]

In theory conscription offered an equitable, democratic, and certain means of attaining recruits. At the same time, it promised to forge the nationalism necessary to pursue total war. The idea of conscription, on the one hand, would teach citizens their duty to the state. Its enforcement, on the other, would demonstrate the state's authority to raise an army. In practice, conscription would force citizens to realize that, in times of war, the requirements of the state superseded local, individual interests. Thus conscription, as Orestes Brownson explained, asserted not only national unity and authority but also "the duty of the citizen to defend his country when called upon."[3]

Individuals liable to the draft in 1862, however, were less interested in the theory of conscription than they were in its practical implications. In states like Pennsylvania, where conservative Democrats wielded significant influence, the idea of conscription threatened long-cherished notions of popular sovereignty and personal autonomy that even war had not displaced. Potential draftees, especially those unable to purchase substitutes, viewed conscription in practical and provincial terms. "The draft will make misery in many families," Isaac B. Tyson, a small mill owner, explained to Governor Curtin. Complaining that his daughter-in-law "will get out of her mind" should his son be conscripted, he added that he relied on his other son to help him run the mill. "If I must lose him," he pleaded, "I am broke up." John Schenk, a Cumberland County farmer, voiced similar fears. Although he supported the idea of conscription, he suggested the law be amended to ensure that at least one man per farm be retained. "I have nabours [that are] subject to draft and are left alone," he wrote. "One man has had two hands [who] both left and went to the army. Now," he wondered, "if he whare to be drafted how would [the] crop be put out?" An anonymous writer from Reading agreed that the law ignored the farmers' special concerns. "Now please listen to me," he wrote to the governor. "There are hundreds here who are willing to go without being drafted. They just want a little more time for to finish their work first, then they will go wherever you want them to go." Taking his criticism one step further, this "sincere friend" cautioned the governor against hasty action. "Everywhere they have provided themselves with ammunition, guns, and rifles," he warned, "and they dare any number to come and draft them before they have their work finished."[4]

Supporters of conscription fully expected conservative Democrats to oppose the measure, but they also expected the law itself to force recalcitrant communities to comply. "There are hundreds of able-bodied Irishmen at the Broad Top Coal Region," a Huntington Township postmaster reported, "who are unwilling to enlist in defense of our country. . . . I therefore hope, that you will make a heavy draft in this township." The Republican editor of the *Mauch Chunk Gazette* agreed that conscription—"a just and right measure"—would "compel townships and counties which have not been willing to do their share of the work . . . to furnish their full and equal proportion now." Despite the logic of this view, these observers underestimated the deep-rooted ethnic and class-related tensions that drove certain communities to oppose Republican war measures—especially conscription.[5]

The fervid election campaign that coincided with this first attempt to conscript exacerbated these tensions and aggravated opposition to the law. Democratic spokesmen, for example, identified conscription as an abolitionist, class-oriented measure that would not have been necessary had propertied Republicans enlisted in the fight. "In order to obtain recruits, let our prominent, influential, and wealthy citizens . . . shoulder their muskets and say 'come with us,' " the *Wayne County Herald* suggested. "They take the lead in receiving benefits from the government and why not in its defense?" The *Luzerne Union* argued likewise. Reporting a fictitious conversation between two local residents, the editor made clear his distaste for Republican war measures. "I always thought the army was too small—that blood didn't flow fast enough," the first resident argued in support of increasing the size of the army. When his colleague asked why he had not enlisted since he was so determined to crush the rebellion, he offered a quick and unembarrassed reply. "Ah that's not the way with us fellows who favor a big army! We like to stay at home and hiss on the rest." The Boston *Pilot,* an Irish Catholic and Democratic paper popular in the coal regions, made similar complaints. Pointing out that Irish and German immigrants had contributed more than their share of soldiers, the editor explained that the "denationalized character" that prevailed among "old know-nothings and Abolitionists" had slowed enlistments. "In the case of conscription," he argued, "it ought to be made heavily on both these classes."[6]

The coming election of 1862 also encouraged Democrats and Republicans to manipulate the process of conscription for their own political advantage. Because soldiers in the field could not vote in 1862, conscription could shape the outcome of the election. Democrats, fearing that the draft would decimate their electoral base, worked hard to postpone it. Republicans, on the other hand, hoped to capitalize on a swift and determined enforcement of the law. "There is another reason why the draft should soon be made and the persons drafted sent to a rendezvous, which is this," one Republican explained to Governor Curtin: "those who have [already] gone are nearly all from the republican and loyal democratic ranks," he asserted, "and the draft would now come off sections which have withheld their support from the war." Benjamin Bannan agreed with this strategy. "We may lose the Congressional district if the draft is not made and the men got off before the election," he reported, "especially since the draft would fall heaviest on democratic districts." Henry Hain, another Schuylkill County Republican, urged even more drastic action. "Hurry the first draft and call for another," he exhorted the governor, "or else we will not have enough men left of Republican and Union men to elect one inspector."[7] These partisan tactics not only undermined the nationalizing aspects of conscription but fueled overt resistance to its enforcement.

Opposition to conscription, especially to the enrolling officers who compiled the lists of eligible draftees, erupted in a number of Democratic townships and grew more fierce as the election approached. The dimensions and significance of that resistance, however, remain difficult to measure. Local newspapers rarely covered episodes of resistance in detail and followed their political party's line whenever they interpreted these incidents. Republican editors, for example, magnified the slightest tremors into evidence of organized resistance and viewed any group of Democrats as a potential threat to the government. Democratic editors, on the other hand, usually pictured resisters as hapless, disorganized victims of an overbearing state. Although they abhorred violent demonstrations, these editors dismissed what outbursts occurred as insignificant and sometimes justifiable re-actions. Because government reports were usually based on sec-ondhand evidence supplied by Republican property holders, they are no less biased sources; they better document the writers' political values than overt resistance to the draft.[8] Nevertheless, the perceptions that colored these reports of resistance largely determined the federal government's official response. In a very real political sense, then, these perceptions and expectations of draft resistance often proved more potent than the resistance itself.

Although the *Easton Argus* in Democratic Northampton County reported that enrollment officers were "received respectfully" and that a "good-humored purpose to submit gracefully" marked the local scene, the editor was not at all sure what would happen when the draft itself took place. "We hear many rumors of organized resistance," he acknowledged, but, as he put it, this could "all be idle talk." When enrollers made their way into the nearby coal regions, however, the populace proved less good-humored and graceful. From the very first days of enrollment, in fact, observers in Schuylkill, Luzerne, and Carbon Counties complained of local efforts to impede the process.[9]

Despite the colorful rhetoric employed by Republican news-papers and official reports of draft resistance, opposition gen-erally took the form of evasion: the likely draftee took to the woods or refused to cooperate with officials. "Where persons lock the doors and refuse to give their names and the proprietor of the building also refuses," one marshal inquired, "what is the duty of the Enrolling officer?" Although there is evidence of community support for resisters, these men generally acted as individuals and developed tactics that they did not consider to be outside the law. When resistance took more organized forms, in fact, it was women, and not potential draftees, who actively opposed enrollers. "The women have an idea that the law does not reach them," the Pittston *Gazette* explained, "and that what-ever assaults they may make will not be interfered with."[10] When twenty-five women assembled in Mauch Chunk and stoned two enrolling officers, however, four were arrested and jailed without bail. Officials in Pittston jailed another woman on a similar charge and were on the trail of three other female offenders.

According to the *Gazette* one Pittston woman even went so far as to "intimidate the Marshal by thrusting into his face a small child which had the smallpox in a most loathsome form."[11]

If this resistance proved neither life-threatening nor well organized, it nevertheless expressed contempt for the law and inhibited the enroller's efforts to enforce it. Consequently, officials procured military assistance to ease the process. For example, when a military guard accompanied the enrollment officer in Archbald, a Luzerne County mining village dominated by Irish Democrats, violence erupted. Although it remains unclear whether that violence first emanated from the crowd or from the armed guard, local Republicans used the episode to justify their belief that without armed force no draft could be made in the coal regions.

The Archbald incident occurred on September 22, 1862, after three different enrollers failed to complete their task. The fourth took the precaution of gathering a posse that included two U.S. cavalrymen. Even the presence of this armed guard, however, did not dissuade a crowd of Irish women, who forcefully drove the officer and his posse out of "Shanty Town," an Irish enclave.[12]

The trouble did not end there. Although American and German residents "cheerfully" cooperated with enrollers, the Irish women allegedly stormed a German shoe shop and "commenced a violent assault with stones, clubs, etc." Despite the fierce violence described by the *Scranton Republican,* the enrolling officer managed to walk off unharmed. Making his way to the entrance of the coal mines, the officer enrolled a few more men before hostilities again erupted. When he entered the office of a coal company, however, a real tumult ensued. The men, who had hovered behind their rock-throwing wives and sisters, now joined in the fight. Painting a scene of wanton destruction, the paper linked this episode to the miners' alleged sympathy for the South. "While one party of brawny Irishmen was trying to break the fastenings of the door," the paper reported, "the main body was bombarding the building and a tempest of missiles was rained against the walls and through the windows almost equal in intensity to the storm of shot and shell which their compatriots at the South hurled against Fort Sumter." This group of "wild

Irishmen"—which numbered 500 according to the Republican press and 150 according to the Democratic—eventually broke into the office, but the enroller safely escaped.[13]

The *Luzerne Union* reported what it called "The Women's Riots of Archbald" somewhat differently. Although its reporter agreed that these women acted in a "crazy manner," he added that "several miners, who at other times have some influence, tried to persuade the women to let [the enroller] depart in peace." Apparently he had offered to surrender the enrollment lists to the crowd and had promised never to return in exchange for his release. When his associates would not allow him to meet these terms, the enroller was once again at the mercy of the women, who allegedly wrestled him to the ground trying to "get his pants off." Only with the help of an assistant did the enroller escape his pursuers. "None of the men of this place interfered," this reporter concluded, except to save the enroller from these "aggravating and embarrassing" circumstances.[14]

When this officer again tried to make the enrollment in Archbald about one week later, an armed military guard and a Catholic priest accompanied him. "Little or no trouble was encountered," the *Luzerne Union* reported, "except on the part of a few women who were promptly arrested." It was only after the entourage returned to their hotel that evening that violence erupted. After townspeople clashed with the military, a riot broke out. Before the trouble could be settled, a member of the guard fatally shot one man and wounded several others. "It is said that stones were thrown at the military before the firing," the paper added, "but whether the assault was sufficient to warrant a promiscuous firing into the crowd may yet be the subject of investigation."[15]

In Schuylkill County the story followed similar lines. In those parts of the county dominated by immigrant Democrats, especially Cass Township, enrollers were impeded by women hurling stones or were evaded altogether. When threats against their lives allegedly forced two enrollers to leave Cass, however, the drama intensified. "If the enrollments are incomplete the balance of the county ought to demand a correct enrollment," Benjamin Bannan advised, "even if it takes a battalion of soldiers to enforce it. . . ." Blaming Breckinridge Democrats for the trouble, Bannan added that it would be a "blessing to the community" if a few these leaders were hanged.[16]

The threat of imminent conscription and the heated election campaign exacerbated long-standing class, ethnic, and political tensions in Cass and the surrounding coal regions. The *Miners' Journal* reported that several farmers in the vicinity had been assaulted and that unknown persons had broken into the house of a local priest. Irish miners in Cass blamed their Protestant neighbors—and the enrolling officer—for the damage and apparently attempted to avenge the attack. The sheriff, accompanied by a seventy-member armed guard, nevertheless averted riot. "Forbearance has well-nigh ceased to be a virtue," Bannan lamented. "A severe example is needed to teach the disorderly element of Cass that there is a power—the law—which it must respect."[17]

By mid-October the enrollment and draft were completed. When officials attempted to deliver the drafted men to the rendezvous, however, tensions reached crisis proportions. Committees of miners announced plans to stop the collieries on Saturday, October 25, the day conscripts were to report for duty. At the same time, the Irish renewed their case against local Protestants, who, according to the Philadelphia *Enquirer*, "found it necessary to leave the township and desert their property." In the midst of these struggles, opponents of conscription managed to stop a train loaded with draftees on their way to Harrisburg, allegedly offering protection to any man wishing to desert.[18] Local officials apprised Governor Curtin of the situation, and he in turn reported the story to Secretary of War Edwin Stanton. "Notwithstanding the usual exaggeration," Curtin prefaced his report, "I think the organization to resist the draft in Schuylkill, Luzerne, and Carbon Counties is very formidable. I wish to crush the resistance so effectively," he continued, "that the like will not occur again." The War Department immediately authorized Curtin to employ all the available military force in his department but tabled his request for one thousand regulars. Two days later, Curtin renewed his appeal, increasing his estimate of the crowd from one thousand to five thousand strong. "We all think that the resistance to the draft is the first appearance of a conspiracy and, unless crushed at once, cannot say how far it may extend."[19]

With the military en route to Schuylkill County, officials also called on the Catholic clergy to soothe tensions. In Tremont, an Irish coal town, the local pastor impressed upon miners "the necessity of preserving the Union and enforcing the laws." According to the Philadelphia *Enquirer*'s report, his argument proved so compelling that "one or two of the would-be rioters, who were disposed to be insolent, were overawed." The Right Reverend Bishop Francis Wood also played a role in averting riot. Meeting privately with local clergymen, Wood instructed them to preach that Sunday "on the evils of resisting constituted authorities of the land" and to threaten those "still determined to be troublesome" with excommunication. When the riot failed to materialize, the Boston *Pilot* congratulated the Catholic clergy on their success. By the influence of religion alone, the paper boasted, "a wide-spread disaffection was totally extirpated; exasperated men went quietly about their usual vocations, and the law was protected without the uplifting of an arm, or the striking of a blow." Governor Curtin supported this assessment. "The decision and promptness but more the presence of Bishop Wood," he informed Stanton, ". . . relieved us all."[20]

Alexander McClure, state administrator of the draft, viewed the situation differently. Although he no doubt also thanked the bishop, he later revealed that it was not religion, but the failure to enforce the draft, that saved Cass Township from destruction. Acknowledging that the draft had fallen most heavily on those he called the "Molly Maguires who ruled the mines," McClure feared that violent conflict would accompany any military effort to deliver these conscripts. Indeed, newspapers reported that miners in Cass Township had already stationed themselves along the railroad tracks to give notice of any approaching troops. McClure, however, convinced the governor that the troops should remain in Pottsville and not advance into Cass. In the meantime, according to his memoirs, McClure telegraphed a coded message to President Lincoln, explaining his reluctance to provoke riot.[21] The following day, Assistant Adjutant General Townsend met McClure with the remark that the president wished to "see the law enforced or at least appear to have been executed." Townsend then added that Lincoln closed his instructions with the phrase, "I think McClure will understand." Although Townsend had no knowledge of what had transpired, McClure understood the president to mean that he should seek a peaceful yet honorable solution to disturbances in Cass. McClure therefore ordered Benjamin Bannan, who served as the local draft commissioner, to proceed to Harrisburg with enough affidavits to prove that Cass had met its quota. Consequently, McClure relieved the "Molly Maguires" conscripts from their duty to the Union.[22]

Although there is no reason to doubt the fact of opposition to conscription, McClure's anecdote overlooks certain aspects of the law enforcement procedure that might better explain the roots of resistance to conscription in the coal regions. Because enrolling officers often relied on tax records or employment rolls to make their lists, they included a number of aliens who were not subject to the law.[23] When a Wilkes-Barre resident reported resistance to enrollment in Luzerne County, for example, he explained that, in the heavy mining districts, "thousands of aliens have been enrolled and to hear these [exemption cases] will require . . . ten days." These careless methods resulted, no doubt, from the draft officials' inexperience and the communities' hostility to enrollers. Nevertheless, it was in communities housing large numbers of aliens that resistance was most likely to erupt. When McClure admitted that the "Molly Maguire conscripts" were not held to service, he implied that organized, treasonous miners overawed the government. It is more likely, however, that these conscripts were released because they had been improperly enrolled in the first place.[24] Whatever their motivation, these recalcitrant miners demonstrated the limits of the 1862 Conscription Law—limits that the Conscription Act of 1863 would forcefully overcome.

When the Congress designed the Conscription Act in the early months of 1863, it made sure that enforcement mechanisms were written into the law. "I think we shall all agree," New York's Congressman Olin explained, "that the time has come . . . when . . . the Government shall arm itself with every power that lies in the strong arms and loyal hearts of her people." For Olin, as for other supporters of the law, the Conscription Act would "clothe the Government at once with the power necessary for self-defense. . . ."[25] Section five of the act empowered the president to appoint a Provost Marshal General, who answered directly to the president, and to appoint provost marshals in every congressional district. The act gave these district provost marshals the power to arrest all deserters, spies, and any person they judged to be resisting the draft, obstructing enrollment, or "counselling" drafted men to desert. The Provost Marshal General's Bureau, then, could bypass state and local governments to enforce the draft and root out treason.[26] Although Congressman White, an Ohio Democrat, contended that this clause would "afford an apology for illegal arrests," his Republican colleagues dismissed this argument. "It is high time the Federal Government exerted every power. . . expressly granted to it," Olin responded. "And if the Government cannot exercise these powers, the sooner we know it the better."[27]

When Samuel Yohe, provost marshal for Pennsylvania's Eleventh Congressional District, reflected on his efforts to enforce conscription, he acknowledged the revolutionary aspects of the law. Reporting that his constituents were "strangers to the strident measures necessary in times of civil revolution," he added that they felt "a strong desire to save themselves." In this basically Democratic district composed of Carbon, Northampton, Wayne, Monroe, and Pike Counties, native-born and immigrant residents challenged the federal government's right to impose conscription. "The thoughts and feelings of our people," Yohe confessed, "were centered upon one grand object . . . and that object was self. . . ."[28]

The Eleventh District proved to be a nightmare for enrolling officers, who sometimes resigned rather than enter Democratic subdistricts. Simon Grabner, for example, complained of a "copperhead" who threatened "to blow the provost marshal's brains out" should he cross over Blue Mountain, and who allegedly offered a group of laborers "ten gallons of good brandy if they would take the [enrolling] marshal and tar and feather him." In Monroe County, four resisters in Polk Township were arrested for forcing enrollers to abandon their work, and in Westfield Township the story was similar. "No one man or twenty can enroll Westfield Township," Samuel Allen reported. According to enrollers, he added, "there was at least two hundred congregated yesterday to mob him." After another officer was "kicked and choked and his papers destroyed," Allen asked for military help. "A small cavalry force would be the best," he explained.[29]

Especially in these rural subdistricts, enrollers feared the emergence of what they called "secret organizations" to resist the draft and generally obstruct the Republican administration's war efforts. Frequent reports of such organizations—referred to as the Knights of the Golden Circle or the Knights of Liberty—crossed the provost marshal's desk, supporting the Republicans' charge that an organized network orchestrated opposition. In Monroe County, Joseph Oliver blamed resistance in Stroudsberg on the machinations of a secret organization, while Joseph Wetherwill explained resistance in Barrett Township in similar terms. "Now this is a Copperhead den in the fullest sense of the term," he informed Samuel Yohe, "for there is a secret order here called the Knights of the Golden Circle . . . avowing their determination to resist the Enrollment or Draft." Noting that this "secret" order met weekly, paraded "with music of fife and drum," and drilled regularly, he added that members "wear a badge of blue ribbon with a large Copper attached to it."[30] Although Democrats claimed that there was nothing sinister about this group and that it functioned along the same lines as the Republican party's Union League, the deputy provost marshal strongly disagreed. "The public [in Monroe County] is dreadful," Samuel Allen complained, "and threats are openly made to ravage and burn out every Republican if any attempt is made to carry out the law."[31]

The specter of a treasonous organization of Irish miners also alarmed officials in the Eleventh District. According to E. H. Rauch, the deputy provost marshal in Mauch Chunk and a leading Republican, Irish miners in the middle coal fields of Carbon County had banded together into a secret labor organization known as the "Buckshots." Noting that the group was well armed—Rauch and his men had found some fifteen guns in a search of houses in one town—he added that the order had strong support in Jeansville, Audenried, Coleraine, and other mining towns in Carbon County, as well as in Hazleton in neighboring Luzerne County. Buckshots in Jeansville, for example, misled "enrollers by false names and other dodges peculiar to the Irish," and in Banks Township the Irish were similarly "troublesome." Indeed, throughout the coal regions Rauch found it difficult to extract the necessary information from the Irish, and, when it came time to notify drafted men, the task proved almost impossible. Had it not been for the "Englishmen, Protestant Irish, and leading citizens of American birth" who came to the provost marshal's aid, Rauch and his men would not have located the draftees. "The leading coal operators declare their determination to expel from their mines all 'Buckshots' and other bad characters," Rauch informed Yohe, "which they can only do if protected by the military."[32]

In Luzerne County, in the Twelfth Congressional District, Provost Marshal Bradford also argued that well-organized resistance to the draft made it impossible to enforce conscription without military aid. When Bradford failed to amass the troops he allegedly required, he appointed special agents to uncover "the necessary evidence to convict the parties who are advising resistance to the enrollment and furnishing arms to the ignorant class to resist with."[33] According to Ario Pardee, a leading coal operator in Hazleton, Conrad Horn was a likely suspect. Horn, a well-known Democrat and a gunsmith, it was rumored, had provided arms to miners. The rumor had some foundation, Pardee informed Bradford, "from the fact that in searching some Irish houses this morning at Harleigh Mines for the purpose of arresting some men who committed an outrage . . . we found several new rifles of Horn's make and . . . four muskets." Although the Democratic press later ridiculed this evidence, asking how it could be treasonous for a gunsmith to sell guns, this strong belief in organized resistance made it possible for Bradford to secure his military force.[34]

Although a small detachment of the Invalid Corps and the 49th Pennsylvania Militia were stationed throughout the Twelfth District, Bradford still doubted his ability to enforce the enrollment. In fact, the arrival of the military only added to his problems with one subdistrict. "Since the arrival of Captain Kern with his command," Bradford complained to Colonel Bomford, "the men have organized and parade the streets of the town, have hauled down an American flag, dragged it in the road after them and hurrahed for Jeff Davis bidding defiance to all authority." Although he called for 50 more men on July 12, ten days later he believed he needed at least 200 men to complete the enrollment. The excitement was so great, he informed Bomford, that he dare not move any of the 120 men guarding his headquarters. He added, "I am satisfied that an attack by a mob would follow."[35]

Bomford, however, was not persuaded by Bradford's fear, and he counseled him to avoid confrontations. In fact, he recommended that General Couch deny Bradford's request for an additional 1,000 men. When Major A. H. Mayer, an inspecting officer, learned of Bradford's request, he grew incensed. "You have been time and time again ordered to keep your men together," he rebuked Bradford, "and under no circumstances allow yourself to be precipitate or impudent in calling on the military force under your orders."[36] Bradford, stung by the criticism, hastened to explain his position. "I have the honor also to report that on Saturday next, August 1," he informed Mayer, "there is to be a general turnout of all the Miners in the valley and what they call a Miners' Union anniversary at this place, and at least four thousand Irishmen will be here. But I believe the name of the meeting is only nominal for I have myself seen Irishmen buying powder etc. and they boast that $4,000 has been expended for arms for them."[37]

Having clarified the basis of his apprehension, Bradford asked to have at least 500 men for the "anniversary" celebration, adding that a section of artillery would be "very efficient." By September, Bradford had amassed two companies of the Invalid Corps and four companies of the 21st Pennsylvania Cavalry, but he still did not "deem it safe to commence the draft" without at least one more regiment of infantry. The Twelfth District, he explained to C. C. Gilbert, the Acting Assistant Provost Marshal for Pennsylvania's Eastern Districts, "is a mining district adjoining Schuylkill County and beyond all question, there is more opposition to the Government in this and the Schuylkill District, than in any other part of the state."[38]

Although Charlemagne Tower, provost marshal for Schuylkill County, shared Bradford's assessment, he proved immediately more skilled and sophisticated in his use of federal power. Where Bradford seemed frightened and insecure in the face of opposition, Tower almost relished the idea of a showdown so that he might demonstrate once and for all the meaning of nationalism in a time of war. As leader of the eighty-man Tower Brigade, which had seen three months service early in the war, Tower had impressed a war correspondent "merely by the tone of his voice—loud and clear as the blast of a trumpet." He had proved himself an "excellent disciplinarian," who "had his men in perfect drill." As provost marshal, Tower used these skills to make it clear that resistance to the draft would not be tolerated in the Tenth District. "Nothing but a sufficient military force vigorously directed to crush opposition," he informed the Provost Marshal General in May, "will prevent the re-enactment of last years scenes and riots."[39]

Enrolling officers in Schuylkill County experienced the same resistance that slowed the process in Carbon and Luzerne Counties. Charlemagne Tower, however, determined from the first to demonstrate the power of federal authority. When Peter Kutz attempted to enforce the enrollment in Hegins Township on June 4, 1863, three residents—Abraham Bressler, Israel Stutzman, and Christopher Stutzman—"put him in such fear of his life or bodily harm that he was obliged to desist . . . and go home." Tower, convinced that this "instance of assault" should not go unpunished, undertook to arrest the culprits.[40]

Deputy Provost Marshal Uriah Gane, together with James Bowen, Sergeant William Parks, and three men of the provost guard, set out to make the arrests. When Bressler refused to open the door, the posse posted themselves round his house. "You are my prisoner and I arrest you in the name of the Provost Marshal," Sergeant Parks reportedly announced. Calling out "Marshal" a few times more, Parks confused the posse, and Bressler was able to make an escape. In the meantime the door was opened, Parks fired his revolver inside, and Gane rushed in and arrested Abraham Reed, a man he thought to be Bressler. Returning to Pottsville, the posse allegedly passed Bressler in a carriage, but he refused to stop. After warning him four times to halt, Parks fired his revolver twice but failed to hit him. Bressler was, nevertheless, arrested a few days later.[41]

The Bressler incident did not end here. In mid-June Uriah Gane and James Bowen were arrested and charged with committing assault and battery upon Abraham Reed with the intent to kill him. Although both defendants argued that they were not guilty "by virtue and under color of authority derived from and exercised by and under the President of the United States," the Court was not sympathetic. To make matters worse, a writ of habeas corpus had been issued in Bressler's favor, although Bressler had already been delivered to U.S. marshals in Philadelphia. The habeas corpus fight underscored the tension that existed between the provost marshal's office and the county courts, and the Bressler case instituted a test of wills over the question of federal authority versus home rule. Tower's earlier observation that "it will not avail me to look to citizens as a *posse comitatus*," since "the many will not feel with me," seemed particularly apt.[42]

The county court made clear its opposition to arbitrary authority:

> The writ of *habeas corpus* would be an empty privilege if the writ could be defeated by pretext set up by [the Provost Marshal] that he held the prisoner by color of authority of another jurisdiction. . . . Was Bressler guilty of a criminal offense against the laws of the United States? The return does not say so, but says that in the "military warrant or order" Bressler is charged with an offense against the laws of the United States. What authority is there for this military order or warrant? . . . This warrant is no more authority than the verbal declaration of the Provost Marshal. Does this offense fall within the offense specified in the [Enrollment] Act? . . . Is this Act constitutional?

The court went on to ask, "Suppose the Provost Marshal should issue his military warrant against an unoffending citizen? The same return could be made and the jurisdiction of the Court ousted."[43] Indeed, later, in November 1863, the Pennsylvania Supreme Court found the law unconstitutional, but it reversed that decision in January 1864 after Republicans gained a majority on the bench.

Even Edward O. Parry, a Republican and an attorney for the Provost Marshal's office, concurred with the county court's decision. Parry found Tower's decision to ignore the court wrong in principle and likely to impede the interests of the federal government. "I cannot see that it can do any good," he informed Tower, "but on the contrary will cause great and unnecessary irritation in the public mind and give the opponents of the government an opportunity to say that the U.S. officers are seeking to evade the powers of the state courts." Parry correctly predicted that the Democrats would use this incident "with great effect."[44]

Parry's argument swayed Tower not at all. Unwilling to bow to local authorities, especially in a case that tested the federal government's power, Tower held fast to his course. "The court . . . impedes me," he complained to Colonel Fry, "and the next step it will take . . . will be to imprison me. . . . Am I authorized to arrest the court?" Tower inquired. "Let me beg of you . . . ," he implored, "to permit me to show . . . the power of the United States."[45]

Although Tower never arrested the court, the Bressler case served his purpose of demonstrating the force of government. "The arrests which I have made . . . the military force which has been sent me, and the assurances given me that as much as I require should come when needed," he wrote to Colonel Bomford, "have had good effect. I have gotten men to accept and go enrolling," Tower boasted, "with prospects of success in three of my worst sub-districts."[46]

Despite Tower's masterful performance in the face of a hostile Democratic court and the military force at his disposal, opposition to conscription and enrollment evasion continued in Schuylkill County. As in 1862, however, such activity often had more to do with the execution of the law than with opposition to the Union. "Much of the opposition to the draft," the Philadelphia *Public Ledger* pointed out in the fall of 1863, for example, "arises not so much from the terms of the act . . . but from the conduct of the Board of Enrollment." James Howe, a Schuylkill County resident, found himself drafted in 1863, and his mother paid his way out despite her claim that her son was not yet twenty. "I am sure," Attorney William J. Turner wrote to Colonel Fry, "that you would gladly correct an erroneous proceeding on the part of your subordinates who may, in some cases, and this is one of them, have been incited to undue zeal by the opposition which the enforcing of the Conscription Act had encountered in the mining districts of Pennsylvania."[47]

When Malachi Gorman and Stephen Tierney fraudulently attempted to avoid conscription, their lawyer also questioned the enrollment board's procedures. Apparently the two had produced substitutes and commutation money only after they unsuccessfully claimed exemptions as underage aliens. The board accepted their money, but Tower held the two to service. Although Tower refused to reconsider his action, their attorney nevertheless attempted to win their freedom or at least to get their money back. "It is true they might have been a little impudent to the Provost Marshal," he explained, "yet I question the right of a Provost Marshal to hold citizens for doing an injury to his feelings." Eventually Gorman and Tierney were discharged, but even their congressman could not get the commutation money back.[48]

Citizens in Rahn Township registered more serious complaints about the board and the process of enrollment in Schuylkill County. There would be no opposition to enrollment officers, the citizens agreed, if the enrollment were corrected and volunteers properly credited. Rahn's residents were not off the mark. When James Bowen succeeded Charlemagne Tower as Provost Marshal in mid-1864, he reported to Colonel Fry that the original enrollment was "a very imperfect Enrollment" that had included "a large number of names . . . who were not subject to military duty."[49]

Democratic Congressman Meyer Strouse similarly complained that a draconian enrollment in the coal regions had provoked opposition to the law. "At the request of a number of my constituents," Strouse wrote to Abraham Lincoln in 1863, "I take the liberty to call your attention to . . . gross errors in the enrollment . . . which if not rectified, may lead to great and serious dissatisfaction." Strouse reported that in Democratic Cass Township, the number enrolled exceeded the vote polled by 158, while in Republican Pottsville, the number was 453 less. "From this enrollment," Strouse concluded, "it will be seen that while the Republican Districts are only enrolled at the rate of sixty-six men to one hundred votes, the Democrats are enrolled at the rate of 175 to one hundred votes."[50]

Charlemagne Tower's response to this charge illuminated not only his perception of his duty to his country, but his intention to use his federal appointment to rid the coal regions of "troublesome" miners. "No constituents of Strouse here, except those determinedly opposed to the government, request Meyer Strouse to do anything. His statements, as to the apparent inconsistencies," the provost marshal continued, "may or may not be true. It is certainly not worthwhile that I should allow my attention to be diverted from my business by anything Meyer Strouse may say or do. If there are such apparent inconsistencies," he concluded, "those persons acquainted with the subdistricts here know the cause of them well." The coal regions, as Tower went on to explain, "where not one man in twenty can read or write," were populated by aliens who followed the Democratic directive to "stay at home . . . and put down this infernal abolition Government. In making the enrollment," he stated, "of course as many of these newly arrived aliens as could be got hold of were enrolled although not entitled to vote until they were here five years." Thus the provost marshal unwittingly supported Strouse's evidence and, indirectly, produced a reason for draft resistance that had little to do with conspiracies, southern sympathy, or labor organization. "There are some errors in [the enrollment lists] no doubt," Tower later explained, "but to amend the lists by scanning the claims to alienage would require . . . three months."[51]

A full 75 percent of all those drafted in Schuylkill County resided in the mining districts, and one-third of those were either improperly enrolled or aliens. Thus the draft fell hardest on those districts where the enrollment seems to have been most carelessly canvassed. The large number of aliens in these districts—men who would not be held to service and who probably believed that they should not even be enrolled—suggests that the enrollment process itself encouraged Irish miners to evade the draft (see table 4).[52] Although critics emphasized the Irishmen's clannishness, ignorance, and overconcern for the present as the reasons behind this opposition, Schuylkill's Irish residents had proved no less loyal to the Union before the imposition of conscription than other residents. Indeed, throughout 1861 the *Miners' Journal* had applauded the miners for their patriotism. "In this county," the paper reported in April, "the Colliery Operators have been greatly crippled by the number of men

TABLE 4. Execution of the Draft in Mining and Farming Regions in Schuylkill County

	Mining Townships	Mining Boroughs	Mining Total	Farming Townships	Farming Boroughs	Farming Total	Total
Deserted	387	297	684	72	10	82	766
Offered Substitute	132	205	337	137	78	215	552
Exempted	154	217	371	88	53	141	512
Paid Commutation	114	150	264	135	27	162	426
Aliens/Misenrolled	456	349	805	84	16	100	905
Mustered In	12	12	24	18	9	27	51
Arrested	19	7	26	5	1	6	32
Total	1,274	1,237	2,511	539	194	733	3,244

Note: Figures based on Lists of Drafted Men, Tenth District, Pennsylvania, RG 110, National Archives. Total is lower than the countywide figure, 3,313, since not all townships are included here.

who have volunteered." One month later it was "happy to state that there is no class of our fellow citizens more imbued with the spirit of patriotism . . . than the Catholics, nine-tenths of whom are adopted citizens." Despite their past service, however, opposition to enrollment had been blamed on the Irish community itself and not the enrollment process.[53]

But if the Irish in Schuylkill County did lead the ranks of those arrested for deserting or failing to report, they also accounted for 6 percent of those drafted men mustered into service—more than any other foreign-born group in the county. And if the Irish evaded service in large numbers, they were certainly not the only residents to shirk their military duty. As his record of delivering soldiers to the rendezvous attests, Charlemagne Tower had trouble with nearly every social group in Schuylkill County. "The daily reports of the draft in the Tenth District," Colonel Fry wrote to Major C. C. Gilbert after the September 1864 draft, "show that nearly all the men fail to report." Although Tower's records claim that 1,096 men had been held to service in 1863, muster rolls demonstrated that only 701 completed the journey to the General Rendezvous.[54]

Throughout the summer of 1863 the enrollment continued to languish in Schuylkill County, especially in the mining sub-districts. Determining that it was time to demonstrate and advance the authority of the federal government, Charlemagne Tower proceeded to bypass standard enrollment procedures, further alienating and alarming county Democrats—especially Irish miners. "I wish you would . . . get every coal operator and every employer of any kind up there," he wrote to Republican coal operator Edward Silliman, "to make out and hand me a list of all the men between twenty and forty-five years of age who are employed by him. . . ." Straightforward as the plan appeared, the operators wanted proof that their lives and property would be protected before they would agree to comply. To assuage their fears, Tower proposed to Colonel Bomford that he "visit each colliery . . . with sufficient armed force and demand of the proprietor and his clerk a list of workmen there. . . . To do all this," he added, "I now ask for one hundred more men to come here . . . with ten day's rations in bulk."[55]

Early in July, Tower began to assemble the forces he would require for his march on the coal mines. Two companies of Invalid Corps, led by Captain Harry Rockafeller, and 79 men under Sergeant Sherwood, joined the force of 56 men already stationed in Schuylkill County—making a total of 290 men and seven officers. "They are well encamped on a height northwest and overlooking [Pottsville]," Tower informed Colonel Bomford. "The whole force now here is needed," he reported, "and ought to remain here until after the draft is entirely through with. Resistance to the draft is threatened in this county," Tower reiterated, "and strongly in many parts of it."[56]

Although Tower apparently relished the task of storming the coal mines and appropriating employment rolls, Colonel Bomford counseled caution, advising Tower to "be content with holding your ground and labor when the opposition is feeble."[57] His advice only spurred Tower to make his position all the more clear. Tower began to forward reports, like that of Railroad Superintendent R. A. Wilder ("one of our most intelligent citizens"), that in Schuylkill, Luzerne, and Carbon Counties an armed force of miners one thousand strong could assemble at twelve hours notice to resist the draft. "I suggest," Tower noted, "that full preparations should be made so that at the instance a resistance shows itself . . . martial law may be declared here."[58]

Tower's insistence that Schuylkill County was on the verge of riotous draft resistance cannot be sustained by documentary evidence, though. Even in Cass Township, where, according to Tower, miners drilled daily in preparation, only one violent episode found its way into his records. In August 1863 a group in Cass allegedly hostile to the draft knocked a sergeant from his horse and took off with his sword, revolver, and money. The perpetrators of this crime were neither identified nor caught. General Whipple nevertheless ordered the arrest and imprisonment of seven hostages to secure "the good behavior of the vicinage hereafter." The Cass Township hostages, Tower explained, "were crass and saucy to a considerable extent each day but the power and decision shown among them have kept them from any attack."[59] Certainly Tower could not have based his claims of imminent violent resistance on this incident. It is more likely that a series of strikes that had begun in Cass in 1862 set the stage for the deployment of the military in 1863 and 1864. "The mines at several collieries in Schuylkill County have already stopped work," Tower explained in one of his many pleas to Colonel Fry. "I trust you will pardon me if I urge it upon you once more that a large increase of the military force now here and addition to it of three or four small howitzers are immediately necessary."[60]

Unless labor conflict and labor organization are considered to be evidence of impending violent resistance to conscription, the conventional picture of draft resistance in the coal regions is misleading. The regions' reputation for violent opposition rests on the farmers' aggressive evasion of enrollers, the stopping of the train in Cass Township in October 1862, and the riot in Archbald around the same time. The rise of local and regional labor unions around 1860 and the outbreak of successful strikes beginning in 1862, however, complicate the issue. Although wartime labor activity predated the imposition of conscription, and in fact culminated at least two decades of struggle, provost marshals in all three districts interpreted this activity as evidence of organized opposition to the war. If this link may have made logical sense, especially given the Union's demand for coal, there is strong evidence to suggest otherwise—that draft resistance and labor organization were concurrent but separate issues, each arising from specific historical conditions. The reemergence of organized miners during the war had more to do with the development of a propertyless, wage-earning class employed in an economically centralized industry than it had to do with disloyalty. Likewise, the provost marshals' decision to retain a standing army in the coal regions long after the enrollment had been made had more to do with the coal operators' desire to undermine labor organization than it had to do with opposition to conscription.

NOTES

1. For a discussion of "total war" see Russell F. Weigley, *Towards an American Army* (New York, 1962), 79–99; Allan Nevins, *The War for Union: War Becomes Revolution, 1862–1863* (New York, 1960). The quotation is from Nevins, vol. 1, page 166.

2. The draft was ordered on Aug. 4, 1862. Nevins, ibid., 1:163–65.

3. For a general discussion of conscription see James Geary, "A Lesson in Trial and Error: The United States Congress and the Civil War Draft, 1862–1865," Ph.D. diss., Kent State University, 1976; Eugene C. Murdock, *One Million Men: The Civil War Draft in the North* (Madison, Wis., 1971); Murdock, *Patriotism Limited, 1862–1865: The Civil War Draft and the Bounty System* (Kent, Ohio, 1967); Frederick Morse Cutler, "The History of Military Conscription with Especial Reference to the United States," Ph.D. diss., Clark University, 1922; Jack F. Leach, *Conscription in the United States: Historical Background* (Rutland, Vt., 1952). Quotation is from Boston *Pilot*, Sept. 13, 1862.

4. Isaac B. Tyson to Andrew Curtin, Aug. 4, 1862; John Schenk to Curtin, Sept. 8, 1862; "Sincere Friend" to Curtin, Sept. 21, 1862, all in Department of Military Affairs, Office of the Adjutant General, RG 19, Pennsylvania State Archives, Harrisburg, Pa. (cited hereafter as PA RG 19).

5. Alexander McClure to Eli Slifer, July 31, 1862, Aug. 4, 1862, Slifer-Dill Papers, Historical Society of Pennsylvania, Philadelphia, Pa.; J. A. Moose to McClure, Sept. 5, 1862, PA RG 19; *Mauch Chunk Gazette*, Aug. 21, 1862.

6. *Wayne County Herald*, Aug. 7, 1862; *Luzerne Union*, Aug. 25, 1862; Boston *Pilot*, Aug. 16, 1862.

7. Major A. H. Mayer to Curtin, Sept. 12, 1862; Benjamin Bannan to Curtin, Sept. 23, 1862; Henry Hain to Curtin, Sept. 17, 1863, PA RG 19.

8. I was led to this conclusion after checking newspaper reports and reports contained in *The War of the Rebellion: A Compilation of the Official Records of the Union and Confederate Armies* (Washington, D.C., 1889–1901) (cited hereafter as *OR*) against more detailed evidence in the Papers of the Provost Marshal General's Bureau, RG 110, and the United States Army Continental Commands, RG 393, National Archives. See Grace Palladino, "The Poor Man's Fight: Draft Resistance and Labor Organization in Schuylkill County, Pennsylvania, 1860–1865," Ph.D. diss., University of Pittsburgh, 1983, for a demonstration of this argument.

9. *Easton Argus,* Aug. 28, 1862.

10. A. Murdock to Eli Slifer, Oct. 25, 1862, PA RG 19; Pittston *Gazette,* Sept. 4, 1862.

11. *Luzerne Union,* Sept. 10, 1862; Pittston *Gazette,* Sept. 4, 1862.

12. *Scranton Republican,* cited in the Pittston *Gazette,* Oct. 2, 1862.

13. Ibid. *Luzerne Union,* Oct. 15, 1862, placed the number at 150.

14. *Luzerne Union,* Oct. 1, 1862.

15. Ibid., Oct. 15, 1862.

16. *MJ,* Oct. 11, 1862.

17. Ibid.

18. Philadelphia *Enquirer* cited in *Wayne County Herald,* Oct. 30, 1862.

19. Andrew Curtin to Edwin M. Stanton, Oct. 22, 1862, ser. 1, vol. 19, pt. II, *OR,* 468; Stanton to Curtin, Oct. 23, 1862, *OR,* 473; Curtin to Stanton, Oct. 23, 1862, *OR,* 473.

20. Philadelphia *Enquirer,* cited in *Wayne County Herald,* Oct. 30, 1862; Boston *Pilot,* Nov. 8, 1862; Curtin to Stanton, Oct. 27, 1862, *OR,* 500.

21. Alexander McClure, *Old Time Notes of Pennsylvania* (Philadelphia, 1905), 1:546.

22. Ibid., 548.

23. *Philadelphia Enquirer* cited in Boston *Pilot,* Nov. 8, 1862. See also Grace Palladino, Ph.D. diss., 184–88. In Schuylkill County one-third of all those drafted from the coal regions in 1863 were either aliens or otherwise improperly enrolled.

24. James P. Dennis to Curtin, Sept. 9, 1862, PA RG 19.

25. *Congressional Globe,* 37th Cong., 3d sess., 1863, vol. 41, pt. 2:1214 (cited hereafter as *CG*).

26. The text of the law can be found in *United States Statutes at Large,* 13:731–37. See also *Final Report Made to the Secretary of War by the Provost Marshal General in Executive Documents of the House of Representatives,* 39th Cong., 1st sess., 1866, vol. 4, pt. 1:1251.

27. *CG,* 1219, 1225.

28. Samuel Yohe to James B. Fry, "Historical Report," Eleventh District, Pennsylvania, RG 110, National Archives.

29. Simon Grabner to Yohe, June 11, 1863, Letters Received, ibid.; Charles C. Bernhouse to Yohe, June 8, 1863, ibid.; Samuel Allen to Yohe,

July 22, 1863, ibid. See also LeRoy Jennings Koehler, *The History of Monroe County, Pennsylvania, during the Civil War* (Monroe County, Pa., 1950).

30. Joseph Oliver to Yohe, June 9, 1863, Letters and Telegrams, Eleventh District, Pennsylvania, RG 110, National Archives; Joseph Wetherwill to Yohe, June 11, 1863, Letters Received, ibid. See Frank Klement, *Dark Lanterns: Secret Political Societies, Conspiracies, and Treason Trials in the Civil War* (Baton Rouge, La., 1984), for the Knights of the Golden Circle.

31. Samuel Allen to Yohe, July 27, 1863, Letters Received, Eleventh District, Pennsylvania, RG 110, National Archives.

32. E. H. Rauch to Yohe, July 13, 1863, July 22, 1863, Nov. 16, 1863, ibid.

33. S. N. Bradford to Col. Bomford, June 22, 1863, Letters Received, Twelfth District, Pennsylvania, RG 110, National Archives; "Tri-Monthly Report," June 21 to June 30, ibid.

34. Ario Pardee to Bradford, June 22, 1863, Letters Received, ibid.

35. Bradford to Col. Bomford, July 12, 1863, July 22, 1863, ibid.

36. Bomford to Bradford, July 24, 1863, ibid.; Major A. H. Mayer to Bradford, July 28, 1863, ibid.

37. Bradford to Mayer, July 28, 1863, ibid.

38. Bradford to C. C. Gilbert, Sept. 15, 1863, ibid.

39. Hal Bridges, *Iron Millionaire: Life of Charlemagne Tower* (Philadelphia, 1952), 71–75; Charlemagne Tower to James B. Fry, May 25, 1863, Letters Received, Eastern Districts, Pennsylvania, RG 110, National Archives.

40. Affidavit of Peter Kutz, 1863, Manuscripts, Historical Society of Schuylkill County, Pottsville, Pa.; Tower to Fry, June 10, 1863, Tower Papers, Butler Library, Columbia University, New York (cited hereafter as TP, CU).

41. "The *Commonwealth* v. *Uriah Gane*, Sept. Sessions, 1863, Proceedings," Manuscripts, Historical Society of Schuylkill County, Pottsville, Pa.

42. Charlemagne Tower to Fry, May 25, 1863, Letters Received, Eastern Districts, Pennsylvania, RG 110, National Archives.

43. Judge Ryon's Opinion, Manuscripts, Historical Society of Schuylkill County; Palladino, Ph.D. diss., 163–65; J. L. Bernstein, "Conscription and the Constitution: The Amazing Case of *Kneedler* v. *Lane*," *American Bar Association Journal* 53 (1967): 708–12.

44. Edward Parry to Tower, June 16, 1863, TP, CU.

45. Tower to Fry, June 26, 1863, Letters Forwarded, Tenth District, Pennsylvania, RG 110, National Archives.

46. Tower to Bomford, June 20, 1863, Letters Received, Eastern Districts, Pennsylvania, RG 110, National Archives.

47. *Public Ledger*, Sept. 23, 1863. W. J. Turner to Fry, Nov. 10, 1863, Letters Forwarded, Tenth District, Pennsylvania, RG 110, National Archives.

48. C. C. Gilbert to Fry, Dec. 27, 1863, Letters Sent, Eastern Districts,

Pennsylvania, vol. 1, RG 110, National Archives, 110. Lin Bartholomew to Gilbert, Oct. 27, 1863, Letters Received, Eastern Districts, Pennsylvania, RG 110, National Archives; Fry to Meyer Strouse, Letters Sent, ibid.

49. Citizens of Rahn Township to James Bowen, June 29, 1864, Letters and Telegrams Received, Tenth District, ibid.

50. Meyer Strouse to Abraham Lincoln, Sept. 19, 1863, in Tower Papers, Historical Society of Schuylkill County, Pottsville, Pa.

51. Tower to Fry, Sept. 30, 1863, ibid.; Tower to Gilbert, Dec. 4, 1863, Letters and Telegrams Received, Tenth District, Pennsylvania, RG 110, National Archives.

52. This argument is more fully demonstrated in Palladino, Ph.D. diss., chapter 6. Cf. Albert Moore, *Conscription and Conflict in the Confederacy* (New York, 1963), 18: "Where the law pressed most heavily, opposition to it was strongest." Categories in table 4 are based on William A. Gudelunas, Jr., and William G. Shade, *Before the Molly Maguires: The Emergence of the Ethno-Religious Factor in the Politics of the Lower Anthracite Regions, 1844–1872* (New York, 1976). *Mining Townships:* Blythe, Branch, Butler, Cass, East Norwegian, Frailey, Foster, New Castle, Reilly, Rush, Schuylkill, Tremont. *Mining Boroughs:* Ashland, Middleport, Minersville, Mount Carbon, Port Carbon, Pottsville, St. Clair, Tamaqua. *Farming Townships:* Barry, E. and W. Brunswick, Eldred, Hegins, Hubley, E. and W. Manheim, Pine Grove, Porter, Rahn, Union, Upper and Lower Mahantango, Washington, Wayne, West Penn. *Farming Boroughs:* Auburn, Cressona, Orwigsburg, Pine Grove Borough, Port Clinton, Schuylkill Haven.

53. *MJ,* Apr. 27, 1861, May 11, 1861, Aug. 17, 1861.

54. Fry to Gilbert, Oct. 3, 1864, Endorsements, Tenth District, Pennsylvania, RG 110, National Archives; Gilbert to Tower, Mar. 9, 1864, ibid.

55. Tower to Silliman, June 11, 1863, Letters Forwarded, ibid.; Tower to Bomford, June 25, 1863, Letters Received, Eastern Districts, Pennsylvania, RG 110, National Archives.

56. Tower to Bomford, July 7, 1863, Letters Received, ibid.

57. Bomford to Tower, July 16, 1863, Letters Received, Tenth District, Pennsylvania, RG 110, National Archives.

58. Tower to Fry, July 18, 1863, Letters Forwarded, ibid.

59. Tower to Bomford, Aug. 18, 1863, ibid.

60. Tower to Fry, July 18, 1863, ibid. It should also be noted that Tower's records include numerous mentions of draft evaders who hid out in the sparsely settled mountainous terrain of the coal regions, but no violence is recorded in connection with them.

6

Labor Organization
in the Wartime Economy
1862–65

"Unless we are egregiously mistaken," Jonathan Fincher, a machinist and editor of *Fincher's Trades' Review*, pointed out in 1863, labor and capital "are one and inseparable." It was the capitalists and not the toiling masses who denied this unity, for it was the capitalists who arrogated to themselves "all the prerogatives of self-government and self-protection." Nevertheless, as Fincher noted, "it takes two to make a bargain," and capitalists could only claim superiority when workers conceded it. "If tameness, submission, or the faintest recognition of their stolen prerogatives, on our part, be tolerated," he concluded, "that is our fault—not theirs."[1]

Fincher's vision of an industrial republic wherein labor met capital as an equal and worthy opponent, if not a partner, was hardly novel by the mid-nineteenth century. From the days of the American Revolution, groups of working people had recognized their rights as free citizens and defended those rights against capital's encroachments. It was not until the Civil War that these contests assumed more than local significance, however, and not until the Civil War that a broad spectrum of workers could confront their employers from a position of strength. It was the war itself that generated the social and economic circumstances necessary to test the validity of their particular republican vision.[2]

War-induced demand for labor and materials provided the economic leverage that allowed northern workers to assert their rights. The army and navy proved reliable customers for coal

121

and iron products, and their seemingly insatiable demand for ready-made clothing, armaments, and supplies of all kinds translated into steady employment for workers throughout the North. Coincidentally, the army's ever-increasing demand for soldiers promised higher wages for the dwindling civilian work force.[3] Capitalizing on these propitious circumstances, northern workers "combined" in local and, sometimes, national unions. By 1863, in fact, coopers, tailors, cabinet makers, clerks, blacksmiths, and iron molders, among many others, had organized to protect their rights in the workplace and increase their wages. "The proceedings of all these societies," Fincher noted in a discussion of New York City unions, "indicates a determination and self-reliance on the part of journeymen, which plainly tells capital that in a conflict with labor it will find 'the stag at bay a dangerous foe.'" Noting that the summer of 1863 seemed to be "the proper moment," Fincher urged northern workers "to battle existing oppression and future aggression [or wear] the chains of servitude."[4]

Mindful of the fact that the burdens of war—increased taxation, inflation, and conscription—fell most heavily on their shoulders, working people agreed that the time had come to press their claims against those of capital. "In the early part of 1863 strikes prevailed in many industries," the U.S. Commissioner of Labor later commented; iron molders, typographers, longshoreman, and tailors all waged frequent and sometimes lengthy "turnouts." "We believe strikes can be avoided only by combination and cooperation," Fincher countered critics in 1863. "When employers will acknowledge that the man in his employ is his equal, socially and politically, although not pecuniarily— then will strikes be unknown. Until then," he concluded, "we must meet power with power."[5]

Capitalists failed to recognize any justice in this observation. From their point of view, and that of a number of state legislatures, labor "combinations" proved no more than conspiratorial, coercive entities and strikes, merely one form of riot. When, for example, canal workers in Carbon County turned out in 1862, observers censured their activity. Workers at a nearby dam, one newspaper reported, "were perfectly willing to work at the wages received, but the crowd came on and compelled them to join in the 'strike.' Thus they became *rioters* and not strikers for higher wages."[6] When Philadelphia ice gatherers struck for higher wages, their employers quickly thwarted their efforts. "The proprietors at once feigned alarm," Fincher reported, "and bolted for the police." Although these bosses had previously "combined" to fix wages, Fincher pointed out, it was only when working people attended "to their own interests in the same manner" that a crime occurred. "What is defined as treason in its application to working men," a St. Louis typographer noted, "is nothing more than a 'regulation of trade' with others."[7]

Because anthracite played a vital role in the Union's war effort, fueling not only the steamships that blockaded the South, but iron manufactories in the North, the Civil War offered Pennsylvania miners their first real chance to organize successfully. War-related demand for coal rendered "combinations" and strikes especially effective. At the same time, however, military demand enabled coal operators to link work-related struggles to disloyalty.[8]

For coal operators and other industry investors who expected to make a tidy profit from the war, the social discontent registered by labor organization and strikes proved personally threatening. Not only was the nation itself menaced by civil war, but now miners were seriously challenging the coal operators' authority. Mine bosses, store clerks, and operators themselves served as targets in labor struggles that were sometimes violent on both sides. But the reason coal miners organized their forces was not to aid the Confederacy nor to expropriate collieries— it was to claim their rights as producers. Their attempts to organize unions and enforce strikes, like those of workers throughout the North, were rooted in a social structure shaped by industrial capitalism, nourished by republican notions of freedom and equality, and given strength by the particular economic conditions generated by the war.

With some of the bleakest years in the history of the coal trade behind them, Pennsylvania's anthracite producers looked forward to a prosperous season in 1862. "Business is in a decidedly improved condition," the Pittston *Gazette* pointed out;

brisk activity in all three coal fields confirmed this impression. Operators manifested their optimism by investing in improved breakers, screens, and transport facilities, while speculators bought up coal lands, proving their confidence in the trade. "It cannot be otherwise," the *Gazette* boasted. "The Creator seems to have designed coal as the great staple of the earth and constant increase in its consumption is rapidly working out its destiny."[9]

If prosperity promised long-awaited profits to coal operators and land speculators, it also promised wage increases to miners, who, since 1857, had earned about a dollar a day over a nine-month season. Operators may have grown "prematurely gray" from the low prices brought by coal, but miners and laborers had suffered along with them, taking their pay in store orders and suspending work whenever coal glutted the market. "Let there be a full understanding between the employers and the men," the *Miners' Journal* advised when it became clear that better times were at hand, "that whenever an advance takes place in the price of coal . . . it is to be shared with the miners and laborers."[10] The commonsense logic of this appeal, however, escaped a good many operators, who continued to pay depression-level wages.

When the navigation season opened in the spring of 1862, miners throughout the anthracite region demanded a wage increase. Larger operators in the northern and middle fields acceded to the demand, but small operators, feeling themselves the victim of unfair competition, held back. In late April miners in Pittston publicized their differences with these operators. "On Monday last," the Pittston *Gazette* reported, the miners "formed a procession with fife and drum and stars and stripes [and] paraded the streets. What they demand . . . ," the paper added, "is to have their coal weighed at 23 cwt to the ton, and payments in cash every month." Although the *Gazette* assured its readers that the trouble between the miners and operators was by no means serious, it noted that both held strongly to their position. By the end of the month, the miners had won their demands.[11]

In Schuylkill County, where numerous small collieries competed with a half-dozen well-organized concerns, a more protracted struggle ensued. Before the operators would concede a raise, miners and laborers at the Heckscherville colliery in Cass Township threatened the entire operation by stopping the pumps that kept the mines from flooding. Although some newspapers observed that a "disinclination to work" motivated these strikers, miners contended that they could not afford the high prices charged at the company store. Apparently the strike had originated among some miners in the Swatara district, who marched to neighboring collieries, "stopping the engines and drawing the coal from beneath the boilers."[12] When the sheriff and a "small force" failed to disperse the crowds, the governor ordered a battalion up from Philadelphia, not "to force the men to yield to the demands of the employer," the *Enquirer* carefully noted, "but to protect private property." Before the two hundred armed soldiers made their way to Heckscherville, however, the strike was settled. Operators offered miners 10 cents more per ton for cutting coal, and laborers a 25-cent weekly increase.[13]

Although most observers agreed that miners were entitled to these raises, Benjamin Bannan, editor of the *Miners' Journal* and a recognized authority on the anthracite industry, was appalled by the strikers' methods. "The coal operators are enabled to pay good wages which of course they will do," he explained, "but lawless violence will not be permitted. . . . mob law will never be permitted to triumph in this region if it should cost a thousand lives in its suppression. . . ." Despite his warning, miners in Schuylkill County continued to strike in the spring and summer of 1862.[14] At the Vorhees Colliery in Norwegian Township, for example, a colliery that employed more miners than the five other operations in town, strikers again "stopped the pumps" and threatened to flood out the mine. "If unlawful combinations . . . continue to interfere with the miners so that the supply of coal for government purposes is threatened," Bannan hinted darkly, "we should not be surprised to see a military force sent here and to see the mines taken possession by the Government." Thus as early as June 1862 the miners' attempts to improve their wages were linked publicly to treason.[15]

Although strike activity had proved infrequent during the industry's first two decades, it increased significantly after the 1857 depression. Only after the industry achieved relative stability during the war, however, did strikes prove an effective tool for labor. A number of successful strikes in 1862 demonstrated the miners' enhanced marketplace power—and their determination to employ that power in their own self-interest.[16]

Like other workers in the Civil War era, anthracite miners capitalized on wartime prosperity to increase wages, improve working conditions, and press their claims as coproducers with the operators. In the northern anthracite field, for example, miners in Pittston, Scranton, Providence, and Hyde Park, as well as Wilkes-Barre, Archbald, and Dickson, formed branches of the Miners' Benevolent Association to protect and advance their rights.[17] "The voice of one man is very little and will scarcely be heard particularly when that man is . . . a 'coal black miner' or laborer," miners in Wilkes-Barre explained. "Individually we have been crying long enough against the impositions of the operators and their hirelings," they continued. "We will now try to make ourselves heard collectively."[18]

These unions, which organized locally, met frequently with regional delegates and held regional meetings at least once a year. Although the documentary history of these unions has been all but lost, miners in Archbald left a written record of their weekly meetings which indicates that these locals concerned themselves largely with trade union matters and not with questions of politics, the war, or even conscription. The Archbald union charged monthly dues of 60 cents, employed a secretary and a messenger, and paid death benefits, sick benefits, and also the expenses of delegates who traveled on union business. The union also assessed members special dues in order to aid striking workers throughout the coal regions, in one instance raising $120.[19]

More than merely a mutual aid society, however, the miners' union appointed committees to arbitrate grievances and exercised control over various aspects of production. "This day the society met . . . and the Delegates report that any more than five cars shall not be loaded by two miners in a breast," a typical entry recorded. "Also grievances by Pat Thomas was brought forth by being deprived of the privileges of laboring or mining or any other work in the employ of the Eaton Co. A committee of 8 persons along with the Delegates," the minutes explained, "were appointed to meet on May the 1st to consult on the many

Grievances which has occurred in [the] work of Eaton and Co."[20] The union also worked to standardize charges on work-related items like powder and oil throughout the region and to see that employers provided good, quality products for the men. They also worked to ensure that "strange" miners not be employed and that only loyal union members be awarded places in the mines. Members whose dues were six months in arrears, for example, who did not "pay up their dues . . . will not be allowed to work in the mines."[21] The union also organized work stoppages over questions of wages, hours, working conditions, and the price of oil and powder.[22]

Although these unions operated as secret societies—that is, members were prohibited from discussing union business with nonmembers—they took great pains to promote a respectable and responsible public image. When Archbald's union organized a Fourth of July parade, for example, inviting other districts to participate, union leaders made it clear that "any member . . . who shall be known to be Intoxicated in the Procession shall be stripped of his colours." Such efforts did not go unnoticed. When organized miners in Pittston paraded in 1862, with banners proclaiming "In union there is strength" and badges sporting an "American eagle resting on a union of hands," they earned the community's respect. "The 'Union' has certainly made a favorable impression upon the public," the Pittston *Gazette* reported, "and all wish it that success which it will doubtless meet if controlled with a spirit of fairness and a desire to promote the mutual benefit of its members and coal operators." As long as this combination recognized the established industrial hierarchy and did not use its power "to accomplish anything unfair or arbitrary," the *Gazette,* at least, could be counted on for support.[23]

As strikes continued throughout 1862 and 1863, however, public support for unions was severely tested. After miners employed at the Delaware, Lackawanna, and Western Railroad's collieries struck and demanded the dismissal of an unfair docking master, the union in Scranton faced public disapproval. "Had this strike originated in a demand for increased wages, and had the miners courteously made such a demand and been refused it, we would feel like upholding them," the *Scranton Republican* explained. But the strike grew out of questions of authority and management, not wage scales. "It is well understood that the Miners' Benevolent Associations, which have been of late so thoroughly organized," the paper contended, "are on the nature of unions which undertake to regulate the relations of employer and employed and this general strike is their handiwork. They propose to test the question whether operator[s] shall discharge their hands at will—whether they shall refuse to employ miners who have struck at other mines."[24]

The paper's assessment was not far off the mark. The unions that emerged in 1862 and 1863 and their committees consciously sought to secure the miners' role as coproducers in the industry and to challenge the operators' claims to sole authority in the mines. Heretofore the operators and transport companies had favored high production despite the unsteady market for coal, and miners had suffered at their hands. Now with the industry somewhat stable and demand for coal strong, the miners attempted to enforce work rules that ensured their safety, regulated their hours of employment, and protected their interests on questions of hiring, firing, and weighing tonnage. Pennsylvania's anthracite miners struck for higher wages during these years of civil war, but they also struck to incorporate their class interests into the system of industrial capitalism. Employing trade union strategies based on economic power, these miners attempted to shape an alternative model for industry, in which the rights and prerogatives of labor and capital had equal weight.

If miners organized to improve their economic circumstances, however, their concept of liberty and equality also motivated their activity. Miners assumed that as free men and producers, they had a valid claim to respect both within and outside the workplace. "We deem it high time to ask for prices at which we can live," miners in Wilkes-Barre proclaimed in 1863, and they expected those wages to be paid in cash and at regular intervals. When opponents denigrated their efforts and suggested that "locofoco" Democrats or the Knights of the Golden Circle orchestrated these demands, the miners were incensed. "Are these people paid to vilify us? or are they merely satisfying their aristocratic hatred of the workingman?" a committee asked through the pages of the *Luzerne Union*. "Have the laboring men of this free republic become a scoff, a shame, a stench in the nostrils of the would be aristocracy that they are to be abused and stultified for merely asking their just rights?"[25]

Other evidence of class discrimination also spurred the miners on. Civil War measures like the Conscription Act, with its $300 commutation clause, underscored the popular belief that this was a rich man's war but a poor man's fight. The image of speculators enriching themselves on government contracts while working people were censured for attempting to improve their circumstances did little to dispel this belief. Indeed, the fact that labor combinations were criticized, if not prohibited by law, while capital had always "combined" to protect its interests, confirmed the miners' sense of injustice.[26] "Before any of these [unions] were known in the valley," a Scranton worker pointed out, "the capitalists and their several 'bosses' combined together to keep wages down; if any miner, or any other laboring man feeling aggrieved in any way and quit, he was not allowed to go to work for any one of the many bosses unless he could get permission from the place he had last been employed. Now, in the name of all that is sacred, what was there left for us to do? Were we to sit down under such usage with our mouths closed," he asked, "or should we prepare for the conflict which we knew was inevitable?"[27]

Miners chose the winter of 1862 to inaugurate this phase of the conflict when they refused to accept a wage cut at the close of the navigation season. Operators had "customarily" reduced wages for winter, or "dead," work—that is, mining gangways and preparing the breasts for the coming season. "This winter," the *Miners' Journal* pointed out, however, "the men in all the different coal regions have resolved not to submit . . . and turnouts have been caused by a refusal to work at reduced rates." In the course of these strikes, miners continued to press their claims to exercise authority in the workplace, or, as Benjamin Bannan put it, to "dictate" to the operators. "This would be virtually taking the management of the colliery out of the hands of the owner," he cautioned, "and ought never to be submitted to . . . except at a loss of self-respect."[28] Operators in Wilkes-Barre concurred with this assessment and noted that any increases in wages "should be cheerfully made by each operator and without *combinations* to make prices. Strikes, processions, or intimidation," these operators made clear, "shall have no effect whatever in the establishment of prices or terms."[29]

Although miners won their increase by February 1863, the question of "dictation" was not settled with the strike. "No man with any self-respect in him will consent that others shall dictate to him whom he shall employ and whom he shall discharge," the *Scranton Republican* observed, and the miners could only be the losers when they supported such an "unjust demand." The Pittston *Gazette* agreed. "The prerogative to rule the works, which men have of late assumed, has lost to both men and operators a large amount of money. The rights of labor should be guarded with jealous care . . . ," the paper acknowledged, "but it is folly for either labor or capital to attempt to ride over each other."[30] The *Miners' Journal* proved less circumspect in its criticism and offered a quick remedy for these difficulties. "When rioters undertook to discharge bosses, stop pumps . . . and other outrageous acts . . . the ringleaders ought to have been arrested and punished." Such advice did not intimidate miners; in fact, before the strike settlement was a month old, a committee of miners was arrested for "conspiring by force and intimidation to stop production" when they called for the discharge of a boss at the Audenried colliery. Similar charges were soon brought against a committee in Minersville, and in June miners in St. Clair "stood out demanding the discharge of an objectionable boss."[31]

From the miners' point of view, committees often had good reason to pursue this course. When miners in Heckscherville refused to work for Thomas Verner, for example, they claimed he was notorious for failing to pay his men. Evidence from a committee in Swatara confirms that irregular wage payments often motivated committees to act. "Mr. John Jones is to send out no more mules to work until such time as the men get their wages," a handbill proclaimed, "or by God he will lose his life." Not only wages, but safety, proved an issue in these struggles. When miners at a Glen Carbon colliery refused to work for a certain inside boss, they threatened the manager's life to make their position clear. "It is better one damned bugger should die," they announced, "than a whole crew."[32]

Although miners had good reason to attempt to regulate hiring and firing, their critics interpreted their actions in ethnic terms calculated to discredit their efforts and undermine solidarity among the men. "There is evidently a disposition on the part of a body of Irishmen to gain possession of the collieries," the *Miners' Journal* noted, "and drive out all the English, Welsh, Scotch and Germans . . . who will not unite with them. . . ." The *Sunbury Gazette* confirmed this reading and suggested that Irish miners relied on a "system of terrorism" in their attempts "to control their employers."[33]

Although organized miners of all ethnicities attempted to impose a closed shop, critics condemned the Irish miners' tactics as evidence of their "inherent" clannishness, intemperance, and even their support for the South. Their strategies, however, reflected the social realities of life in the coal regions. If mining, as an occupation, was not the preserve of a single ethnic group, individual coal towns tended to be dominated by particular groups of miners. The conflation of class and ethnicity in these towns, especially in those dominated by large enterprise, shaped the development of ethnic-based labor unions. When the Irish sought to work with other Irish miners, their actions were influenced not only by the social geography of the industry but also by deep-seated tensions between Irish Catholics and British or native-born Protestants that were exacerbated when Welsh bosses weighed Irish tonnage, docked Irish pay, or assigned the Irish places in the mines. More than ethnocentrism informed the Irish miners' control strategy—experience suggested that an all-Irish work force could better defend its rights.[34]

Although labor combinations were rarely welcomed in the coal regions, no matter what ethnic group was involved, no critic proved so harsh as Benjamin Bannan in condemning their emergence. To Bannan, who had lost money as an independent operator in Schuylkill County, there was little difference between organized labor and organized crime or between a strike and a riot. Although his was a most parochial and often paranoid view, nevertheless, Bannan's opinions had greater significance than those of other critics. The *Miners' Journal*, one of the few newspapers of its day to collect and publish industry statistics, served as the operators' trade paper, thus allowing Benjamin Bannan to influence a far wider audience than his local clientele.[35]

By Bannan's lights, labor combinations not only threatened social and industrial order in general but also threatened individual enterprise—especially in Schuylkill County—in particular. Like corporations, labor combinations took unfair advantage of independent competitors, forcing them out of business and rupturing the economic structure of the republican social order. His overt hostility toward miner combinations, then, reflected his ideological conviction that free competition among equals—independent operators, independent miners, independent shippers — offered the only hope for sustained economic growth. It also reflected his deep-seated belief that, at least in Schuylkill County, such free competition ruled the industry.

Bannan's conception of the industry's structure, even in Schuylkill County, however, proved anachronistic by 1860. If corporations had dominated the trade in the northern and middle fields almost from the beginning, large enterprise already dominated production, prices, and wage rates in the southern field.[36] In Schuylkill County, where the separation of landowning, mining, and shipping rights was protected by law, improvement companies and railroad corporations joined forces to blur these distinctions. For example, the one-time rivals, the Schuylkill Navigation Company and the Philadelphia and Reading Railroad, had made their peace by the early 1860s, and the railroad basically monopolized coal shipments in the county. In fact, the P & R Railroad, with the help of the managers of the Charles A. Heckscher Company, were well on their way to acquiring what was left of the independent railways in Schuylkill County.[37]

Despite obvious changes in the structure of the industry, Bannan continued to blame labor combinations, especially combinations of "turbulent" Irish miners, for the demise of individual enterprise. On the one hand, his special antipathy toward the Irish reflected the fact that they manned the most productive collieries in Schuylkill County. On the other hand, it stemmed from his well-publicized nativist sympathies.[38] When, for example, the miners in Cass Township won a raise in 1862, Bannan tarred these strikers with the same brush he had used against them in the 1850s. Democrats, he insisted, had induced "worthless" miners to strike against the wishes of "the better class of workmen." Such "rumsuckers and others who if they made five dollars a day would be as badly off as if they made but seventy-five cents," were obviously the pawns of "grog shop keepers" and "scurvy politicians." And what had been the outcome of knuckling under to desperadoes and meeting their unlawful demands? The Irish, encouraged by spineless operators had, Bannan answered, "leagued together in a secret association known as the Molly Maguires." This association proved especially dangerous, from Bannan's point of view, since Irish miners, unlike their Welsh and English counterparts, lacked rudimentary common sense.[39]

Bannan made good use of his columns in the *Miners' Journal* to brandish his conviction that combinations equaled crime in the coal fields. He offered dramatic and often sensational accounts of violent episodes to prove his contention that Irish miners were "ruffians" who "acted more like savages than like men." When a boss at the Forestville Colliery was allegedly attacked by a miner named McCluslin, for example, Bannan described the "outrage" in detail. The miner, "without having received the slightest provocation," responded to the boss's request to measure his work by turning around and assaulting him, "with his pick striking him once in the head immediately above the eye, once in the face below the eye laying-open his cheek, and once in the hand, the point of his pick passing through it." How the boss survived this attack, which he apparently lived through, and what in fact led up to the skirmish is not at all clear from Bannan's report.[40]

Around the same time, Bannan spotlighted the action of committeemen from St. Clair, who demanded the discharge of an objectionable boss. When mine operator George Repplier "naturally" refused the request, the miners searched out the boss in question. "They had an interview with him and it seems [they] by threats made him promise not only to leave Mr. Repplier's place but the county. He was handed a Bible for the purpose of making him swear upon it to keep the promise and was in the act of taking an oath with the book in his hand when one of the men in the crowd shot him down in the most cold-blooded manner." Bannan predicted that the unfortunate boss would probably lose his arm, but he offered no identification of the assailant. "There have been no arrests and we presume there

will be none, ruffianism and murder having full sweep unmo-
lested in this county. . . ." If the committee staged the shooting,
however, it certainly called the worst kind of attention to itself
in the process.[41]

Bannan consciously linked "unlawful combinations" of miners
to such brutality and managed to mention the "committee"
whenever he related tales of senseless violence. He provided no
direct evidence, however, to connect organized miners to these
crimes. He relied rather on the coincidence of location and well-
publicized "coffin notices" to make his case. Although these
notices sometimes contained statements like "death to traitors"
or "by God you'll lose your life," committee notices could also
be quite straightforward. "We have come to the following agreement," one notice from a committee in Cass read, "that there
will be no work in the different collieries . . . until Heckscherville
colliery starts by some other person than Thomas Verner."[42]
Whether the more dramatic and threatening "coffin notices"
were the work of the committee, the operators, or unorganized
workers cannot be proved. Whether brutal outrages were the
work of organized miners or the product of rival ethnic gangs
also cannot be proved.[43] Such details, however, did not deter
Benjamin Bannan from eagerly reporting every lurid occurrence
and at least tacitly attributing each to labor combinations. "These
are specimens of the poor, injured, oppressed miners of Cass
Township," he wrote in an article describing the demolition of
a widow's beer shop by unidentified assailants, "who stop collieries, beat women, [and] shoot men."[44] No doubt by labeling
strikes, murders, and beatings alike as "outrages," Bannan encouraged his readers to do the same.

Violence, or the threat of violence, however, emanated from
both sides of the industrial conflict. If, as one Welsh miner
reported, "revolvers are ready weapons here with ordinary people," so, too, was it true that coal operators were armed and
had a long tradition of relying on the militia whenever strike
activity threatened production.[45] No agency existed to hear both
sides of industrial disputes—each side waged its own fierce
battle. Although coal miners threatened "blacklegs," store clerks,
and bosses with pistols, they chanced being served a "diet of
rifles" whenever they challenged the operators. Violence was

not the basis of labor organization in the coal regions, although Bannan and his colleagues implied that it was. Nevertheless, the belief that organized violence threatened capital investment and coal production drove men like Bannan to demand a quick and masterful reprisal.

The emergence of miners' unions in Schuylkill County, as in the rest of the anthracite regions, proved to be more the result of centralized, corporate-dominated industry than the cause. Nevertheless, critics continued to argue that labor combinations—and not the industrial capitalist system itself—threatened the economic and social structure of the American republic. For men like Bannan, who sought to maintain a way of life that was rapidly being transformed, these combinations served as useful scapegoats for all that was wrong in the industry. Incapable of recognizing these unions as the miners' functional response to industrial change, Bannan instead blamed outside agitators and Irish ignorance for labor activity. "The large mass of those [miners] who desire to work and support their families must be protected at all hazards from the ruffians that infest a portion of our region," he argued. "Such poor devils are to be pitied," he added, "but it is far better to send them into the army and put them in the front ranks, even if they are killed by the enemy, than that they should live to perpetuate such a cowardly race. . . ."[46]

If Bannan and the operators could not rely entirely on the war itself to rid the coal fields of organized miners, they soon perceived that the Conscription Act might prove useful in the fight to save managerial prerogative. The chronological coincidence of the institution of conscription and miners' strikes in 1863 provided the operators with an ostensibly legitimate reason to invite the Union army into the coal regions. Although observers insisted that the military arrived to enforce the draft and not to break the miners' organizations, Benjamin Bannan, for one, saw nothing wrong in killing two treasonous birds with the same stone. "Now is the time," he wrote, as enrollers were canvassing the coal regions, "for the operators . . . to get rid of the ringleaders engaged in threatenings, beatings, and shooting bosses at the collieries, and put better men in their places."[47] Before the war was over, a coalition of provost marshals, coal operators, and military leaders would put this suggestion into action, court-martialing and imprisoning leaders of the miners' unions and utilizing Union troops to patrol the coal regions, to protect strikebreakers, and to impose the operators' authority in the workplace by force of arms.

NOTES

1. *Fincher's Trades' Review,* Dec. 5, 1863, June 13, 1863.

2. David Montgomery, *Beyond Equality: Labor and the Radical Republicans, 1862–1872* (New York, 1967). For a discussion of wartime strikes, see pages 91–101. A cursory trip through a paper like the New York *Daily News* or *Fincher's Trades' Review* will impress the reader with the number and variety of workers on strike. The U.S. Commissioner of Labor in his report for 1887 listed fifteen major strikes for 1863 involving journeymen tailors in California, longshoremen in Boston and New York, and morocco finishers in Charlestown, Massachusetts. No coal miners' strikes were listed, although Pennsylvania miners were included for 1862. The U.S. Commissioner of Labor, *Third Annual Report: Strikes and Lockouts, 1887* (Washington, D.C., 1888), 1047–48.

3. Montgomery, *Beyond Equality;* Allan Nevins, *The War for Union: War Becomes Revolution, 1862–1863* (New York, 1960), 2:483–511.

4. *Fincher's Trades' Review,* July 11, 1863.

5. Ibid., Dec. 17, 1863.

6. *Mauch Chunk Gazette,* July 24, 1862.

7. *Fincher's Trades' Review,* Jan. 23, 1864, Aug. 23, 1863.

8. Montgomery, *Beyond Equality,* 112–13. See pages 98–100 for legislative attempts to curb wartime strikes.

9. Pittston *Gazette,* Jan. 30, 1862, Feb. 27, 1862; *MJ,* Mar. 22, 1862; *Easton Argus,* Dec. 4, 1862.

10. Clifton K. Yearley, Jr., *Enterprise and Anthracite* (Baltimore, 1961), 166–71, for wages between 1851 and 1870. *MJ,* July 14, 1860. Bannan here notes that wages for laborers had been $4.50 to $5.50 a week since 1858. The quotation is from *MJ,* Mar. 22, 1862.

11. Pittston *Gazette,* May 1, 1862.

12. *MJ,* May 10, 1862; *Philadelphia Enquirer,* cited in Pittston *Gazette,* May 14, 1862; Philadelphia *Public Ledger,* May 10, 1862.

13. *MJ,* May 10, 1862.

14. *MJ,* May 17, 1862, June 14, 1862. The *Democratic Standard* noted that "when miners demanded an increase of wages, the *Miners' Journal* instead of advocating the interests of the miners, called upon the government to send a military force. . . . That paper has been abusing Sheriff Rausch . . . because he did not call out a military force to shoot the people of Cass Township when they refused to work for the wages they were

getting." Cited in the *Catholic Herald and Visitor,* Apr. 18, 1863, in reference to the 1862 strike.

15. According to the manuscript for the United States Census of Manufactures for 1860, the colliery owned by J. S. Vorhies [sic] employed 150 miners who earned $20 a month. The Clark and Llewellyn Colliery employed 2 men and paid $24 a month; J. F. Simmons employed 5 and paid $20; J. Biddle employed 4 at $19; Jacob Rich employed 20 at $16; and the Connecticut and Schuylkill Coal Mining Company employed 40, wages unknown. Wages here are based on dividing stated monthly wages by the number of men employed. *MJ,* June 21, 1862. According to the *Miners' Journal,* July 5, 1862, the government had already seized the P & R Railroad when a strike interrupted service.

16. See chapter 3.

17. References to these organizations can be found in the *Luzerne Union* and the Pittston *Gazette,* but very infrequently. Harold Aurand mentions the Pittston Union. See Aurand, *From the Molly Maguires to the United Mine Workers* (Philadelphia, 1971), 67.

18. *Luzerne Union,* Feb. 4, 1863.

19. Most of my information on Civil War–era unions is derived from announcements in the local press about parades or meetings and from complaints by the operators recorded by the provost marshal. Only the Miners' Benevolent Association of Archbald left a minute book. References here are to a typed transcript in my possession, courtesy of Peter Gottlieb, Historical Collections and Labor Archives, Pennsylvania State University, University Park, Pa.

20. Miners' Benevolent Association of Archbald, Minutes, Apr. 27, 1863 (cited hereafter as MBA Minutes).

21. MBA Minutes, Feb. 10, 1864, Nov. 6, 1863, Mar. 24, 1864, Feb. 23, 1865, May 3, 1864.

22. MBA Minutes, May 19, 1863, Feb. 10, 1864, Sept. 12, 1864. They also stopped work to bury deceased members, Oct. 23, 1863.

23. MBA Minutes, May 19, 1863; parade plans are mentioned on an undated page ca. early June; Pittston *Gazette,* July 17, 1862.

24. *Scranton Republican,* cited in Pittston *Gazette,* Jan. 1, 1863.

25. *Luzerne Union,* Feb. 4, 1863.

26. For opposition to commutation see Hugh Earnhart, "Commutation: Democratic or Undemocratic?" *Civil War History* 12 (1966): 132–42; Robert Sterling, "Civil War Draft Resistance in the Middle West," Ph.D. diss., University of Illinois, 1974; Arnold Shankman, "Draft Riots in Civil War Pennsylvania," *Pennsylvania Magazine of History and Biography* 101 (1977): 190–204; Adrian Cook, *The Armies of the Streets: The New York City Draft Riots of 1863* (Lexington, Ky., 1974); Eugene C. Murdock, *One Million Men: The Civil War Draft in the North* (Madison, Wis., 1971). See also *Fincher's Trades' Review* throughout 1863 for evidence of unequal treatment of labor "combinations" and capital "combinations."

27. *Fincher's Trades' Review,* Mar. 17, 1866.

28. *MJ*, Jan. 3, 1863.

29. *Luzerne Union*, Jan. 21, 1863.

30. *Scranton Republican*, cited in Pittston *Gazette*, Jan. 1, 1863, Jan. 15, 1863.

31. *MJ*, Feb. 28, 1863.

32. Swatara Committee Handbills, Letters Forwarded, Tenth District, Pennsylvania, vol. 1, RG 110, National Archives, 114. Reports of accidents surfaced weekly in the *Miners' Journal*. See also, Yearley, *Enterprise and Anthracite*, 173; Aurand, *From the Molly Maguires to the United Mine Workers*, 37–43; Samuel H. Daddow and Benjamin Bannan, *Coal, Iron, and Oil* (Pottsville, Pa., 1866), 442–45; Andrew Roy, *The Coal Mines* (Cleveland, 1876), 114–53; Alexander Trachtenberg, *The History of Legislation for the Protection of Coal Miners in Pennsylvania, 1824–1915* (New York, 1942).

33. *MJ*, Sept. 12, 1863; *Sunbury Gazette*, cited in *MJ*, Dec. 12, 1863.

34. See chapter 3.

35. Even the Archbald MBA purchased a subscription. MBA Minutes, Mar. 21, 1865.

36. See chapter 2.

37. See Grace Palladino, "The Poor Man's Fight: Draft Resistance and Labor Organization in Schuylkill County, Pennsylvania, 1860–1865," Ph.D. diss., University of Pittsburgh, 1983, 146–47. Although the evidence is sketchy, it appears that the Heckschers locked out the miners in April 1863, deprived the Mine Hill Railroad of tonnage, and then ended the "strike" by offering wage increases after the Mine Hill was forced to sell out to the Philadelphia and Reading Railroad.

38. See chapter 4.

39. *MJ*, Feb. 28, 1863.

40. *MJ*, June 13, 1863. See also Jan. 11, 1863, Feb. 28, 1863, Apr. 11, 1863, May 2, 1863, Aug. 1, 1863, for other "outrages."

41. *MJ*, June 6, 1863.

42. Letters cited in Richard Heckscher to Charlemagne Tower, Feb. 1, 1864, Letters Forwarded, Tenth District, Pennsylvania, RG 110, National Archives.

43. Aurand mentions the Modocs, a Welsh Protestant gang, who fought with Irish gangs in the county. Allan Pinkerton's informant during the Molly Maguire investigation also mentions the Modocs and ethnic gangs. JMF to Pinkerton, Jan. 11, 1875, Pinkerton Detective Agency Papers, reel 4, Manuscript Division, Library of Congress. For example, when the Molly Maguires planned a St. Patrick's Day Parade, the president wanted to hold the celebration in Mahonoy, "as he would like to show the 'Modocs' that there was a few Molly Maguires left yet." In December 1874 the informant reported that a fight in Mahonoy was, according to some Molly Maguires, caused by the "modocs." JMF to Pinkerton, Dec. 12, 1874. Interestingly, F. B. Gowen ignored these reports of rival ethnic groups as far as the Modocs were concerned. See also Wayne G. Broehl, *The Molly Maguires* (Cambridge, Mass., 1964).

44. *MJ*, May 2, 1863. If strikes are not counted as "outrages," then Cass compares well with the rest of the county. The *MJ* reported 36 violent episodes, including murders, fires by incendiaries, and street brawls where rocks were thrown, etc., as follows: Cass, 6 episodes; Ashland, 6; Pottsville, 6; Washington, 5; St. Clair, 2; Minersville, 2; and Mahonoy, Silver Creek, West Penn, New Philadelphia, East Norwegian, Foster, Tamaqua, Port Carbon, and Mount Laffee, 1 each. (Episodes of violence reported within the context of a strike, but not the strike itself, were included. Total for 1863 only.)

45. See chapter 3. The militia was called in during strikes in 1842, 1856, 1857, and 1862. See Yearley, *Enterprise and Anthracite*, 177, and Joseph F. Patterson, "Reminiscences of John Maguire After Fifty Years of Mining," *Publications of the Historical Society of Schuylkill County* 4 (1914): 333. An account book in the Charles A. Heckscher Company Papers notes R. Heckscher's purchase of one revolver "for the mines."

46. *MJ*, Aug. 22, 1863.

47. Ibid.

7

The Return to Order: The Provost Marshal and Organized Labor 1862–65

"I am confident," James B. Fry reported to Edwin Stanton in 1866, "that there is no class of public servants to whom the country is so indebted . . . than to the District Provost Marshals." Colonel Fry, Provost Marshal General and administrator of the draft, well appreciated the difficulty encountered in raising the Union army, especially in those areas where ideas of local autonomy persisted. Because the Conscription Act extended the long arm of the federal government into individual communities — bypassing state and local authority in the process — district provost marshals both embodied and exercised the growing power of a centralized state.[1]

In Pennsylvania's anthracite regions, where potential draftees evaded enrollers and prominent Democrats contested the constitutionality of conscription, provost marshals faced a particularly difficult task. Consequently, these officials implemented strategies that both demonstrated and extended the federal government's authority. In Colonel Fry's opinion, the "healthy influence" and "great moral force" manifested by provost marshals not only maintained "the National cause" but also aided "in the formation and dissemination of a proper public sentiment."[2] In the coal regions, however, this sentiment exceeded questions of nationhood or conscription. Provost Marshals Charlemagne Tower, Samuel Yohe, and Stephen N. Bradford moved well beyond their mandate to enforce the draft: the chronological coincidence of conscription with the miners' efforts to or-

140

ganize and maintain a union in 1863 and 1864 encouraged
these representatives of the federal government to enforce managerial prerogative in the mines. Actions taken by these provost
marshals were later described as defensive moves against violent
resistance to the draft, but they were actually motivated by
employers who were determined to assert the preemptive rights
of capital over the legitimate claims of labor.

When miners "turned out" in 1863 to improve wages and
gain union recognition, they disrupted production in Schuylkill,
Carbon, and Luzerne County collieries. This attempt to capitalize on increased economic power enraged operators, who then
impugned both the miners' sense of patriotism and their sense
of business. But miners were not alone in their efforts to rectify
years of low wages and poor working conditions—operators
also expected war-induced windfall profits to make up for years
of struggle. The emergence of unions and their successful strikes
upset the operators' plans. "These strikes disarrange everything," the Pittston *Gazette* complained. "We should think that
in times like these when all are making money, that some arrangement might be made to avoid these miserable *strikes*."[3]
Beginning in January 1863, organized miners shut down numerous collieries in all three counties, and their success boded
ill for the operators. Small operators had little choice but to
meet the miners' demands since they could not afford the economic consequences of a long and drawn-out struggle. Although
large operators were better able to lock out strikers if necessary—and did so when it served their interests—increasing
buyer demand encouraged both sets of operators to resolve this
strike wave by replacing organized miners with strikebreakers.[4]
"The ringleaders ought to have been arrested and punished,"
Benjamin Bannan complained of strikers in Cass Township, "and
the others discharged from employment. . . ." Civil authorities,
however, could not or would not execute the task. Bannan nevertheless proposed a solution to the stalemate—a solution made
possible by the Conscription Act. Since the federal government
had jurisdiction over the state militia and since it also required
a steady supply of coal, the provost marshal's office could protect
the collieries against striking miners. If necessary, he added, the

provost marshal could declare martial law so that "ringleaders" might thereby be arrested. "A good Provost Guard with a battalion," he explained, "would soon teach the outlaws . . . their duties to the country in which they live."[5]

Before Bannan's suggestion could be acted upon—as it eventually was—district provost marshals first had to secure the armed force necessary to prevent strikes. Although provost marshals in the Tenth, Eleventh, and Twelfth Congressional Districts had called for military protection almost from their first days in office, troops were not always available to them. Charlemagne Tower, for example, complained incessantly of hostile resistance to enrollment and threats to social order, but he managed to amass only two companies of Invalid Corps troops by July. Deputy Marshal E. H. Rauch contemplated arming a civilian guard to maintain law and order, while Stephen Bradford spent most of the summer pleading for military troops to protect his headquarters and enforce the enrollment in Luzerne County.[6]

Beginning in August, however, the provost marshals' pleas for better-equipped troops fell on more sympathetic ears. On the one hand, resistance to enrollment continued throughout the summer; on the other hand, increased strike activity heightened fears of social disorder, which justified augmenting the troops. Although in both the Tenth and Eleventh Districts the most sustained and violent resistance occurred in rural townships, coal townships drew the most attention and the best-equipped troops—especially when a strike was underway. "The state of things [in the coal regions] is disgraceful to Pennsylvania," General Darius Couch informed Adjutant General Kelton, and he added that "a gang of lawless ignorant fanatics have taken pretty much all power over life and property into their hands."[7]

Couch proved to be an important ally for both provost marshals and coal operators. Not only did he share their view that miners were barely civilized, hard-drinking dupes of the Democrats, but he also supported their contention that federal authority should sustain social order if civil authorities were not up to the task. "My intention," he reported to Colonel Fry, "has been to keep a reserve force of three regiments and a battery or more at Reading in order to reinforce at any point where more troops might be required. The ignorant miners have no fear of God, the state authorities or the devil," he explained further, adding that a "strong military power under the General Government alone will keep matters quiet."[8] Couch's defense of a standing army in the coal regions proved a boon for provost marshals, legitimizing their calls for armed force. When, for example, Governor Curtin tried to muster out militia troops then stationed in Schuylkill County, Couch fought him at every turn. "You certainly cannot mean for me to withdraw those troops from Pottsville before others can replace them," he argued, especially since such action would "subject every coal mine there to the risk of being destroyed. Order off these," he warned, and "you may have Pottsville laid in ashes and a thousand barbarities committed." Although the governor withdrew the troops — since they had been raised to protect Pennsylvania from invasion, not to enforce the draft or protect the mines — the coal regions soon secured more reliable military help. On August 20, 1863, the Department of the Susquehanna, a division of the United States Army, established the Lehigh District, a separate military department to maintain law and order in the coal regions. Headquartered first in Reading, then successively in Pottsville, Scranton, and Mauch Chunk, this military district included Schuylkill, Luzerne, and Carbon Counties, as well as Berks, Lehigh, Northampton, and Monroe.[9]

Not every resident of the coal regions appreciated this military support. Democratic spokesmen, for example, alleged that party politics, not social disorder, accounted for the military presence. "We understand that a provost guard . . . [is] kept at Scranton in the service of Provost Marshal Bradford, but what for we have not been informed," the *Luzerne Union* noted in July. "Is it for the purpose of establishing a military surveillance in old Luzerne that is to last till after the election? Or," the paper asked, "is it to provoke some ill-advised persons to make a disturbance which will be used as an excuse for placing the county under martial law?"[10] Although the *Scranton Republican* countered that the draft could not be enforced without the military, the *Union* remained unconvinced. "Our own opinion is that the less fur and feathers apparent on those charged with the duty of making the draft, the easier the whole business will be got along with." Francis W. Hughes, Democratic leader of Schuylkill County, likewise pondered the military occupation of the coal regions. Addressing a Democratic county meeting, Hughes informed the crowd that soldiers were encamped on a hill near Pottsville not to maintain order, "but to overawe the court."[11]

Democrats also argued that Republicans exaggerated the degree of violent resistance to enrollment in order to secure troops. "Perhaps there never was a greater humbug got up in any place," a Scranton resident complained, "than that military display and splurge at Scranton. It is now known and almost universally admitted," he continued, "that the sending of soldiers to Scranton to protect the Provost Marshal, the property of the town, railroad etc. was an imposition on citizens there as well as the soldiers themselves." This Democrat blamed "two mischievous old Irish women" for starting rumors of riot and blamed "railroad and machine shop Black Republican donkeys and flunkies" for circulating them. The Republicans, he continued, came to believe "their own fabulous lies." The editor of the *Luzerne Union* agreed that the provost marshal had overreacted. "A stranger would suppose, were he now to visit [Luzerne County] that we were actually in rebellion against the United States," he argued, "for, in whichever way he may turn, he sees companies, regiments, brigades and divisions of armed soldiers . . . but for what purpose," he wondered, "neither he nor a Hamlet could determine."[12]

Evidence that the provost marshal employed military personnel to strengthen the operators' authority in the mines suggested one "purpose." When Charlemagne Tower utilized the military to arrest colliery clerks, seize employment rolls, and execute the draft, for example, he marveled at the military's ability to inhibit militant miners: "the presence and sundry exhibitions of the military force here have soothed the rebellion greatly," he informed Colonel Fry, "and not only prevented their making any hostile demonstration but even moved them to do more work and more quietly than heretofore."[13] Military occupation certainly furthered the coal operators' struggle to diffuse the solidarity of organized miners. When Benjamin Bannan posed the so-called Copperhead question, "What is the military here for?"

he made the connection explicit. "The sheriff of the County gave this week a practical answer," he reported, "when he applied to General Whipple in writing for a force to enable him to execute a writ at Silver Creek after he and his posse had been driven off by a mob of Irishmen." The writ, an eviction notice, was aimed at organized miners living in company houses. Apparently these miners attempted to impose wage rates and work rules by means offensive not only to the operators but also, Bannan contended, to "the large mass of miners." A military guard would protect these workers "at all hazards from the ruffians that infect a portion of our region" and ensure their right to work at rates lower than that established by the committee. One week following the eviction of "ringleaders," Bannan praised the "salutary effect" of military occupation that, he noted, could be measured by the increased supply of coal. "If the Operators, who have been troubled so long with these bad and turbulent men, do not embrace the present opportunity to establish law and order at their collieries," he warned, "they will receive but little sympathy hereafter should the difficulties continue."[14]

Coal operators throughout Pennsylvania followed Bannan's advice. When managers at the R. Gorrell colliery in Columbia County discontinued a night shift and discharged night workers, the remaining miners struck to protest the closing. General Whipple dispatched troops to the colliery, and, as Bannan put it, "a portion of the men commenced work . . . under the protection of the military." Operators in Northumberland County similarly resolved difficulties with organized miners: When workers at a Locust Gap colliery struck to increase wages and establish a closed shop, they also refused to vacate company housing. The operators, according to Bannan, then "procured the assistance of a company of cavalry, [and] put them out of the houses they occupied, besides arresting eight of the ringleaders."[15]

The military occupation of the coal regions by a standing army thus weakened organized miners' attempts to assert their increased economic power in the industry. The social order so established, however—an order designed to suit the needs of operators and speculators, but not necessarily those of the Union—could not be maintained without the army. Military troops could not resolve conflicts that led to organization among miners except at the point of open confrontation. In fact, their presence exacerbated rather than reconciled the social and political tensions at the root of these conflicts. The use of coercive state power in the coal fields, not merely to enforce the draft but to overawe organized miners, confirmed the miners' distrust of the Republican administration and its use of federal power. It also strengthened the perception that a centralized state would prove hostile to their interests. Consequently, when the army decamped, the struggle raged on, this time more violently than it had begun. Although miners continued to organize the work force where they could, some employed the same brute force that had been used against them; when armed troops no longer patrolled the coal fields, a number of breakers and company houses were burned to the ground. No wonder provost marshals and their colleagues in the coal industry quaked in their boots as the army prepared to leave. No wonder these provost marshals worked so hard to retain the troops long after the enrollment had been enforced.[16]

With the execution of the draft in October 1863, military officials attempted to remove the troops guarding the coal regions. Ario Pardee, a Luzerne County coal operator, a Republican, and, according to Provost Marshal Bradford, "one of the best friends to the Government," requested that a "sufficient force" remain in Hazleton, where his collieries were located. Lieutenant Colonel Caraher of the Invalid Corps denied the request. According to Bradford, Caraher "did not think it necessary to consult the *fears* of every citizen as to the disposition of troops." Despite Bradford's contention that, without troops, "Union men would be driven from their homes," Caraher nevertheless ordered the troops away. "The result was as I expected," Bradford reported to the acting assistant provost marshal for Pennsylvania's eastern districts. "The mines have been stopped, several leading men have been murdered, and Union men in all that region are in danger of their lives and property being taken without warning."[17]

Although some four murders apparently transpired, only one victim, George K. Smith, drew public attention. Smith, an operator of the Honey Brook Colliery in Schuylkill County, had provided employment lists to Charlemagne Tower, who had then dispatched some fifty cavalrymen to complete the enrollment. After draft notices were served in late October, Smith invited the soldiers back to his home in Yorktown, Carbon County, where he proceeded to entertain them, and, at the same time, protect himself. Later that week Smith informed Tower's deputy, Uriah Gane, that county residents were "very indignant at him for having feted the cavalry."[18]

When George Smith was murdered on the night of November 5, 1863, the army had been in and around the middle coal fields for about two weeks. According to an unnamed, pro-Union correspondent, the "outbreak occurred in pursuance of the declaration that the war had gone on long enough and that they were determined to put a stop to it."[19] On November 6, eight Irishmen had allegedly beaten up a soldier, and bosses at the mines nearby feared similar retribution. "It has leaked out somehow," Tower's correspondent wrote, "that Smith's inside Boss was the next victim, then Mumpers [a coal tenant] . . . and after that on the list came myself. They had nothing against me," he pointed out, "but in taking into my house some of the cavalry men, when they came up here to serve notices on the drafted men."[20] Although the army had arrived before the murder of Smith and had perhaps provoked the outrage, Tower seized upon the incident as justification for the salutary use of military force.

Around the same time that Smith entertained the military, E. Greenough Scott wrote to Abraham Lincoln and described the atmosphere in this militarily occupied area. "Why how is it that the place is so deserted?" Scott had asked a soldier. "Because we won't let them come out," the soldier reportedly replied. "When we first got here we ordered every one of them in." When Scott inquired if these people had resisted the soldiers, if there had been any difficulty at all, the soldier replied, "No, but there might have been."[21]

The incident appalled Scott and he went on to describe another incident involving a cavalryman who, with saber drawn, chased a young boy off the street. "How will these ignorant people regard the government—," Scott asked, "as a beneficial friend or a deadly enemy? Can we decently express surprise," he wrote to Lincoln, "if we hear that these poor people whose condition is despair and whose leaders are their passions, with such an example before them commit acts of violence?"[22]

Asked to comment on Scott's letter, Charlemagne Tower pointed out that Scott, a Democrat, "was prepared by feeling, principle, and experience to call that oppression which all hopeful and earnest friends of the Union would and did regard as only proper treatment of people rebelliously disposed."[23] Summing up his view of resistance, Tower again clarified his position. "The killing of Smith, the wounding of his clerk, and the attempt to kill his wife is not a murder." He stated, "It is rebellion and in my judgement ought to be treated as such. I suggest that the flag of the United States should be raised at once on the house of Smith," he urged Colonel Fry, "and a sufficient force be quartered there to keep it flying and overawe all the rebels in and about the hiding places of the three counties."[24]

Not all the military, by any means, shared Tower's enthusiasm for martial law. When, for example, Provost Marshal Bradford requested military support for the Twelfth District, Lieutenant Colonel Caraher labeled him "unnecessarily frightened." Colonel George Giles concurred and added that civil authorities, not the Union army, should enforce civil law.[25] Their viewpoints enraged Tower. "Such a disposition would at once withdraw all the Union armies from the domain of rebeldom," he countered. "No matter whether it is one of the duties of the district Provost Marshal to enforce Civil Law or not," he noted, "it is all important in this day of discontent that the military force of the Country should be on hand everywhere and alive to check tumults and put down rebellion. . . ."[26]

Benjamin Bannan and a number of other journalists supported Tower. "A severer example will have to be made of these ruffians and their leaders, by Government," Bannan insisted, "before order will be restored. . . ." The Philadelphia *Public Ledger*, quoting an article in the *Easton Express*, agreed that the "disturbance" in Carbon County involved much more than murder. "The mine owners are said to be completely under the control of men whom they have to pay . . . as much as $80 in wages," the editor noted, cognizant of the fact that speculating operators had been blamed for the excessively high price of coal.[27] The *New York Times* agreed and added that the "mob orators" who had "inaugurated the reign of terror" had also informed "deluded miners" that "they must not submit to the Lincoln tyranny, that the object [was] to draft every Democrat, that they must stand in the doors and resist every officer connected with the draft who [came] near them."[28] Like coal operators and provost marshals, these journalists linked draft resistance, labor strikes, and the murder of George K. Smith to the same treasonous Democratic plot.

On Tuesday, November 10, three companies of the Invalid Corps and one company of cavalry arrested some forty residents in and around Yorktown and Jeansville—two notorious coal towns. "These Buckshot villains are all as quiet as mice just now," the *Mauch Chunk Gazette* reported, "and will remain so as long as the blue jackets are about, but no longer. They are beastly cowards, every one of them," the paper continued, "and ought to be exterminated. . . ." This paper, published and edited by Deputy Provost Marshal E. H. Rauch, hoped for a quick disposition and suggested that the prisoners be tried immediately and hanged if found guilty. "Proving that one of them belongs to the Buckshots," the *Gazette* explained, "should be deemed sufficient to convict and to execute."[29]

The *Carbon Democrat* was not so sure. Although the editor hoped that the military would bring Smith's assassins to justice, he contended that reports of riot in the region had been exaggerated. He also wondered what charges had been brought against those arrested and whether the prisoners were implicated in the murder or were only deserters from the draft. Two weeks later he continued to wonder. Although the *Gazette* dismissed his questions as mere partisan rhetoric, in this case the *Democrat* had a point.[30] Even the provost marshal was not sure of the charges—since their assignment would prove instrumental for prosecution. If those arrested were charged with murder, their cases would be tried by civil authorities, and neither the provost marshal nor the operators trusted this plan. "We must be very cautious about substituting military law for civil [law]," General Couch explained to General Sigel. He added, however, that "the good people in [the coal regions] are desirous of having martial law declared and would bless you if you could hang one hundred men a day for a week. One thing is clear," he continued, "that these men who have been arrested against whom no charges can be preferred should not at present be set at liberty." Couch, together with the district provost marshal and local Republican lawyers, quietly resolved the problem: "if any of the party or all had conspired to resist the draft, or harbored deserters, or resisted the military forces in the execution of their lawful duty," Couch explained, "undoubtedly they could be tried by military courts." The *Mauch Chunk Gazette* translated this strategy for the public. "It will be proven, at the proper time," the paper contended, "that a most formidable organization against the government exists, and that numerous acts of murder, arson, assault, threats, etc. are the natural results of Copperhead teaching."[31]

Couch and his associates had good reason to court-martial those arrested since the so-called Buckshots included miners who had organized strikes in Carbon County. Although Deputy Rauch went to great lengths to identify members of this group as organized opponents of the draft, he stated, nevertheless, that the "character of the 'Buckshots' is not to resist officers or soldiers, but only to assassinate well-disposed citizens." Leading coal operators, he informed Provost Marshal Yohe, had openly declared their determination to expel these Buckshots from the mines and required military help to do so. Coal operators had also been in touch with General Couch about the problem. "The operators whom I saw proposed this," he reported to Major Townsend, "that if they could be assured of the protection of the general government . . . they would discharge the bad characters and employ new ones, having eventually a body of men that could be controlled." Couch estimated that it would take three months to execute these "desired reforms." He warned, however, that "if commenced, the troops must not be withdrawn until the work is thoroughly done, otherwise two-thirds of the anthracite region would stop sending coal to market."[32]

Both the Secretary of War and the War Department quickly approved the operators' plan to repopulate the coal regions. "The general government is not unmindful of the great interests at stake," Couch quoted from an official letter, "and is disposed to lend every assistance to the operators in carrying out the proposed reforms." Mindful that "cleaning out the bad characters" would prove a delicate task, Couch suggested to General Lilly, commander in Mauch Chunk, that he, Lilly, and General Sigel meet with the operators "in order to come to a uniform understanding as to the course to be adopted." Couch further instructed Lilly to proceed discreetly. "The letters [to and from the War Department] above referred to," he advised, "are to be seen only by those directly interested and not to appear in print."[33]

Charles Albright, Republican spokesman and attorney, took matters in hand and arranged to meet with the operators. "I have been diligently at work in ascertaining what can be proved," he wrote to General Sigel, "in trying to reduce the work to some kind of system. I have . . . given [the coal men] the necessary points to develop," he noted. Because the murder was not a military matter, resistance to the draft would have to be proved before dissident miners might be court-martialed. "This, it seems to me," Albright concluded, "should be made the starting point."[34]

The strategy devised by this combination of coal operators, army officers, and provost marshals was not confined to Carbon County. The military arrested some one hundred residents in and around Hazleton in Luzerne County and almost seventy prisoners were confined in Fort Mifflin. With companies of New Jersey's Tenth Regiment headquartered in the middle coal regions — specifically, in Beaver Meadow, Tresckow, Yorktown, Audenried, and Hazleton—miners there were not likely to strike. "Everything is working excellently [in the Lehigh Valley]," General Couch assured Major General Halleck, adding that "some of the worst characters having been arrested. . . . others have fled from that region and the operators are again getting their mines under proper control. So soon as the other two anthracite regions, viz. Schuylkill and Wyoming, agree to certain propositions," he added, "the bad characters will be cleaned out . . . the supply of coal increased with less numbers of miners, and matters will probably resume the quiet of before the war."[35]

Late in January 1864, a military commission convened in order to try the Buckshots. According to newspaper reports, the trials focused on the question of organized resistance to conscription. Prosecutors attempted to prove that those arrested claimed membership in the Knights of the Golden Circle (KOGC), a treasonous, conspiratorial, secret organization sworn to "uphold the Constitution as it is and the Union as it was," allegedly led by Robert E. Lee, George McClellan, and Irvin McDowell.[36] Testimony placed various prisoners at draft resistance meetings held in June and October 1863. The defense countered, however, that these were political meetings, where Democrats denounced the draft but urged obedience to the law. Whatever the purpose of these meetings and the nature of the KOGC, most of those arrested could not be convicted on these grounds. In fact, the judge advocate had informed H. O. Ryerson, who presided at the hearings, that "there are but two against whom any evidence can be brought. . . . If all these men are tried and acquitted, as they must be if there is no evidence against them," he cautioned, "it will be considered a triumph of the opponents of the Government." This information probably did not surprise Couch, who was more interested in the process of the trial rather than its outcome. "By the time the trial [would be] over," he had predicted in December, "quiet would not only be established in the mining regions, but the operators will have so gotten the laborers under their control. . . ."[37] The purpose of the trial, or so it seems, was not so much to arrest and confine traitors, but to reform and repopulate the mining regions.

The decision to arrest "ringleaders" in Schuylkill County made this even more clear. In the midst of a strike in Cass Township, Provost Marshal Charlemagne Tower and coal operators worked together to try a similar case in the military court. "The day has now come when something must be done . . . ," Tower informed General Sigel, "without delay and decisively." In order for the operators to regain control of the mines, Tower proposed that at least one company of infantry ("two companies would be better") and about fifty cavalrymen be stationed in Cass. "I recommend this force and the use of it," Tower explained, "to check wrongs and put an end to lawlessness, to supply the place, in fact, of a civil authority which ought to but does not and cannot exist here. . . ." In Tower's view, the army should remain in and around Cass "until a better population, a proper sentiment, and continuous thriving industry shall be denizens there."[38]

Before Tower could arrange for the arrest of these miners, however, he needed evidence to substantiate his case so that it would fall within his jurisdiction as provost marshal. In January 1864 Tower invited operators Peter and Richard Heckscher to meet with him. "These gentlemen know as well as I do," Tower wrote to General Sigel, "that the men who oppose and embarrass them ought to be handled by the civil authorities." But, according to Tower and the Heckschers, civil authorities in Cass proved "the mere creatures of these combined men."[39]

At Tower's suggestion, a number of operators in Schuylkill County formally applied for military assistance to "enable us to regain control of our collieries and enjoy the use of our property in peace." Charles Hewett, Henry Dunne, and Alonzo Snow all supplied evidence of "outrages" perpetrated by "committee men" to make their case. "For the last few years unlawful combinations have existed in parts of the mining districts," Henry Dunne, manager of the Heckscherville Colliery in Cass, complained, whose numbers "are not satisfied to work or not work themselves as they see proper, but they *claim the right to prevent* any man from working or any Colliery from being worked except on their terms and under their dictation." Combinations relied on force, threats, anonymous notes, and similar means of intimidation, Dunne explained, and members elected "committee men" to execute their "most wicked and malicious demands." "They claim the right to fix wages," Dunne continued,

and if not acceded to, to prevent the colliery from being worked. They claim the right to declare that a colliery shall be worked in a certain way or that it shall not be worked at all. They claim the right to compel persons obnoxious to themselves to leave the neighborhood or they shall be removed from their situations as superintendents, outside or inside boss etc., and all those unlawful and unjust assumptions are by them enforced. . . . No coal operator . . . in an infected district such as the neighborhood of Heckscherville [can] use, enjoy, control or work his colliery properly as other citizens of this commonwealth can use, enjoy, or control their property.[40]

Richard Heckscher concurred. "The beginning of these serious troubles dates back as far as the spring of 1862," he explained, "when ringleaders . . . formed a fiendable combination *forcing* all the hands . . . to join in the same or else *compelled* them to leave the[ir] places. . . . " Miners then appointed a committee that sought not only to regulate matters concerning "their own association" but also "to control regularly our whole works." Shortly after the committee was formed, Heckscher pointed out, miners stopped the colliery pumps, "nobody being allowed to work the engines or haul coal . . . merely because we refused to give the wages they demanded."[41]

Charles Hewett pointed out that the committee embodied "a 'Union' of the most formidable character" that was governed by a set of rules

> which are . . . not only illegal but . . . render it almost impossible to conduct the operations of a large colliery with success. For instance, one rule is that no person shall be allowed to work at the collieries unless he belongs to the union and pays an initiation fee . . . also that any man introducing a new man to the works without giving his name to the committee shall be fined. Another rule is that no man shall be allowed to tender for work which another has tendered thus destroying all competition in labor and enabling the men to fix their own price for their work. Also, that no one is to be allowed to work during a strike.[42]

"To show how totally unreasonable they are in their expectations," Hewett continued, ". . . they insisted on our supplying them with coal for their houses at one quarter of its cost price." Although the company had offered it gratis if the men would cut it themselves, or for half-price, the committee would not budge. The "fiendish combination" lost the fight, though. "By refusing them coal and threatening them with arrest if they took it by force (which thanks to the Provost Guard we are now enabled to do) we have compelled them . . . ," Hewett concluded, "to abandon these outrageous demands and accept the very fair offer we made them."[43] Although Hewett admitted that "personal outrages have not been so rife at our works," he argued that, nevertheless, the union had coerced solidarity by "inspiring such fear of its power and such a dread of its displeasure that there is now no opposition to its dictates." The union, he explained, had hoodwinked not only ignorant Irishmen but also "those whose education and intelligence ought to teach them better."[44] That Hewett was arguing that coercive state power be employed to induce fear and dread among miners so that there would be no opposition to the operators' dictates did not seem at all contradictory to him.

Both operators and Tower agreed that only by arresting the ringleaders or "committeemen" would social order be restored to Cass Township, but Tower first needed charges that would link the committees' actions to draft resistance and treason. Although nowhere in the operators' testimony is the issue of draft evasion even raised, nevertheless, early in February 1864, committeemen were charged with "treasonable acts, such as forming leagues to resist the draft [and] embarrass the government by stopping the supply of coal."[45] "I shall . . . follow the suggestion of General Sigel . . . ," Tower wrote to Captain Robert Ramsey, "and see to it that the ringleaders are arrested, especially the members of the 'committee' who have acted in violation of law and order and endangered the operations of the government." After operators supplied the names of those they considered to be "ringleaders," the men were arrested, sent to Reading, and eventually imprisoned in Fort Mifflin. "There will be clean work made of it this time," Benjamin Bannan rejoiced. "The severity of our government in arresting and punishing those guilty of fraud" would serve as a "profound lesson to the Authorities in localities where assassinations, incendiarism, robbery, etc. are rife and are perpetrated with impunity." The editor of the *Democratic Standard,* however, offered a different view of the matter. "Verily it has come to this," he reported, "that a laborer who refuses to work at a rate of wages fixed by monopolists thereby commits a crime which subjects him to arrest by military authorities, [removal] from the county, and [imprisonment] without trial. This," the editor concluded, "is American Freedom under Republican rule."[46]

Notwithstanding the assertion of the *Miners' Journal* that "the evidence against the [committeemen] must be strong or they would not have been taken into custody," Brigadier General Orris Ferry, also a Republican, could not concur. After receiving the charges filed by Captain Harry Rockafeller, Ferry informed General Couch that "the charges and specifications [against seventeen civilians recently arrested at Heckscherville and New Mines] were utterly insufficient on their force to hold anybody to trial either before a military or civil tribunal." Although the Heckschers had called on Ferry, "professing the ability to make out more explicit charges," the general noted that he believed it was his duty to report his views unofficially. "I think the arrest of the men," he stated frankly, "was a grave mistake. They were arrested it seems, because as a committee of the laborers in the mines they undertook to fix a tariff of hours and wages of labor. . . . At the same time," he continued, "*some persons unknown* were putting up notices threatening violence to the laborers who consented to work at different rates from those proposed by the Committee. There is not a particle of evidence against the persons arrested," he reiterated, "upon which any tribunal could base a judgement of guilty of any civil or military offense."[47]

According to Ferry, reports of coal-mine difficulties amounted to "a vast deal of humbug." In Ferry's experience, most of the mines did not encounter anything "approaching violence. In others," he claimed, "the struggle between employers and employed occasionally assumes the bad shape which is frequently witnessed in other places and occupations. . . . The occurrence of the draft," he added, "has afforded a plausible pretense to [political] ends. In this state of affairs," he concluded, "some outbreaks of actual violence have been grossly exaggerated by the coal operators."[48]

Ferry's observations were tacitly supported by Lieutenant Colonel Carlisle Boyd's official report of the arrests. "The working of the Collieries was controlled by committees," he noted, "who are appointed by the operatives. These committees fixed the price of labor, the terms upon which contracts were to be taken and the persons whom the operators were to employ." More important, however, the committee also "assumed the right to fix the quantity of coal which persons having contracts might excavate per day. The object being, of course," Boyd explained, "to keep up the price of coal and labor." Neither the issue of draft resistance, nor its companion charge, that treasonous, southern-sympathizing miners sought to harm the government by withholding coal, surfaced in this report.[49]

According to Boyd, the arrests produced the desired effect of "alarming and manifesting to those who remain that lawlessness will not be permitted and that breaches of the laws, where the civil authorities are powerless, will be taken cognizance of by the Military authorities." Boyd was convinced that the presence of a military force "is absolutely necessary to enable coal operators to carry on the works." Charlemagne Tower concurred: "I very much fear . . . without a force [in Cass Township]," he wrote to Brigadier General Ferry, "that [excitement] will take vent in the burning of collieries and destruction of other property and of lives." But if Tower had convinced everyone else of the propriety of his stance, he did not convince Ferry. "I would not arrest a man unless [he was] an actual participant in scenes of violence," he stated. "But to strike for higher wages, to fix tariffs or prices and to urge their observance by employees . . . are not crimes. Crimes begin when the strikes proceed to violence. . . . These laborers," Ferry concluded of the Cass Township committee, "are an unorganized and unarmed mob in mortal terror of the smallest detachment of federal troops."[50]

Ferry's objections notwithstanding, the military reestablished "social order" in Schuylkill County by arresting and imprisoning committeemen. Two companies of the Invalid Corps, which were commanded by Harry Rockafeller, had been "very efficient and useful in restoring order," Charlemagne Tower reported, "and in inclining the men to good reason and work." When these troops were mustered out, a portion of New Jersey's Tenth Regiment replaced them, and another company of infantry arrived as well. "It is now fully ascertained," Benjamin Bannan reported in the *Miners' Journal*, "that nothing but the presence of the military will keep order in [Cass] Township and enable collieries to be worked without molestation."[51] With the military on hand to inhibit labor organization, Charlemagne Tower resigned his commission in April 1864. "The state of things has passed away which existed here [that] nearly a year ago induced me to accept the appointment of Provost Marshal of the Tenth District," he explained to Edwin Stanton. Three months later Tower pocketed a hefty profit when he sold his interest in the Honey Brook Coal Company.[52]

At the same time that Provost Marshals Tower, Yohe, and Bradford employed the police power of the state to undermine labor organization in the coal regions, the supply—and especially the price—of coal advanced steadily. Although consumers blamed both miners and operators for the price increase, industry supporters contended that organized miners limited supplies and thereby raised the price of coal. In fact, provost marshals and their military and industrial allies justified the arrest and imprisonment of organized miners partly on these grounds. With the operators back in control, General Couch explained in December 1863, coal would be "produced more surely and . . . more plentifully, the price of which will probably decrease until it reaches the proper point."[53]

As numerous newspapers pointed out, however, it was not short supplies that raised the price of coal in 1863. "In New York coal is selling at $10 per ton and dealers predict that it will be held at $15 before next spring," the *Luzerne Union* reported in November. "And yet," the paper continued, "the statistics of the coal companies show an increase of more than 20 percent in the quantity mined this year over last." The Pittston *Gazette* concurred: "Notwithstanding the immense increase in the production of coal this year over last season, prices continue upward." Apparently, increased demand for increasing supplies had pushed up the price of coal.[54]

Production in Schuylkill County also rose in 1863, increasing more than 700,000 tons over the previous year by November. "This is an extraordinary increase," Benjamin Bannan boasted, "and we have no doubt it will reach three-quarters of a million by the close of the fiscal year." The miners' strikes of 1863, then, had not diminished supplies significantly.[55]

Neither were the wage increases extracted by striking miners responsible for the price increase. To be sure, wage increases raised production costs, but prices advanced more dramatically than wages did. Local residents of the coal region, who purchased their coal at the mines, particularly questioned the rate of increase. One observer noted that operators charged $1.25 per ton of broken coal in 1862 and found this rate to be "remunerative." Throughout the summer of 1863, local residents paid about $1.75 a ton, an increase they considered justifiable in light of labor scarcity and a wage increase. By fall, however, another 25 cents had been added to the price, and by November, this observer pointed out, citizens were "obligated to pay $2.50 at the mines, which is just double the sum, *admitted by the operators* to be entirely satisfactory before the present season." Although this writer likened the operators' tactics to those of a bandit, he stopped short of attacking their integrity. "They would not purposely apply the thumbscrew," he felt sure, but he did add that the prices charged far exceeded "what the advance in labor would demand or reasonable profits would justify."[56] Labor journalist Jonathan Fincher proved less circumspect in his criticism. "The history of the coal fraud of 1863 is yet to be written," he exclaimed through the pages of his *Trades' Review*. "If the price of coal advanced $2 and $3 per ton when wages advanced ten cents per ton," he wrote following a strike, "what will these Shylocks fasten upon the consumer should [the miner] ask a fair equivalent for his labor to say nothing of his risk?"[57]

Even after the operators succeeded in breaking the power of the union, however, they continued to argue that organized miners' excessively high wages caused price increases. Newspapers in New York, Philadelphia, and Boston informed the public that miners earned wages upward of $400 a month. But if some miners did command such rates, they were contract miners who hired and paid a crew. In general, miners earned between $3.00 and $4.00 a day in 1864—about $80 to $100 a month. Considering the high cost of living in 1864, these were not excessive rates. "So much for the outrageous demands of the operatives at the mines of which we have heard so much," Fincher noted after publishing a wage list, "and against whom the Government is asked to exert its power."[58] Trade unionist William Sylvis agreed with Fincher and blamed transportation rates, not wages, for high prices. "The average price paid by companies taking coal from the mines is only about $2.50 per ton, loaded on the cars and boats ready for transportation." The trip to Philadelphia, however, added about $10.00 to the cost. "It is very easy to guess [into] whose pockets this large sum goes," Sylvis maintained, "and yet these very men, robbers I should say, who, by one of the closest combinations known in the land, are the first to cry out against and oppose unions as combinations among workingmen."[59]

Although Benjamin Bannan agreed that transporters and "Foreign Jew Gamblers in New York" contributed to excessive prices, he added another explanation. "The demand is ahead of the supply," he noted in August 1864, around the same time that production had slowed down, "and outsiders, who must have coal, bid higher than those who are receiving it in order to get the coal and up goes the price." For Bannan it was a simple question of supply and demand, since, after all, "if a man has a commodity for sale and a purchaser offers $6 for it, he is not likely to sell it at $5." When miners applied the same reasoning, however, their patriotism was challenged and the full force of federal authority compelled them to sell their labor at rates lower than their market power might command.[60]

In fact, operators in Schuylkill County openly acknowledged the fact that short supplies in the spring of 1864 grew "out of the fact that the present contractors decline to pay market prices to operators." Benjamin Bannan went to great lengths to prove that contractors made a greater profit than operators, as if this justified the operators' cutbacks on government coal.[61] When Schuylkill County's miners made a similar charge, Bannan called for the military. Indeed at the very time that committeemen were imprisoned in Fort Mifflin, Schuylkill County's coal dealers amiably announced that "if the Government contractors will pay a fair market price for coal, there will be no difficulty in procuring a sufficient supply for all the wants of Government."[62] No cries of military necessity, no armed troops met this disclosure, even after critics charged that operators had locked out miners in order to decrease supplies. Obviously miners in Schuylkill County were held to much higher standards of patriotism than operators and dealers were.

Strikes continued in the anthracite region as long as prices advanced—miners and other workers continued to demand their share of the industry's profits. Employers continued to rely on armed force to bring these workers to terms. As late as February 1865, miners and railway workers employed by the Delaware, Lackawanna, and Western Railroad and the Delaware and Hudson Canal Company in the northern coal fields fought the same fight that their colleagues in the middle and lower fields lost in 1863 and 1864. A member of the Brotherhood of

Locomotive Engineers outlined the story for the readers of
Fincher's Trades' Review. "The real cause of this difficulty," he
explained, "is the hatred and enmity to the B. of L. E. by the
officials of this road. . . . These same officials tried to break up
the Miners' Association last July. . . . The Railroad company
stocked a large quantity of coal then reduced the wages of the
miners so much that they (the Co.) were certain the miners
should stop work, and thought they could at the same time make
it appear to be the fault of the miners alone. If as the officials
say," he concluded, "these societies are an injury to the capitalists
of this valley, they must blame themselves alone for their exis-
tence."[63]

Company officials did not share this view. Notwithstanding
the high wages paid to workmen, a superintendent of the D &
H Canal Company informed Provost Marshal Yohe, "a large
number of our men have 'struck' and threaten to kill any who
may continue at work." The company could replace these workers, he noted, but only if the military would protect them. He
then requested a force of one hundred cavalrymen to be stationed in Honesdale with orders to operate anywhere on the
railroad lines between Honesdale and Scranton. "We think you
will have no difficulty in getting the necessary orders from Washington by telegraph to accomplish this object," the superintendent continued, "as similar aid has been offered by the War
Department in other localities. By complying with this request,"
he added, "you will be doing this company a great favor which
I assure you will be duly appreciated and remembered." Provost
Marshal Yohe readily complied with the request, and within two
weeks the superintendent was happy to report that "our troubles
with our laborers [have] passed for the present." With the help
of General Cadwalader and the cooperation of Provost Marshal
Bradford in the Twelfth District, "several ringleaders were arrested and sent to Philadelphia, and this restored peace at once."[64]

When the commander of the Lehigh District was ordered to
release cavalry troops that guarded much of the coal regions in
February 1865, he complied, but only reluctantly. "Strikes, riots,
and resistance to the draft have only been kept down by the
presence of a military force," he argued, adding that "the price
of coal per ton is already exorbitant."[65] But it was organized

capital more than organized labor that had raised the price of coal, and *both* had halted production when it suited their interests. Indeed, coal operators were less concerned with these issues than they were with the miners' attempt to shift the balance of power in the industry by organizing the work force and enforcing a closed shop. Coal operators, with the direct assistance of provost marshals and the United States Army, invoked the police power of the state to undermine labor organization. This military and industrial "combination," however, sought neither to protect nor to advance the interests of the Republic, but rather to protect and advance the rights of capital against the claims of labor.

NOTES

1. Colonel James B. Fry to Edwin Stanton, *Final Report,* Mar. 17, 1866, Reports and Decisions of the Provost Marshal General, RG 110, National Archives, Microfilm Publication M621.

2. Ibid., 335.

3. Pittston *Gazette,* July 30, 1863.

4. *MJ,* Feb. 28, 1863.

5. Ibid.

6. Rauch to Yohe, July 15, 1863, Letters Received, Eleventh District, Pennsylvania, RG 110, National Archives; Bomford to Yohe, July 23, 1863, ibid.; see also chapter 5.

7. Couch to Fry, Aug. 5, 1863, Letters Sent, vol. 1, U.S. Army Continental Commands, part I, Department of the Susquehanna and Pennsylvania, RG 393, National Archives, 62.

8. Couch to Kelton, Aug. 2, 1863, ibid., 59–60.

9. Couch to Curtin, Aug. 6, 1863, cited in Couch to S. W. Cullen, Aug. 7, 1863, ibid., 65. For the Lehigh Military District, see William Itter, "Conscription in Pennsylvania during the Civil War," Ph.D. diss., University of Southern California, 1941, 141–42.

10. *Luzerne Union,* July 15, 1863.

11. *Scranton Republican,* cited in *Luzerne Union,* ibid.; *MJ,* July 11, 1863.

12. *Luzerne Union,* Sept. 9, 1863.

13. Tower to Fry, Aug. 20, 1863, Letters Forwarded, Tenth District, Pennsylvania, RG 110, National Archives.

14. *MJ,* Aug. 15, 1863, Aug. 22, 1863.

15. *MJ,* Sept. 12, 1863, Dec. 5, 1863.

16. As late as June 6, 1865, the *Miners' Journal* reported that the Lehigh District, under Charles Albright's command, had 1,500 troops at its disposal.

17. Bradford to Gilbert, Nov. 9, 1863, Letters Received, Twelfth District, Pennsylvania, RG 110, National Archives.

18. Tower to Fry, Nov. 7, 1863, Letters Received, Eastern Districts, Pennsylvania, RG 110, National Archives.

19. Tower to Gilbert, Nov. 7, 1863, ibid.

20. Ibid.

21. E. Greenough Scott to Abraham Lincoln, Oct. 31, 1863, Letters Forwarded, Tenth District, Pennsylvania, RG 110, National Archives. Lewis Audenried, a Republican and a coal land owner and operator, accompanied him and verified the incident.

22. Ibid.

23. Tower to Gilbert, Apr. 30, 1863, Letters Forwarded, Tenth District, Pennsylvania, RG 110, National Archives.

24. Tower to Fry, Nov. 7, 1863, Letters Received, Eastern Districts, Pennsylvania, RG 110, National Archives.

25. Tower to Gilbert, Nov. 17, 1863, ibid.

26. Ibid.

27. *MJ*, Nov. 7, 1863; Philadelphia *Public Ledger*, Nov. 14, 1863.

28. *New York Times*, Nov. 7, 1863.

29. *Carbon Democrat*, Nov. 14, 1863; *Mauch Chunk Gazette*, Nov. 12, 1863.

30. *Carbon Democrat*, Nov. 14, 1863, Nov. 21, 1863, Dec. 5, 1863; *Mauch Chunk Gazette*, Dec. 10, 1863.

31. John S. Schultze to Captain H. L. Johnson, Judge Advocate, ca. Jan. 25, 1864, Letters Sent, vol. 1, RG 393, National Archives, 196; Couch to Sigel, Nov. 14, 1863, Letters Sent, vol. 1, RG 393, National Archives, 151–52; see also General Order 141; *Mauch Chunk Gazette*, Dec. 10, 1863.

32. Rauch to Yohe, Nov. 16, 1863, Letters Received, Acting Assistant Provost Marshal General, RG 110, National Archives; Couch to Townsend, Nov. 13, 1863, Letters Sent, RG 393, National Archives.

33. Couch to Lilly, Nov. 24, 1863, Letters Sent, RG 393, National Archives.

34. Albright to Sigel, Dec. 3, 1863, Letters Received, RG 393, National Archives.

35. *Mauch Chunk Gazette*, Nov. 26, 1863, Dec. 10, 1863, Dec. 3, 1863; Couch to Halleck, Dec. 10, 1863, Letters Sent, vol. 1, RG 393, National Archives, 167.

36. For a discussion of the Knights of the Golden Circle see Frank Klement, *Dark Lanterns: Secret Political Societies, Conspiracies, and Treason Trials in the Civil War* (Baton Rouge, La., 1984).

37. *Mauch Chunk Gazette*, Jan. 28, 1864, Feb. 4, 1864, Feb. 11, 1864; Ryerson to Couch, Feb. 22, 1864, Letters Received, RG 393, National Archives.

38. Tower to Sigel, Feb. 2, 1864, Letters Forwarded, Tenth District, Pennsylvania, RG 110, National Archives.

39. Tower to Sigel, Jan. 16, 1864, ibid.

40. Charles Hewett to Tower, Feb. 2, 1864, Letters Forwarded, Tenth District, Pennsylvania, RG 110, National Archives; Henry Dunne, Affidavit, Feb. 1, 1864, ibid.; Statement of Alonzo Snow, Feb. 1, 1864, ibid.

41. Richard Heckscher to Tower, Feb. 1, 1864, ibid.; see also William Hindson, Affidavit, Feb. 4, 1864, ibid.

42. Hewett to Tower, Feb. 2, 1864, ibid.

43. Ibid.

44. Ibid.

45. Couch to Col. Joseph Holt, Mar. 15, 1864, Letters Sent, vol. 1, RG 393, National Archives, 253.

46. Tower to Ramsey, Feb. 6, 1864, Letters Forwarded, Tenth District, Pennsylvania, RG 110, National Archives; *MJ*, Feb. 20, 1864. Ringleaders identified by Hewett included Peter Brennan, James Bressler, Daniel Hoffman, Patrick Meehan, Robert Wren (president), James Marlow, Edward O'Brien, Edward Stanton, James Griffith, Thomas Peters, John Evans, and John Reese. The last three named, who also have Welsh surnames, allegedly were "forced against their will" into the committee. Hewett to Tower, Feb. 2, 1864. Ringleaders identified by Richard Heckscher included Owen Smith, Richard Kavenaugh, Patrick Keelegher, Samuel Herrick, George Mealy, Patrick Grady, John Gallagher, Phil McGovern, Barney Colan, Frank Riley, Ed Kivington, David Kelly, Daniel Maley, John Knovilein, Laurence Smith, James Maley, and William Murphy. Dunne identified Owen Doyle, James Brennan, Thomas Ryan, Philip Nash, and Michael Conners.

47. *MJ*, Feb. 20, 1864; Ferry to Couch, Mar. 25, 1864, Letters Received, RG 393, National Archives.

48. Ferry to Couch, ibid.

49. Boyd to Beardsley, Mar. 15, 1864, Letters Received, RG 393, National Archives.

50. Ibid.; Tower to Ferry, Mar. 21, 1864, Letters Forwarded, Tenth District, Pennsylvania, RG 110, National Archives; Ferry to Couch, Mar. 25, 1864, Letters Received, RG 393, National Archives.

51. *MJ*, Apr. 2, 1864.

52. *MJ*, July 16, 1864.

53. Couch to Townsend, Dec. 22, 1863, Letters Sent, vol. 1, RG 393, National Archives, 175.

54. *Luzerne Union*, Nov. 11, 1863; Pittston *Gazette*, Nov. 12, 1863.

55. *MJ*, cited in Pittston *Gazette*, Nov. 12, 1863. Figure is for coal carried over the P & R Railroad.

56. Pittston *Gazette*, Oct. 15, 1863.

57. *Fincher's Trades' Review*, Aug. 15, 1863.

58. Ibid.

59. *Fincher's Trades' Review*, Sept. 17, 1864. Sylvis's letter is dated Sept. 8, 1864.

60. *MJ*, July 16, 1864.

61. Ibid.

62. *MJ*, Apr. 30, 1864; Sylvis to Editor, *Fincher's Trades' Review*, Oct. 29, 1864.

63. *Fincher's Trades' Review*, Feb. 18, 1865.

64. C. F. Young to Yohe, Feb. 14, 1865, Letters Received, Eleventh District, Pennsylvania, RG 110, National Archives; Bradford to Captain McNally, Feb. 6, 1865, Letters Sent, vol. 4, Twelfth District, Pennsylvania, RG 110, National Archives; Schultze to Bradford, Feb. 1, 1865, Letters Sent, vol. 2, RG 110, National Archives, 475–76; Schultze to Adjutant General, Feb. 20, 1865, Letters Sent, vol. 2, RG 393, National Archives, 526.

65. Schultze to Adjutant General, ibid.

8

Conclusion

"I have always said . . . that the great majority of laboring men in Schuylkill County, nay in all the mining districts," Charles Heckscher remarked in his farewell address as president of the Forest Improvement Company, "are well-disposed, orderly, reasonable and desirous to promote the true interests of themselves and their families . . . ." This well-disposed majority, though, he confessed, "has repeatedly allowed itself to be over-awed and directed by the sinister suggestions and fatal advice of a designing criminal minority." His nephew, Richard Heckscher, echoed these sentiments. "Root out the bad characters which I and you know are amongst you. Leave them, do not associate with them," he advised the miners assembled. "If you wish to become good citizens educate your children . . . and [if you wish] to be able to buy handsome frocks for your old woman be industrious. . . ." Encouraging the members of his audience to avail themselves of the "blessed times and high wages" afforded by civil war, he reminded them, somewhat reluctantly, that these conditions "will not last forever."[1]

Although both speakers congratulated the miners for their "right-thinking" individualist ways, each alluded to the "regrettable differences" that had estranged the community for the past three years. At the same time, each applauded the operators' "firm and determined" stand that had suppressed—but in no way resolved—the conflict. Significantly, neither acknowledged the means employed to enforce the operators' stand or the federal troops that made this very celebration of industrial harmony and productivity possible. Their rhetoric notwithstanding, it was the police power of the national state and the manipulation of federal law, not the operators' principled defense

166

of "individualism," that had "rooted out" so-called undesirable miners.

Because the Heckschers, like their counterparts and supporters throughout the coal regions, promoted the idea that "sinister suggestions" and cultural depravity generated wartime strikes, they effectively divorced evidence of social conflict from the industrial system itself. In so doing they rejected any notion that conflict emanated from conditions of social and economic inequality, or that the wage system they employed did not equitably reward or protect those who invested labor rather than capital in the industry. Neither were they willing to recognize any connection between the rise of centralized industry, the price competition to control the market, and the miners' dissatisfaction with the industrial system. But if they castigated labor "combinations" as criminal entities intent on destroying republican industry, they barely criticized coal "combinations" that had directed industry policy since the 1840s. Even in Schuylkill County, where state law protected individual enterprise, Charles Heckscher and his colleagues managed to circumvent the law, never questioning capital's right to combine when economic self-interest required it.

And their economic self-interest did require it. The overproduction induced by intense competition ensured that only those operators able to capitalize on large-scale production and beneficial shipping arrangements would prosper. The exhaustion of easily accessible coal also pushed operators to "combine," since the technological requirements of deep mining demanded capital investment beyond the means of most individuals. The same critics who reviled organized miners, however, were either unconcerned or unaware that the Heckschers mined and sold coal from their own lands (through legal subterfuge) and that they entered into arrangements with the Philadelphia and Reading Railroad to lower transportation costs—even joining in arrangements to extend the railroad's control over independent lateral roads in the county. Stalwart proponents of "republican" industry nevertheless cited the Heckschers' success to bolster their individualistic, market-oriented economic ideology. When the Heckschers called upon the federal government to protect their control of their interests, these same republicans cheered their efforts.

But if champions of individualism were unable to perceive the trend of economic centralization, a number of miners were not so incapable. Men employed by the Heckschers, like those employed in large collieries elsewhere, learned a different lesson. Their experience taught them that combination, not individual effort, secured stability in an otherwise anarchistic and usually unprofitable business. And miners, like the men who employed them, similarly attempted to centralize their economic power through organization and to assert that power through strikes if necessary. Whenever they came close to achieving that goal, though, their efforts were nullified by the armed force of the sheriff, the local militia, or the federal government.

Before, during, and after the Civil War, miners fought for a more democratic industrial system, a system predicated on the needs and aspirations of labor as well as capital. In the 1860s, as in the 1840s and 1850s, miners struck for increased wages, for safe working conditions, and for an end to the store-order system of payment. These were not irrational demands or demands calculated to destroy economic prosperity, and the records extant suggest that safety issues remained a primary concern of organized miners. Nevertheless, employers argued that any attempts to "control the works" threatened prosperity by curtailing their proprietary rights to manage the industry according to their particular interests. The operators' behavior in the face of organized miners, including their prompt resort to a "whiff of grapeshot," indicates that they considered it a discretionary right, not a social or economic obligation, to pay fair wages in cash, to keep mines in safe working order, to weigh tonnage accurately, or to hire foremen who kept safety in mind as much as production. Given the highly competitive nature of the industry, operators also depended on their "right" to pay the lowest wages possible and their "right" to discharge organized miners in favor of those more desperate for work. The national government not only endorsed, but enforced, those rights.

No doubt the perception that ethnic depravity and political disloyalty motivated strikers strengthened the operators' position. With the help of outspoken critics like Benjamin Bannan, they targeted ethnicity rather than inequality as the key to labor unrest. Linking the emergence of labor unions to the Irish miners' alleged clannishness, intemperance, and slavish devotion to the Democrats, these critics ignored the important fact that Irish miners were most likely to be employed by large centralized collieries. Neither did they acknowledge the fact that supposedly respectable Welsh, English, and native-born miners similarly employed also organized. Ethnic ties may well have helped to build solidarity among groups of miners, but it was not these ties alone that encouraged miners to organize. Indeed, when the operators managed to repopulate the coal regions with Eastern European immigrants later in the century, they hurled the same epithets when these allegedly more docile workers also organized to defend their rights.[2]

Coal miners were not the only workers to criticize the industrial system during the Civil War, and coal operators were not the only industrialists to rely on federal troops to discourage their efforts. During a strike in 1864, for example, company officials requested the War Department to seize and operate the Philadelphia and Reading Railroad. "Your action brought the strike at once to a crisis," president Charles E. Smith informed Major General George Cadwalader, "and hastened a result favorable to us."[3] When working people in Louisville, Kentucky, organized that same year, the local provost marshal proclaimed that "no combinations shall be formed" in establishments "where articles are manufactured for the naval and transport service of the United States," and he advised employers to provide his office with the names of persons involved in any such activity. "In putting down this attack upon private rights and the interests of the service by organizations led by bad men," he added, "the General commanding [officer] confidently relies upon the support of the city authorities and of all right-minded men." This provost marshal, like his colleagues in the coal regions, claimed that issues of national defense, not managerial prerogative, were at stake, but *Fincher's Trades' Review* did not agree. "Forcing these purse-proud employers into terms is treason—," editor Jonathan Fincher complained, adding that "a social difference between employers and employed is sufficient to call for government interference while a horde of other capitalists are dragging the government to ruin."[4] Fincher also reported evidence of military interference on the side of capital in other cities: New York City; Albany, New York; Cumberland, Maryland; and St. Louis, Missouri. "God help us if the Government, which we have worshipped with such devotion, is to waste its energies by so bare a prostitution of its power," he complained in the summer of 1863. "If outrages like these are to be embraced in the future duty of soldiers, conscription must indeed become a 'military necessity,' " he added, "for no brave man will, spaniel-like, voluntarily kiss the foot that kicks him."[5]

The end of the war in no way heralded the end of labor conflict in Pennsylvania's anthracite regions.[6] In fact, two short months after the Confederacy's surrender, miners chose to strike rather than accept wage cuts proposed by the operators. Although Benjamin Bannan complained that "ruffianism" was again on the rise, this time he criticized the operators, who had imposed what he called drastic cuts. "Forty percent on miners and thirty on laborers is all the reduction that ought to be asked," he advised, "until present prices of living are reduced to a greater extent." He even went so far as to say, in a later column, that "the interests of labor must be protected as well as the interests of the producers, because no business can flourish where labor is not properly remunerated."[7]

Bannan's temperate tone in this instance, together with his general antipathy to monopolies and his later support for the Greenback party, suggests that he believed that the operators had employed coercive state power during the war, not to centralize their authority, but to protect his brand of independent "republican" industry.[8] In fact, his dedication and faith in individual enterprise hardly waned despite obvious changes in the industry. In 1864, for example, when an improvement company had begun developing coal lands, he vigorously protested this "outrage" upon the rights of individual operators, upon the business community, and upon the people. "In fact," Bannan exhorted, as if this were something new, "it is *rank treason to the county* and our members who participate in the outrage . . . ought to be indicted as conspirators. . . ."[9] If he expected the provost marshal to act upon this suggestion though, as he had acted upon so many others, Bannan was to be sorely disappointed. When the legislature further relaxed legal impediments to economic centralization in 1865, Bannan again voiced his dismay. "Speculators opened the door for the introduction of coal mining companies," he reported, "by secret legislation unknown to the people." Two years later he continued to lament the rise of coal companies and the social consequences of speculation, and he cursed the cowardice of Schuylkill's operators who refused to pursue a "manly" independent policy. "If we did not cringe to injustice and threats or fawn for favors and promises," he argued, "we would not for a moment suffer any corporation or monopoly to threaten us against all law and justice. The people are always masters," he concluded, "until they become slaves." The spirit of speculation, he added sadly, had diverted attention away from the "safe and honest fruits of business."[10] Unfortunately, his insights had come two decades too late.

Bannan's eloquent disappointment with this turn of economic events, his continued faith in "safe and honest" business, cannot be easily reconciled with the history of the anthracite industry. Speculation had nourished the industry's development and financed its expansion; the operators' manipulation of wages had helped produce whatever "fruits" the industry had thus far enjoyed. Neither was the industry's conduct following the war any more "honest." The performance of the New York and Schuylkill Coal Company — the successor to the Forest Improvement Company — makes it clear that "safe and honest" business had little to do with economic success in the anthracite regions.[11]

When President Otto Wilson Davis reported that water threatened to drown the company's mines in February 1867, he praised his employees for their prompt and voluntary assistance to the company. In the same breath, however, he remarked that rumors of imminent insolvency had materially benefited the company, enabling "us to make contracts at much less rates than our neighbors." Adding that some "expedients" were necessary to keep down the price of labor, Davis suggested a surefire plan. "As the price of a barrel of flour has by custom and common consent been made the barometer of wages," he explained, "I would recommend that we sell flour at less than cost for the next sixty days."[12] When news of an impending regional strike threatened to upset these plans, he devised a similarly useful strategy. Suggesting that he immediately meet the miners' wage demands, he added that the company should not start up any more collieries. The company then could "weed out every man here and employ men from the other collieries about— which would be no difficulty and when we have a complete change made then return to present wages. Such a course would cost us only a few hundred dollars," he explained, "and as a lesson for the future would be invaluable."[13] In the meantime the company relied on its private police force to maintain order.[14]

Davis's actions and Bannan's attitudes demonstrate a crucial difference between the interests and aspirations of supporters of individual enterprise and supporters of economic centralization. If independents continued to envision thriving local business based on free access to the industry, which would serve a community of producers with a shared interest in economic prosperity, centralizers looked to control the work force to ensure the high productivity and low prices on which their prosperity was based. Ultimately, supporters of individual enterprise recognized that they had more in common with wage earners than with large centralized operators, and they attempted to align themselves with the miners in the late 1860s and early 1870s. Nevertheless, the consequences of their earlier alliance with centralized operators during the Civil War negated these efforts; they were to find that the same power of the national state used then could be invoked whenever local agencies could not maintain "order"—regardless of local middle-class support for strikers. When organized capital called on the state or federal government to defend managerial prerogative during the strikes of 1877, the Homestead strike of 1892, or the Pullman strike of 1894, among others, evidence of local support for the strikers did not deter government action.[15] And when Slavic miners employed in Hazleton organized a strike in 1897, and the sheriff's posse opened fire on these "ignorant," "depraved," and "riotous" miners, leaving nineteen dead and thirty-eight wounded, the governor sent militia troops to Hazleton the following day despite the community's outrage.[16]

The system of industrial capitalism that developed in the nineteenth century generated a political and economic structure antithetical to long-cherished notions of a republican social order. It neither produced the equitable economic rewards central to the wage earners' concept of republicanism or the economic prosperity and political consensus essential to the republicanism envisioned by independent entrepreneurs. On the contrary, it engendered an economic structure that promoted centralization of resources and centralized control and also depended on the employer's ability to secure labor at the lowest possible cost. This structure thus repudiated any commitment to the shared interests of labor and capital and at the same time reduced wage earners to commodities. If this system generated dynamic economic growth in the process, it was growth characterized by conflict and cyclical depression, protected by a political state that recognized and defended capital's interests as its own. The recurring need to employ coercive state power to resolve industrial conflicts—whether through state militia, federal troops, state-chartered private police, or federal injunction—demonstrates that organized capital relied on the state to cripple working-class opposition to the revolutionary extension of corporate power.

But if organized capital expected that this access to state power could eradicate opposition, history proved otherwise. The continual emergence and reemergence of labor organizations despite capital's hostility and cyclical defeats demonstrate that organization proved a logical consequence of the system of industrial capitalism and not an aberration. The economic and social inequality inherent in this system and the conflict that resulted from it not only induced but required working people to organize if they hoped to reap economic or social benefit from their labor. The combined power of organized capital and the state, however, so clearly illustrated during the Civil War, significantly constrained organized labor's ability to muster its forces. But if this combination subverted both the structure and the promise of a producers' republic, it could not destroy the ideal.

NOTES

1. *MJ*, Jan. 21, 1865.
2. For information on other ethnic groups of miners see Sister M.

Accurisa, "Polish Miners in Luzerne County, Pennsylvania," *Polish American Studies* 8 (1946): 5–12; Rowland Berthoff, "The Social Order of the Anthracite Region, 1825–1902," *Pennsylvania Magazine of History and Biography* 89 (1965): 261–91; Victor Greene, *The Slavic Community on Strike* (South Bend, Ind., 1968); Bela Vassady, Jr., "Themes from Immigrant Fraternal Life: The Early Decades of the Hazleton-Based Hungarian Verhovay Sick Benefit Association," in *Hard Coal, Hard Times: Ethnicity and Labor in the Anthracite Region*, ed. David L. Salay (Scranton, Pa., 1984), 17–34; and Peter Roberts, *Anthracite Coal Communities* (New York, 1904).

3. John L. Blackman, Jr., "The Seizure of the Reading Railroad in 1864," *Pennsylvania Magazine of History and Biography* 111 (1987): 49–60. The quotation is on page 55.

4. *Fincher's Trades' Review*, June 11, 1864.

5. Ibid., June 20, June 27, 1863, Mar. 26, Apr. 23, May 14, June 25, 1864. The quotation is from June 20, 1863.

6. Most of the secondary literature on anthracite miners begins with the formation of the Workingmen's Benevolent Association in 1868, and for that reason I have not cataloged the rise of this union or the related "Molly Maguire" episodes and trials in the 1870s. See Harold Aurand, *From the Molly Maguires to the United Mine Workers* (Philadelphia, 1971); Wayne G. Broehl, *The Molly Maguires* (Cambridge, Mass., 1964); Anthony Bimba, *The Molly Maguires* (New York, 1932); Edward Pinkowski, *John Siney, The Miners' Martyr* (Philadelphia, 1963); Marvin W. Schlegel, *Ruler of the Reading: The Life of Franklin B. Gowen, 1836–1889* (Harrisburg, Pa., 1947); and Charles E. Kileen, "John Siney: The Pioneer of American Industrial Unionism and Industrial Government," Ph.D. diss., University of Wisconsin, 1942, among others.

7. *MJ*, June 3, 1865. Around the same time that Bannan complained of increased lawlessness, the *Miners' Journal* recorded the fact that a Richard Heckscher pleaded guilty to assault and battery on a woman. *MJ*, June 10, 1865. For his comments on wage cuts and the cost of living see *MJ*, June 24, July 8, July 15, 1865.

8. For Bannan's later position see David Montgomery, *Beyond Equality: Labor and the Radical Republicans, 1862–1872* (New York, 1967), 345.

9. *MJ*, Mar. 19, 1864.

10. *MJ*, July 29, 1865, Mar. 9, 1867.

11. In 1865 the New York and Schuylkill Coal Company listed Otto Wilson Davis as president and Peter Heckscher as treasurer and secretary. Moses Taylor, John Phelps, Percy Pyne, Charles A. Heckscher, Samuel Sloan, and Richard Heckscher were named directors.

12. Davis to Parker, Feb. 21, 1867, Charles A. Heckscher Company Papers, Moses Taylor Collection, Manuscript Division, New York Public Library.

13. Davis to Parker, Mar. 11, 1867, ibid.

14. Davis to Parker, Mar. 30, 1867, and May 27, 1867, ibid. For a discussion of private police forces see Stephen R. Couch, "The Coal and Iron Police in Anthracite Country," in Salay, ed., *Hard Coal, Hard Times,*

100–119; Aurand, *From the Molly Maguires to the United Mine Workers*, 24–26; Jeremiah Patrick Shalloo, *Private Police: With Special Reference to Pennsylvania* (Philadelphia, 1933).

15. Clifton K. Yearley, Jr., *Enterprise and Anthracite* (Baltimore, 1961), 186–93; Aurand, *From the Molly Maguires to the United Mine Workers*, 67–72.

16. See Jerry M. Cooper, *The Army and Civil Disobedience: Federal Military Intervention in Labor Disputes, 1877–1900* (Westport, Conn., 1980); George A. Turner, "Ethnic Responses to the Lattimer Massacre," in Salay, ed., *Hard Coal, Hard Times*, 126–52; Victor Greene, "A Study in Slavs, Strikes, and Unions: The Anthracite Strike of 1897," *Pennsylvania History* 31 (1964): 199–215; Aurand, *From the Molly Maguires to the United Mine Workers*, 137–41.

Bibliography

PRIMARY SOURCES

Manuscripts

Buchanan, James. Papers. Historical Society of Pennsylvania, Philadelphia.

Buckalew, Charles R. Papers. Manuscript Division. Library of Congress, Washington, D.C.

Cameron, Simon. Papers. Historical Society of Dauphin County, Harrisburg, Pennsylvania.

Carey, Henry C. Papers. Edward Gardiner Carey Collection. Historical Society of Pennsylvania, Philadelphia.

Chase, Salmon. Papers. Library of Congress, Washington, D.C.

Department of Military Affairs, Office of the Adjutant General. Record Group 19. Pennsylvania State Archives, Harrisburg.

Girard Estate Papers. Historical Society of Pennsylvania, Philadelphia.

Charles A. Heckscher Company. Papers. Moses Taylor Collection. Manuscript Division. New York Public Library, New York.

Hoffman, John N. Files. Division of Agriculture and Natural Resources. National Museum of American History, Washington, D.C.

Larcom, Sir Thomas. Papers. Microfilm. Library of Congress, Washington, D.C.

Lincoln, Abraham. Papers. Manuscript Division. Library of Congress, Washington, D.C.

Loeser, Charles. Papers. Historical Society of Schuylkill County, Pottsville, Pennsylvania.

Marble, Manton M. Papers. Manuscript Division. Library of Congress, Washington, D.C.

McPherson, Edward. Papers. Manuscript Division. Library of Congress, Washington, D.C.

Miners' Benevolent Association of Archbald. Minutes. Pennsylvania

State University Labor Collection, University Park, Pennsylvania.

Miscellaneous Manuscripts. Historical Society of Schuylkill County, Pottsville, Pennsylvania.

Papers of the Provost Marshal General's Bureau. Record Group 110. National Archives, Washington, D.C.

Pinkerton Detective Agency. Papers. Microfilm. Library of Congress, Washington, D.C.

Records of the Office of the Judge Advocate General. Record Group 107. National Archives, Washington, D.C.

Scranton Family Papers. Lackawanna County Historical Society, Scranton, Pennsylvania.

Slifer-Dill Papers. Historical Society of Pennsylvania, Philadelphia.

Stevens, John A. Papers. New-York Historical Society, New York.

Stevens, Thaddeus. Papers. Manuscript Division. Library of Congress, Washington, D.C.

Swisher, Carl B. Papers. Manuscript Division. Library of Congress, Washington, D.C.

Tower, Charlemagne. Papers. Butler Library, Columbia University, New York.

Tower, Charlemagne. Papers. Historical Society of Schuylkill County, Pottsville, Pennsylvania.

United States Army Continental Commands. Part I. Department of the Susquehanna and Pennsylvania. Record Group 393. National Archives, Washington, D.C.

Wright, Hendrick B. Papers. Wyoming Geological and Historical Society, Wilkes-Barre, Pennsylvania.

Public Documents

"Acts of Incorporation of the New York and Schuylkill Coal Company Formerly the Forest Improvement Company." New York, 1864.

Bergner, George, pub. *The Legislative Record Containing the Debates and Proceedings of the Pennsylvania Legislature for the Sessions of 1860–65.* Harrisburg, Pa., 1860–65.

The Congressional Globe. 37th Cong., 3d sess., 1863, vol. 41, pt. 2.

Gowen, Franklin B. "Argument in the Case of the *Commonwealth* v. *Thomas Munley.*" Court of Oyer and Terminer of Schuylkill County. Pottsville, Pennsylvania, 1876.

Lane, John Q., and S. W. Petitt. "Argument before the Investigating Committee of the Pennsylvania Legislature, July 28–31, 1875, Anthracite Monopoly." Philadelphia, 1875.

Lehigh Coal and Navigation Company. *Annual Report,* 1830–55.

Lincoln, Charles Z., ed. *Messages from the Governors.* Albany, New York, 1909.

"Memorial Against an Act to Incorporate the Schuylkill Coal Company to the Senate and House of Representatives of the Commonwealth of Pennsylvania," n.p., ca. 1822. John N. Hoffman Files, National Museum of American History, Washington, D.C.

Pennsylvania. General Assembly. Senate. Committee on the Judiciary. *Report in Relation to the Anthracite Coal Difficulties.* Harrisburg, 1871.

———. Supreme Court. "Opinion of Honorable John M. Reed in Favor of the Constitutionality of [The Conscription Act]." Philadelphia, 1863.

"Petition of David Brown and Others for an Act of Incorporation for Sinking a Shaft at Their Colliery in Schuylkill County." Pottsville, Pennsylvania, 1856.

Proceedings of the Pennsylvania Democratic State Convention. 1856.

Report of the Inspector of Mines of the County of Schuylkill for the Year Ending December 31, 1869. Harrisburg, Pennsylvania, 1870.

Reports of the Inspectors of Coal Mines of the Anthracite Coal Regions of Pennsylvania for the Year 1870. Harrisburg, Pennsylvania, 1871.

Reports of the President and Managers of the Philadelphia and Reading Railroad to the Stockholders. Philadelphia, 1862.

United States. Census Office. Eighth Census, 1860. *Population of the United States in 1860.* For Schuylkill County, Pennsylvania. Original unpublished returns.

———. Census Office. Eighth Census, 1860. *Manufactures in the United States in 1860.* For Schuylkill County, Pennsylvania. Original unpublished returns.

———. Commissioner of Labor. *Third Annual Report: Strikes and Lockouts, 1887.* Washington, D.C., 1888.

———.House of Representatives. *Executive Documents.* 39th Cong., 1st sess., 1866, serial 1251, vol. 4, pt. 1.

———. House of Representatives. *Labor Troubles in the Anthracite Regions of Pennsylvania, 1887–1888.* 50th Cong., 2d sess., 1889, House Report 4147, vol. 4.

———. War Department. *The War of the Rebellion: A Compilation of the Official Records of the Union and Confederate Armies.* Washington, D.C., 1889–1901.

Newspapers

Carbon County Gazette. Mauch Chunk, Pa.

Catholic Herald and Visitor. Philadelphia, Pa.

Easton Argus. Easton, Pa.
Fincher's Trades' Review. Philadelphia, Pa.
Gazette. Pittston, Pa.
Irish American. New York, N.Y.
Lehigh Pioneer. Mauch Chunk, Pa.
Luzerne Union. Wilkes-Barre, Pa.
Mauch Chunk Gazette. Mauch Chunk, Pa.
Miners' Journal. Pottsville, Pa.
Mining Register and Democrat. Pottsville, Pa.
New York Times. New York, N.Y.
North American. Philadelphia, Pa.
Patriot and Union. Harrisburg, Pa.
Pilot. Boston, Mass.
Pottsville Emporium. Pottsville, Pa.
Press. Philadelphia, Pa.
Public Ledger. Philadelphia, Pa.
Wayne County Herald. Honesdale, Pa.
Weekly Democrat. Johnstown, Pa.

SECONDARY SOURCES

Articles and Pamphlets

Accurisa, M. "Polish Miners in Luzerne County, Pennsylvania." *Polish American Studies* 8 (1946): 5–12.
Alden, H. M. "Coal Fields of Pennsylvania." *Harper's* 28 (1863): 455–67.
Allison, Robert. "Early History of Coal Mining and Mining Machinery in Schuylkill County." *Publications of the Historical Society of Schuylkill County* 4 (1912): 134–55.
"The Anthracite Coal Trade of Pennsylvania." *North American Review* 42 (1836): 241–56.
Aurand, Harold W. "Workingman's Benevolent Association." *Labor History* 7 (1966): 19–34.
Baker, Jean. "A Loyal Opposition." *Civil War History* 25 (1979): 139–55.
Bernstein, J. L. "Conscription and the Constitution: The Amazing Case of *Kneedler* v. *Lane.*" *American Bar Association Journal* 53 (1967): 708–12.
Berthoff, Rowland. "Peasants and Artisans, Puritans and Republicans: Personal Liberty and Communal Equality in American History." *Journal of American History* 69 (1982): 579–98.
———. "The Social Order of the Anthracite Region, 1825–1902."

Pennsylvania Magazine of History and Biography 89 (1965): 261–91.

Blackman, John L., Jr. "The Seizure of the Reading Railroad in 1864." *Pennsylvania Magazine of History and Biography* 111 (1987): 49–60.

Chandler, Arthur. "Anthracite Coal and the Beginnings of the Industrial Revolution in the United States." *Business History Review* 47 (1972): 149–81.

Collins, Bruce. "The Ideology of the Antebellum Northern Democrats." *Journal of American Studies* 11 (1977): 103–21.

Curry, Richard. "The Union As It Was: A Critique of Recent Interpretations of the 'Copperheads.' " *Civil War History* 13 (1967): 25–39.

Earnhart, Hugh. "Commutation: Democratic or Undemocratic?" *Civil War History* 12 (1966): 132–42.

Ershkowitz, Herbert, and William G. Shade. "Consensus or Conflict? Political Behavior in the State Legislatures during the Jacksonian Era." *Journal of American History* 58 (1971): 591–621.

Fields, Barbara J. "Ideology and Race in American History." In *Region, Race, and Reconstruction,* ed. J. Morgan Kousser and James M. McPherson, 143–78. New York, 1982.

Geary, James W. "Civil War Conscription in the North: A Historiographical Review." *Civil War History* 32 (1986): 256–67.

Greene, Victor. "A Study in Slavs, Strikes, and Unions: The Anthracite Strike of 1897." *Pennsylvania History* 31 (1964): 199–215.

Gudelunas, William A., Jr. "Nativism and the Demise of Schuylkill County Whiggery: Anti-Slavery or Anti-Catholicism?" *Pennsylvania History* 45 (1978): 225–36.

———. "The Lower Anthracite Region Votes: An Electoral History of a Turbulent Region." *Proceedings of the Canal History and Technology Symposium* 4 (1985): 45–68.

Henretta, James. "The Study of Social Mobility: Ideological Assumption and Conceptual Bias." *Labor History* 18 (1977): 165–78.

Hobbs, Herrwood E. "A Lawyer Goes to War." *Publications of the Schuylkill County Historical Society* 7 (1961): 100–103.

Hoffman, John N. "Anthracite in the Lehigh Region of Pennsylvania, 1820–45." In *Contributions from the Museum of History and Technology* (Washington, D.C., 1968): 91–104.

Hopkins, George F. "A Cursory Review of the Schuylkill Coal Region in Reference to Its Introduction into New York and the Other Atlantic Cities." New York Public Library. New York, 1823.

Huston, James L. "A Political Response to Industrialism: The Republican Embrace of Protectionist Labor Doctrines." *Journal of American History* 70 (1983): 35–57.

Itter, William A. "Early Labor Troubles in the Schuylkill Anthracite District." *Pennsylvania History* 1 (1934): 28–37.

Kidd, William. "A Few Things Interesting to Coal Burners." n.d. Littell File, Lackawanna County Historical Society, Scranton, Pa.

Knies, Michael. "Industry, Enterprise, Wealth, and Taste: The History of Mauch Chunk, 1791–1831." *Proceedings of the Canal History and Technology Symposium* 4 (1985): 17–45.

Levin, Bernard. "Pennsylvania and the Civil War." *Pennsylvania History* 10 (1943): 1–10.

Levine, Peter. "Draft Evasion in the North during the Civil War, 1863–1865." *Journal of American History* 67 (1981): 816–34.

Lewis, W. David. "The Early History of the Lackawanna Iron and Coal Company: A Study in Technological Adaptation." *Pennsylvania Magazine of History and Biography* 96 (1972): 424–68.

Luraghi, Raimondo. "The Civil War and the Modernization of American Society: Social Structure and Industrial Revolution in the Old South before and during the War." *Civil War History* 18 (1972): 230–50.

MacDonough, Oliver. "The Irish Famine Emigration to the United States." *Perspectives in American History* 10 (1976): 357–448.

Man, Albon P. "Labor Competition and the New York Draft Riots of 1863." *Journal of Negro History* 36 (1951): 375–405.

Marvel, William. "New Hampshire and the Draft Riots of 1863." *Historical New Hampshire* 36 (1981): 58–72.

"The Molly Maguires." Historical Society of Schuylkill County. Pottsville, Pa., 1969.

Patterson, Edith. "Schuylkill County Deals with the Draft." *Publications of the Historical Society of Schuylkill County* 7 (1961): 63–68.

Patterson, Joseph F. "Old W.B.A. Days." *Publications of the Historical Society of Schuylkill County* 2 (1910): 355–84.

———. "Reminiscences of John Maguire After Fifty Years of Mining." *Publications of the Historical Society of Schuylkill County* 4 (1914): 305–36.

Paxson, Isaac. "Reminiscences of Schuylkill Haven in the Civil War." *Publications of the Historical Society of Schuylkill County* 2 (1910): 418–44.

Saxton, Alexander. "Blackface Minstrelsy and Jacksonian Ideology." *American Quarterly* 27 (1975): 3–28.

Schlegel, Marvin W. "The W.B.A.: The First Union of Anthracite Miners." *Pennsylvania History* 10 (1943): 243–67.

Shade, William G. "Revolutions May Go Backwards: The American Civil War and the Problem of Political Development." *Social Science Quarterly* 55 (1974): 753–67.

Shalhope, Robert E. "Republicanism and Early American Historiography." *William and Mary Quarterly* 39 (1982): 334–56.

Shankman, Arnold. "Francis W. Hughes and the 1862 Pennsylvania Election." *Pennsylvania Magazine of History and Biography* 95 (1971): 383–93.

———. "Draft Riots in Civil War Pennsylvania." *Pennsylvania Magazine of History and Biography* 101 (1977): 190–204.

Virtue, G. O. "The Anthracite Mine Workers." *Bulletin of the Bureau of Labor* 2 (1897): 728–74.

Books

Aurand, Harold. *From the Molly Maguires to the United Mine Workers: The Social Ecology of an Industrial Union, 1869–1897.* Philadelphia, 1971.

Baer, Christopher T. *Canals and Railroads of the Mid-Atlantic States, 1800–1860.* Wilmington, Del., 1981.

Baker, Jean H. *Affairs of Party: The Political Culture of the Northern Democrats in the Mid-Nineteenth Century.* Ithaca, N.Y., 1983.

Benson, Lee. *The Concept of Jacksonian Democracy: New York as a Test Case.* Princeton, 1961.

Bimba, Anthony. *The Molly Maguires.* New York, 1932.

Bogen, Jules I. *The Anthracite Railroads: A Study in American Railroad Enterprise.* New York, 1927.

Bowen, Eli, ed. *The Coal Regions of Pennsylvania.* Pottsville, Pa., 1848.

Bradley, Erwin S. *The Triumph of Militant Republicanism.* Philadelphia, 1964.

Bradsby, Henry C. *History of Luzerne County, Pennsylvania.* Chicago, 1893.

Brenckman, Frederick. *History of Carbon County.* Harrisburg, Pa., 1913.

Bridges, Hal. *Iron Millionaire: Life of Charlemagne Tower.* Philadelphia, 1952.

Broehl, Wayne G. *The Molly Maguires.* Cambridge, Mass., 1964.

Clawson, Dan. *Bureaucracy and the Labor Process: The Transformation of U.S. Industry, 1860–1920.* New York, 1980.

Coleman, J. Walter. *The Molly Maguire Riots: Industrial Conflict in the Pennsylvania Coal Region.* Washington, D.C., 1936.

Coleman, John F. *The Disruption of the Pennsylvania Democracy, 1848–1860.* Harrisburg, Pa., 1975.

Commons, John R., et al. *History of Labor in the United States,* vol. 1. New York, 1918.

————. *A Documentary History of American Industrial Society,* vol. 8, Cleveland, 1910.

Conway, Alan, ed. *The Welsh in America: Letters from the Immigrants.* Minneapolis, Minn., 1961.

Cook, Adrian. *The Armies of the Streets: The New York City Draft Riots of 1863.* Lexington, Ky., 1974.

Cooper, Jerry M. *The Army and Civil Disobedience: Federal Military Intervention in Labor Disputes, 1877–1900.* Westport, Conn., 1980.

Crippen, Lee F. *Simon Cameron: Ante-bellum Years.* New York, 1972.

Daddow, Samuel H., and Benjamin Bannan. *Coal, Iron, and Oil.* Pottsville, Pa., 1866.

Davis, Stanton L. *Pennsylvania Politics, 1860–1863.* Cleveland, 1935.

[Delaware and Hudson Company.] *A Century of Progress: History of the Delaware and Hudson Company, 1823–1923.* Albany, N.Y., 1925.

Dewees, Francis P. *The Molly Maguires: The Origin, Growth and Character of the Organization.* New York, 1969 [Philadelphia, 1877].

Du Bin, Alexander, ed. *Massey, Lea, and Heckscher Families.* Philadelphia, 1948.

Dublin, Thomas. *Women at Work: The Transformation of Work and Community in Lowell, Massachusetts, 1826–1860.* New York, 1979.

Duggan, Joseph C. *The Legislative and Statutory Development of the Federal Concept of Conscription for Military Service.* Washington, D.C., 1946.

Dusinberre, William. *Civil War Issues in Philadelphia, 1856–1865.* Philadelphia, 1965.

Evans, Chris. *History of the United Mine Workers of America from the Year 1860 to 1890,* vol. 1. Indianapolis, 1900.

Evans, Frank B. *Pennsylvania Politics, 1872–1877.* Harrisburg, Pa., 1966.

Foner, Eric. *Free Soil, Free Labor, Free Men: The Ideology of the Republican Party before the Civil War.* New York, 1970.

————. *Politics and Ideology in the Age of the Civil War.* New York, 1980.

Friedel, Frank. *Union Pamphlets of the Civil War, 1861–1865.* 2 vols. Cambridge, Mass., 1967.

Friedman, Jean E. *The Revolt of the Congressional Democrats.* Ann Arbor, Mich., 1979.

Fry, James B. *New York and the Conscription: A Chapter in Civil War History.* New York, 1885.

Gallagher, John P. *A Century of History: The Diocese of Scranton, 1868–1968.* Scranton, Pa., 1968.

Glasco, Laurence Admiral. *Ethnicity and Social Structure: Irish, Germans, and Native-Born of Buffalo, New York, 1850–1860.* New York, 1980.

Goodrich, Carter. *The Miner's Freedom: A Study of the Working Life in a Changing Industry.* Boston, 1925.

Gray, Wood. *The Hidden Civil War: The Story of the Copperheads.* New York, 1942.

Greeley, Horace. *The American Conflict.* New York, 1866.

Greene, Homer. *The Blind Brother, A Story of the Pennsylvania Coal Mines.* New York, 1887.

Greene, Victor. *The Slavic Community on Strike.* South Bend, Ind., 1968.

Gudelunas, William A., Jr., and William G. Shade. *Before the Molly Maguires: The Emergence of the Ethno-Religious Factor in the Politics of the Lower Anthracite Region, 1844–1872.* New York, 1976.

Gutman, Herbert. *Work, Culture, and Society in Industrial America.* New York, 1977.

Hanagan, Michael, and Charles Stephenson, eds. *Proletarians and Protest: The Roots of Class Formation in an Industrialized World.* Westport, Conn., 1986.

Hartz, Louis. *Economic Policy and Democratic Thought: Pennsylvania, 1776–1860.* Cambridge, Mass., 1948.

Harvan, George. *The Molly Maguire Trials in Carbon and Schuylkill Counties, Pennsylvania.* Lansford, Pa., 1969.

Harvey, Oscar Jewell, and Ernest Greg Smith. *A History of Wilkes-Barre, Luzerne County, Pennsylvania.* Wilkes-Barre, 1930.

Hesseltine, William B. *Lincoln and the War Governors.* New York, 1948.

Hirsch, Susan E. *Roots of the American Working Class: The Industrialization of Crafts in Newark, 1800–1860.* Philadelphia, 1978.

A History of Schuylkill County, Pennsylvania. New York, 1881.

Hitchcock, Frederick. *History of Scranton and Its People.* New York, 1914.

Hobsbawm, Eric J. *The Age of Capital, 1845–1875.* New York, 1979.

Hodas, Daniel. *The Business Career of Moses Taylor.* New York, 1976.

Hollister, Horace. *History of the Lackawanna Valley.* Philadelphia, 1885.

Holt, Michael F. *Forging a Majority: The Formation of the Republican Party in Pittsburgh, 1848–1860.* New Haven, Conn., 1969.

Howe, Daniel. *The Political Culture of the American Whigs.* Chicago, 1979.

[The Hudson Coal Company]. *The Story of Anthracite.* New York, 1932.

Hyman, Harold, and William Wiecek. *Equal Justice under Law: Constitutional Development, 1835–1875.* New York, 1982.

Jones, Chester Lloyd. *The Economic History of the Anthracite-Tidewater Canals.* Philadelphia, 1908.

Jones, Eliot. *The Anthracite Coal Combinations of the United States.* Cambridge, Mass., 1914.

Kelley, Robert. *The Cultural Pattern in American Politics: The First Century.* New York, 1979.

Klement, Frank. *Dark Lanterns: Secret Political Societies, Conspiracies, and Treason Trials in the Civil War.* Baton Rouge, La., 1984.

———. *The Limits of Dissent: Clement L. Vallandigham and the Civil War.* Lexington, Ky., 1970.

Kleppner, Paul. *The Cross of Culture: A Social Analysis of Midwestern Politics, 1850–1900.* New York, 1970.

Koehler, LeRoy Jennings. *The History of Monroe County, Pennsylvania, during the Civil War.* Monroe County, Pa., 1950.

Korson, George. *Black Rock: Mining Folklore of the Pennsylvania Dutch.* Baltimore, 1960.

Laurie, Bruce. *Working People of Philadelphia, 1800–1850.* Philadelphia, 1980.

Leach, Jack F. *Conscription in the United States: Historical Background.* Rutland, Vt., 1952.

Lewis, Arthur H. *Lament for the Molly Maguires.* New York, 1964.

Lonn, Ella. *Desertion during the Civil War.* Gloucester, Mass., 1966.

———. *Foreigners in the Union Army and Navy.* Westport, Conn., 1969.

McCague, James. *The Second Rebellion: The Story of the New York City Draft Riots.* New York, 1968.

McClure, Alexander K. *Old Time Notes of Pennsylvania.* 2 vols. Philadelphia, 1905.

MacDonald, Fergus. *The Catholic Church and the Secret Societies in the United States.* New York, 1946.

MacFarlane, James. *The Coal Regions of America: Their Topography, Geology, and Development.* New York, 1873.

McPherson, James. *Ordeal by Fire: The Civil War and Reconstruction.* New York, 1982.

Milton, George Fort. *Abraham Lincoln and the Fifth Column.* New York, 1942.

Montgomery, David. *Beyond Equality: Labor and the Radical Republicans, 1862–1872.* New York, 1967.

———. *Workers' Control in America: Studies in the History of Work, Technology, and Labor Struggles.* Cambridge, 1979.

Moore, Albert. *Conscription and Conflict in the Confederacy.* New York, 1963.

Moore, Barrington. *Social Origins of Dictatorship and Democracy: The Making of the Modern World.* Boston, 1966.

Morrison, Samuel, et al. *Dissent in Three American Wars.* Cambridge, Mass., 1970.

Mumford, John K. *Anthracite.* New York, 1925.

Murdock, Eugene C. *One Million Men: The Civil War Draft in the North.* Madison, Wis., 1971.

———. *Patriotism Limited, 1862–1865: The Civil War Draft and the Bounty System.* Kent, Ohio, 1967.

Nevins, Allan, ed. *The Diary of Philip Hone,* vol. 1. New York, 1927.

———. *The War for Union: War Becomes Revolution, 1862–1863.* 2 vols. New York, 1960.

Nichols, Roy Franklin. *The Democratic Machine, 1850–1854.* New York, 1967.

———. *The Disruption of American Democracy.* New York, 1948.

Pessen, Edward. *Jacksonian America.* Urbana, Ill., 1985.

Pinkowski, Edward. *John Siney, The Miners' Martyr.* Philadelphia, 1963.

Powell, Howard Benjamin. *Philadelphia's First Fuel Crisis: Jacob Cist and the Developing Market for Pennsylvania Anthracite.* University Park, Pa., 1978.

Prude, Jonathan. *The Coming of Industrial Order: Town and Factory Life in Rural Massachusetts, 1810–1860.* Cambridge, 1983.

Rhodes, James Ford. *History of the United States.* New York, 1919.

Roberts, Peter. *Anthracite Coal Communities.* New York, 1904.

———. *The Anthracite Coal Industry.* New York, 1901.

Roy, Andrew. *A History of the Coal Miners of the United States.* Westport, Conn., 1970 [1907].

———. *The Coal Mines.* Cleveland, 1876.

Rupp, Daniel I. *History of Northampton, Lehigh, Monroe, and Schuylkill Counties.* Harrisburg, Pa., 1845.

Salay, David L., ed. *Hard Coal, Hard Times: Ethnicity and Labor in the Anthracite Region.* Scranton, Pa., 1984.

Schalck, Adolf W., and D. C. Henning. *History of Schuylkill County, Pennsylvania*. Harrisburg, Pa., 1907.

Schlegel, Marvin W. *Ruler of the Reading: The Life of Franklin B. Gowen, 1836–1889*. Harrisburg, Pa., 1947.

Shalloo, Jeremiah Patrick. *Private Police: With Special Reference to Pennsylvania*. Philadelphia, 1933.

Shankman, Arnold. *The Pennsylvania Anti-War Movement, 1861–1865*. Rutherford, N.J., 1980.

Shannon, Fred A. *The Organization and Administration of the Union Army, 1861–1865*. 2 vols. Gloucester, Mass., 1965.

Shaw, Douglas V. *The Making of an Immigrant City: Ethnic and Cultural Conflict in Jersey City, 1850–1877*. New York, 1976.

Silbey, Joel H. *A Respectable Minority: The Democratic Party in the Civil War Era*. New York, 1977.

Trachtenberg, Alexander. *The History of Legislation for the Protection of Coal Miners in Pennsylvania, 1824–1915*. New York, 1942.

Tyrell, Ian R. *Sobering Up: From Temperance to Prohibition in Ante-Bellum America, 1800–1860*. Westport, Conn., 1979.

Unger, Irwin, ed. *Essays on the Civil War and Reconstruction*. New York, 1970.

Wallace, Anthony F. C. *St. Clair*. New York, 1987.

———. *The Social Context of Innovation*. Princeton, 1982.

Wallace, Francis B. *Memorial of the Patriotism of Schuylkill County in the American Slaveholders' Rebellion*. Pottsville, Pa., 1865.

Ware, Norman. *The Industrial Worker, 1840–1860*. Chicago, 1964.

Weeden, William B. *War Government, Federal and State, in Massachusetts, New York, Pennsylvania, Indiana*. Boston, 1906.

Weigley, Russell F. *Towards an American Army*. New York, 1962.

Wieck, Edward. *The American Miners' Association*. New York, 1940.

Wilentz, Sean. *Chants Democratic: New York City and the Rise of the American Working Class*. New York, 1984.

Wiley, Samuel T. *Biographical and Portrait Cyclopedia of Schuylkill County, Pennsylvania*. Philadelphia, 1893.

Wright, Hendrick B. *Historical Sketches of Plymouth, Luzerne County*. Philadelphia, 1873.

Yearley, Clifton K., Jr. *Enterprise and Anthracite: Economics and Democracy in Schuylkill County, 1820–1875*. Baltimore, 1961.

Zerbey, Joseph Henry. *History of Schuylkill County*. 6 vols. Pottsville, Pa., 1934–35.

Unpublished Materials and Dissertations

Aurand, Harold W. "The Anthracite Mine Workers, 1869–1897: A Functional Approach to Labor History." Ph.D. diss., Pennsylvania State University, 1969.

Binder, Frederic M. "Pennsylvania Coal: An Historical Study of Its Utilization to 1860." Ph.D. diss., University of Pennsylvania, 1955.

Bowman, John B. "Terrorism on the Canal." Paper at Historical Society of Schuylkill County, Pottsville, Pa., n.d.

Cutler, Frederick Morse. "The History of Military Conscription with Especial Reference to the United States." Ph.D. diss., Clark University, 1922.

Fields, Barbara, and Leslie Rowland. "Free Labor Ideology and Its Exposition in the South during the Civil War and Reconstruction." Paper delivered at the Organization of American Historians, Annual Meeting, 1984.

Freifeld, Mary Ellen. "The Emergence of the American Working Classes." Ph.D. diss., New York University, 1980.

Geary, James. "A Lesson in Trial and Error: The United States Congress and the Civil War Draft, 1862–1865." Ph.D. diss., Kent State University, 1976.

Hirsch, Mark. "Coal Miners and the American Republic: Trade Union Ideology in the Anthracite Regions of Pennsylvania, 1875–1902." Ph.D. diss., Harvard University, 1984.

Itter, William. "Conscription in Pennsylvania during the Civil War." Ph.D. diss., University of Southern California, 1941.

Kileen, Charles E. "John Siney: The Pioneer of American Industrial Unionism and Industrial Government." Ph.D. diss., University of Wisconsin, 1942.

Miller, Kirby. "Emigrants and Exiles: The Irish Exodus to North America from Colonial Times to the First World War." Ph.D. diss., University of California at Berkeley, 1976.

Miscellaneous Civil War Writings and Clippings. Scrapbook. Historical Society of Schuylkill County, Pottsville, Pa.

Roads, Jay Oliver. "The Coal Region of Schuylkill County." Unpublished manuscript, Historical Society of Schuylkill County, Pottsville, Pa., 1943.

Shegda, Michael. "History of the Lehigh Coal and Navigation Company to 1840." Ph.D. diss., Temple University, 1952.

Sterling, Robert. "Civil War Draft Resistance in the Middle West." Ph.D. diss., University of Illinois, 1974.

Tipton, Harry J. "Chronology of Coal Mining." Unpublished manuscript, Pottsville Free Public Library, Pottsville, Pa., n.d.

Ward, Leo. "Unrest in the Coal Regions: A Paper on the Resistance to the Draft during the Civil War." Paper at Historical Society of Schuylkill County, Pottsville, Pa., 1971.

Index

Albright, Charles, 6, 70, 86, 151, 162n. 16
Allen, Samuel, 105, 106
Anthracite coal, reluctance to use, 18
Archbald: enrollment resistance in 100–101; miners' union in, 126–27, 137n. 19
Ashland, strike in, 58
Associated Mechanics of Schuylkill County, 55

Bank of the United States, 44
Bannan, Benjamin, 23, 25, 28, 30, 32, 38, 43, 47, 49, 54, 59, 60, 72, 73, 74–76, 77–78, 81, 85, 86, 87, 98, 101–2, 104, 125, 129, 131–34, 135, 141–42, 144–45, 148, 155, 157, 158, 160, 168, 170–71
Bast, Gideon, 52, 68n. 35
Bates Union, 53
Beaver Meadow, strike in, 58
Belmont, August, 95
Benevolent associations, 65, 126, 137n. 19
Biddle, Charles, 11
Black, Jeremiah, 83
Bomford, Col. James D., 107, 108, 111, 115
Borda, Eugene, 30, 34, 41n. 26, 56, 57
Boston *Pilot*, 97, 103
Bowen, Eli, 43, 85
Bowen, James, 109, 112
Boyd, Lt. Col. Carlisle, 156–57
Bradford, Stephen N., 107, 108, 140, 142, 143, 146, 148, 161
Brady, Thomas, 49, 52

Breckinridge, John C., 82, 84, 101
Bressler, Abraham, 109, 110
Broad Top Coal Region, 97
Brotherhood of Locomotive Engineers, 160–61
Brown, David, 32
Brownson, Orestes, 96
Buchanan, James, 82–83, 84
Buckshots, 106, 149, 150, 151

Cadwalader, Gen. George, 161, 169
Cameron, Simon, 31, 85
Caraher (a lieutenant colonel), 146, 148
Carbon County, 72, 89
Carbon County Gazette, 27, 45, 74
Carbon Democrat, 58, 149
Carbon Guards, 57
Carey, Henry, 81
Cass Township coal district, 54, 60–61, 62, 63, 101, 112, 116, 132
Catholic church: and enrollment, 103; and politics, 75, 79; and temperance, 75–76
Charles A. Heckscher Company, 30–31, 60–61, 132
Chase, Salmon, 31, 41n. 27
Child labor, in the mines, 38
Cist, Jacob, 18
Civil War: conscription necessary for, 95–96, 97–98; enlistments for, 85, 95, federal military occupation of coal region during, 4, 5–6, 10, 13, 102–3, 107–8, 115–16, 125, 142–43, 145–46, 147–48, 149–50, 153, 157, 161; opposition to con-

191

scription during, 3–6, 11–12, 95–117 passim, 140

Coal: price of, 8, 25, 27–28, 33–35, 47, 53, 56, 59, 148, 158, 159, 160, 167; tonnage of, 18, 19, 30, 158

Coal industry: and agriculture, 44–45; collective production control suggested, 33–34; and company stores ("store-order system"), 38, 47, 48, 51, 52, 57, 125; improvement companies in, 29–32; independent operators in, 8–9, 19, 22–23, 24–25, 27–28, 29, 32–34, 35–37, 47; markets for, 18; prosperity in, 16–17, 123–24, 141; provost marshals' interests in, 12, 157; respectability of, 43; shipping price war in, 25–27; transport companies in, 8, 19, 23, 24–25, 159–60; wage cuts attempted, 129, 170

Coal miners: benevolent associations for, 65, 126; immigration of, 45, 54, 72–73; numbers of, 47; property ownership among, 61, 62; strike tradition among, 54; unemployment among, 57; unionizing among, 9, 12–13, 16–17, 53, 55, 62, 63–66, 126, 128, 135; wages for, 9, 17, 37–38, 46–47, 51, 52–54, 56, 59, 61, 65, 81, 124, 125, 128, 129–30, 137n. 15, 158–59, 167. See also Strikes, by coal miners

Coal Mining Association of Schuylkill County, 34

Cochran, Edward, 49

Coleman, J. W., 5

Collieries, owned by Heckscher family, 30–31, 60–61

Conscription Act of 1863, 11–12, 104, 129, 135, 140, 141

Conscription Law (1862), 104

Couch, Gen. Darius, 108, 142–43, 149, 150–51, 155, 158

Curtin, Gov. Andrew, 4, 96, 98, 102, 103, 143

Davis, Jefferson, 107

Davis, Otto Wilson, 171, 174n. 11

Delaware and Hudson Canal Company, 24, 27, 34, 35, 39–40n. 7, 160, 161

Delaware, Lackawanna, and Western Railroad, 34, 36, 127, 160

Democratic party: denouncement of military presence in mining regions, 143; farmers' support for, 72, 76; miners' support for, 4, 7, 10–11, 66, 70–71, 73, 78, 79, 81–82, 89; opposition to conscription by, 96, 97, 98, 140, 152; pragmatism of, 82; and restoration of the Union, 70–71

Democratic Standard, 155

Department of the Susquehanna (Union Army), 5, 143

Douglas, Stephen, 84

Dunne, Henry, 153

Easton Argus, 86, 87, 88, 99

Easton Express, 148

Emancipation Proclamation, 86, 95

Emporium. See Pottsville Emporium

Ethnicity: and loyalty, 85; and voting patterns, 80, 81

Farmers: impact of coal industry on, 44–45; loyalty to Democrats, 72, 76; opposition to conscription among, 5

Ferry, Brig. Gen. Orris, 155–56, 157

Fincher, Jonathan, 121, 122, 123, 159, 169–70

Fincher's Trades' Review, 121, 159, 161, 169

Forest Improvement Company, 29–30, 166, 171

Fort Mifflin, 151, 155, 160

49th Pennsylvania Militia, 107

Foster, Thomas, 84

Foster Township, 62

Fry, Col. James B., 111, 112, 113, 116, 140, 142, 144, 148

Gane, Uriah, 109, 147

German (Pennsylvania Dutch) farmers, loyalty to Democrats among, 76

Gilbert, C. C., 108, 114

Giles, Col. George, 148

Gorman, Malachi, 112

Gorrell, R.: colliery of, 145
Gowen, Franklin B., 3, 86, 138n. 43
Grabner, Simon, 105

Hain, Henry, 98
Halleck (a major general), 151
Harrisburg *Patriot and Union*, 84
Hart, Roswell, 36
Hauto, George F., 19
Hazard, Erskine, 19
Hazel, borough of, 62
Hazleton coal district, 54, 172
Heckscher, Charles A., 30, 31,
    41n. 27, 166, 167, 174n. 11. *See also*
    Charles A. Heckscher Company
Heckscher, Peter, 153, 174n. 11
Heckscher, Richard, 30, 31, 34,
    41nn. 27, 33, 153, 166, 174nn. 7,
    11
Heckscherville Colliery, 153
Heilner, Henry, 52
Hewett, Charles, 69n. 44, 153,
    154–55
Homestead strike (1892), 13, 172
Hone, Philip, 43
Honey Brook Coal Company, 157
Honey Brook Colliery, 146
Horn, Conrad, 107
Howe, James, 111
Hughes, Francis W., 82–83, 144

Invalid Corps, 107, 108, 142, 146,
    149, 157
Irish coal miners: and all-Irish work
    force, 131; blame placed on, 62, 66,
    131, 132–33, 169; enrollment
    among, 113–14; loyalty to Demo-
    crats among, 72–73, 79, 81–82;
    strike tradition among, 54–55; and
    temperance, 75–76
Itter, William, 5

Jeansville coal district, 54, 58, 62, 106
Johns, William H., 34, 41n. 33
Johnston, Gov. William, 84
Jones, John, 130

Kelton, J. C., 142
Kern (a captain), 107
King, Horatio, 82

Knights of Liberty, 106
Knights of the Golden Circle, 106,
    128, 152
Kutz, Peter, 109

Labor combinations, opposition to,
    131–32
Labor unions: growth during wartime,
    122; organized among miners, 9,
    12–13, 16–17, 53, 55, 62, 63–66,
    126, 128, 135
Lackawanna Coal and Iron Company,
    36
Lackawanna Township, 62
Larer, Daniel, 85
Lausanne, Irish miners in, 62
Lee, Robert E., 152
Lehigh Canal, 26
Lehigh Coal and Navigation Com-
    pany, 19, 23–24, 26, 27, 39–40n. 7
Lehigh Coal Company, 19
Lehigh (middle) coal field (Luzerne
    and Carbon Counties), 8, 18, 19,
    23, 46, 151
Lehigh District, military organization
    of, 143, 161, 162n. 16
Lehigh Pioneer, 17, 24, 25
Leyburn, A. W., 52
Lilly (a general), 151
Lincoln, Abraham, 6, 70, 82, 85, 86,
    87, 88, 95, 103, 112, 147, 148
Loeser, Charles, 32
Luzerne County, 72, 104
Luzerne Union, 71, 86, 87, 88, 89, 97,
    101, 128, 143, 144, 158

McAllister, Richard, 84
McClean and Company, 57
McClellan, George, 152
McClure, Alexander, 103–4
McDonnell, James, 3
McDowell, Irvin, 152
Mauch Chunk coal district, 19
Mauch Chunk Democrat, 3
Mauch Chunk Gazette, 57, 58, 78, 84,
    97, 149, 150
Mayer, Maj. A. H., 108
Miner, Charles, 18
Miners. *See* Coal miners

Miners' Benevolent Association, 126, 128, 137n. 19
Miners' Journal. See Pottsville *Miners' Journal*
Minersville, strike activity in (1842), 49
Mining Register and Democrat, 32, 33, 53, 74, 76, 78–79
Modocs, 138n. 43
Molly Maguires: coffin notices of, 63; conscription among, 103, 104; investigation of, 138n. 43; viewed as agitators, 3, 4, 55, 133
Murdock, Eugene C., 4

Nativism, political, 73–74, 75, 76, 79–80
New York and Schuylkill Coal Company, 29, 41n. 27, 171
New York Times, 149
New York Tribune, 89
North American Review, 22
North Branch Canal, 35, 36
Norwegian Railroad, 49

O'Connor, Edward, 49
Official Records of the Civil War, 4
Olin, Abram D., 104, 105
Oliver, Joseph, 106

Palmer, Robert, 49, 52
Pardee, Ario, 107, 146
Parks, Sgt. William, 109
Parry, Edward O., 110–11
Peoples party, 85
Petherick, Thomas, 31
Philadelphia and Reading Railroad, 25, 26–27, 29, 31, 33, 61, 132, 138n. 37, 167, 169
Philadelphia Enquirer, 102, 103, 125
Philadelphia *Public Ledger,* 16, 111, 148
Pierce, Franklin, 74
Pittston, 65
Pittston *Gazette,* 34, 35, 36, 65, 85, 99, 100, 123, 127, 130, 141, 158
Pottsville: enrollment in, 112; strike activity in (1842), 49
Pottsville coal district, 19
Pottsville Emporium, 48, 52, 79

Pottsville *Miners' Journal,* 16, 23, 26, 29, 45, 49–50, 51, 55, 58, 59, 63, 66, 72, 73, 74, 75, 80, 82, 85, 86, 87, 102, 113, 124, 129, 130, 131, 155
Provost marshals: as conscription administrators, 6, 7, 11, 105; opposition to, 11–12; powers of, 11–12, 105, 140–62 passim
Pullman, Illinois, strike (1894), 13, 172
Pyne, Percy, 32, 174n. 11

Railroad, shipping coal by, 25–26
Railroad strike (1877), use of military force during, 13
Ramsey, Capt. Robert, 155
Rauch, E. H., 81, 106–7, 142, 149, 150
Red ash coal, 22, 28
Reed, Abraham, 109, 110
Repplier, George, 133
Republicanism, of miners, 48–49
Republican party: as critic of labor organization, 10–11; support for Civil War by, 70; support for emancipation by, 86
Rice, Henry, 71
Rockafeller, Capt. Harry, 115, 155, 157
Room Run mine, 46
Ryerson, H. O., 152
Ryon, James, 81–82

Safety, in coal mines, 46, 65, 128
St. Clair, strike in, 58
St. Clair Sentinel, 38
Schuylkill Canal and Navigation Company, 25, 26. *See also* Schuylkill Navigation Company
Schuylkill (southern) coal filed (Schuylkill County), 8, 18, 19, 23, 28, 32, 60, 151; first regional strike in (1842), 48; union organized in, 53, 135
Schuylkill County: Democrats in, 72, 81, 85–86; enrollment in, 101, 108–16; Whigs in, 74
Schuylkill Navigation Canal, 19, 26, 53

Schuylkill Navigation Company, 19,
  132. *See also* Schuylkill Canal and
  Navigation Company
Scott, E. Greenough, 147–48
Scranton, George W., 36
Scranton Republican, 100, 127, 130,
  143
Shankman, Arnold, 5
Shannon, Fred A., 5
Sharpe, Charles, 3
Sherwood (a sergeant), 115
Shunk, Frances, 79
Sigel, Gen. Franz, 149, 151, 152, 153,
  155
Silliman, Edward, 115
Slavery: Democratic position on,
  83–84, 87; Republican position on,
  86–87
Smith, Charles E., 169
Smith, George K., 3, 146–47, 149
Snow, Alonzo, 153
Stanton, Edwin, 102, 103, 140, 157
Stevens, John Austin, 31, 41n. 27
Strikebreakers: protection for, 10, 13,
  50, 56; use of, 141
Strikes, by coal miners: conduct of
  miners during, 59; effectiveness of,
  125–26, 141; in 1842 (first re-
  gional), 48–52; in 1846, 52; in
  1858, 58; in 1862 and 1863,
  124–26, 127–28, 130, 141, 158;
  prosecution of strikers following,
  59, 130; reasons for, 48–49, 51, 55,
  60, 128, 168
Strikes, by transport workers, 53, 122,
  160
Strouse, Meyer, 86, 112, 113
Stutzman, Christopher, 109
Stutzman, Israel, 109
Summit Hill mine, 46, 57
Sunbury Gazette, 131
Swatara coal district, 29, 125
Sylvis, William, 159

Taxation, during Civil War, 88
Taylor, Moses, 31, 41n. 27, 174n.11
Taylor, Zachary, 73
Temperance, 75–76
Tenth New Jersey Regiment, 151,
  157

Thomas, Pat, 126
Tierney, Stephen, 112
Tower, Charlemagne, 56, 69n. 44,
  108–9, 110–11, 112–13, 114,
  115–16, 140, 142, 144, 147, 148,
  152–53, 155, 157
Tower Brigade, 109
Townsend (a military officer), 103,
  150
Tremont, enrollment efforts in,
  103
Tucker, John, 31
Turner, William J., 111
21st Pennsylvania Cavalry, 108

Union League, 106
Unions. *See* Labor unions

Verner, Thomas, 130, 134
Vorhees Colliery, 125, 137n. 15

Wadesville, strike activity in (1842),
  50
Wayne County Herald, 88, 97
West Branch coal district, 29
Wetherwill, Joseph, 106
Whig party: as critic of labor organ-
  ization, 10, 76–77, 78–79; and nat-
  uralization reform, 72–73; and po-
  litical nativism, 73–74, 79–80
Whipple, Gen. W. D., 116, 145
White, Chilton A., 105
White, Josiah, 19
White ash coal, 28
Wilder, R. A., 115
Wintersteen, Capt. A. J., 57
Women: economic role of, 37–38; op-
  position to conscription among,
  99–101
Wood, Bishop Francis, 103
Woodward, George, 83
Workingmen's Advocate, 59, 60, 68n. 35
Wright, Hendrick B., 12, 85, 86
Wyoming (northern) coal field (Luz-
  erne County), 8, 18, 19, 23, 24, 34,
  35, 36, 126, 151

Yohe, Samuel, 105, 106, 107, 140,
  150, 161
Yorktown, strike in, 58

Note on the Author

GRACE PALLADINO is an editor of the Samuel Gompers Papers project at the University of Maryland. She received her Ph.D. from the University of Pittsburgh in 1983 and has published articles in *Labor History* and the *Western Pennsylvania Historical Magazine.* She is currently writing a history of the International Brotherhood of Electrical Workers.

Books in the Series
The Working Class in American History

Worker City, Company Town:
Iron and Cotton-Worker Protest in Troy
and Cohoes, New York, 1855–84
Daniel J. Walkowitz

Life, Work, and Rebellion in the Coal Fields:
The Southern West Virginia Miners, 1880–1922
David Alan Corbin

Women and American Socialism, 1870–1920
Mari Jo Buhle

Lives of Their Own:
Blacks, Italians, and Poles in Pittsburgh, 1900–1960
John Bodnar, Roger Simon, and Michael P. Weber

Working-Class America:
Essays on Labor, Community, and American Society
Edited by Michael H. Frisch and Daniel J. Walkowitz

Eugene V. Debs: Citizen and Socialist
Nick Salvatore

American Labor and Immigration History, 1877–1920s:
Recent European Research
Edited by Dirk Hoerder

Workingmen's Democracy:
The Knights of Labor and American Politics
Leon Fink

The Electrical Workers:
A History of Labor at General Electric
and Westinghouse, 1923–60
Ronald W. Schatz

The Mechanics of Baltimore:
Workers and Politics in the Age of Revolution, 1763–1812
Charles G. Steffen

The Practice of Solidarity:
American Hat Finishers in the Nineteenth Century
David Bensman

The Labor History Reader
Edited by Daniel J. Leab

Solidarity and Fragmentation:
Working People and Class Consciousness in Detroit, 1875–1900
Richard Oestreicher

Counter Cultures:
Saleswomen, Managers, and Customers
in American Department Stores, 1890–1940
Susan Porter Benson

The New England Working Class and the New Labor History
Edited by Herbert G. Gutman and Donald H. Bell

Labor Leaders in America
Edited by Melvyn Dubofsky and Warren Van Tine

Barons of Labor:
The San Francisco Building Trades
and Union Power in the Progressive Era
Michael Kazin

Gender at Work:
The Dynamics of Job Segregation by Sex during World War II
Ruth Milkman

Once a Cigar Maker:
Men, Women, and Work Culture in American
Cigar Factories, 1900–1919
Patricia A. Cooper

A Generation of Boomers:
The Pattern of Railroad Labor Conflict
in Nineteenth-Century America
Shelton Stromquist

Work and Community in the Jungle:
Chicago's Packinghouse Workers, 1894–1922
James R. Barrett

Workers, Managers, and Welfare Capitalism: The Shoeworkers
and Tanners of Endicott Johnson, 1890–1950
Gerald Zahavi

Men, Women, and Work: Class, Gender, and Protest
in the New England Shoe Industry, 1780–1910
Mary Blewett

Workers on the Waterfront:
Seamen, Longshoremen, and Unionism in the 1930s
Bruce Nelson

German Workers in Chicago:
A Documentary History of Working-Class Culture
from 1850 to World War I
Edited by Hartmut Keil and John B. Jentz

On the Line:
Essays in the History of Auto Work
Edited by Nelson Lichtenstein and Stephen Meyer III

Upheaval in the Quiet Zone:
A History of Hospital Workers' Union, Local 1199
Leon Fink and Brian Greenberg

Labor's Flaming Youth:
Telephone Operators and Worker Militancy, 1878–1923
Stephen H. Norwood

Another Civil War:
Labor, Capital, and the State
in the Anthracite Regions of Pennsylvania,
1840–68
Grace Palladino

Coal, Class, and Color:
Blacks in Southern West Virginia, 1915–32
Joe William Trotter, Jr.